An Introduction
to the Study of Paul

Third Edition

Other titles in the T&T Clark Approaches to
Biblical Studies series include:

An Introduction
to the Study of Paul

Third Edition

David G. Horrell

B L O O M S B U R Y
LONDON • NEW DELHI • NEW YORK • SYDNEY

Bloomsbury T&T Clark
An imprint of Bloomsbury Publishing Plc
Imprint previously known as T&T Clark

50 Bedford Square	1385 Broadway
London	New York
WC1B 3DP	NY 10018
UK	USA

www.bloomsbury.com

BLOOMSBURY, T&T CLARK and the Diana logo are trademarks of Bloomsbury Publishing Plc

First published 2000, reprinted 2003, 2004
Second edition published 2006, reprinted 2007
(twice), 2008, 2009, 2011, 2012 (twice)

British Library Cataloguing-in-Publication Data
A catalogue record for this book is available from the British Library.

ISBN: HB: 978–0–56765–624–7
PB: 978–0–56765–625–4
ePDF: 978–0–56765–627–8
ePUB: 978–0–56765–626–1

Library of Congress Cataloging-in-Publication Data
Horrell, David G.
An introduction to the study of Paul / David G. Horrell. – Third edition.
Pages cm – (T&T Clark approaches to biblical studies)
Includes bibliographical references and index.
ISBN 978-0-567-65624-7 (hardcover) – ISBN 978-0-567-65625-4 (pbk.) – ISBN
978-0-567-65627-8 (epDF) – ISBN (invalid) 978-0-567-65626-8 (ePUB)
1. Paul, the Apostle, Saint. 2. Bible. Epistles of Paul–Criticism, interpretation,
etc. I. Title.
BS2650.52.H67 2015
227.06′1–dc23
2014031523

Typeset by RefineCatch Limited, Bungay, Suffolk

Contents

Figures

Abbreviations

BCE	Before the Common Era
CE	the Common Era
cf.	*confer* (Latin), meaning 'compare'
DGH	my initials: denotes my own translation
KJV	King James Version
LXX	Septuagint (the Greek translation of the Hebrew scriptures)
NIV	New International Version
NRSV	New Revised Standard Version
P. Oxy.	the Oxyrynchus Papyri
RSV	Revised Standard Version

Preface to the Third Edition

In a kind review of the second edition of this book, which was published six years after the first edition, Peter Oakes commented that six years seemed about the right time-gap between editions. I have let a few more years slip past this time, but am grateful for the encouragement from Dominic Mattos, at Bloomsbury T&T Clark, to produce a third edition. I am naturally pleased that the book seems to be appreciated as a 'way in' for those beginning their studies of Paul and I remain convinced that the book's value lies primarily in its attempt to introduce students to the diversity of scholarly perspectives on Paul and to alert them to the evidence and issues that underpin this diversity. Authors who focus on giving their own view of Paul often do not alert readers to the alternative ways of understanding the same evidence. I hope I give my readers a reasonable introduction to Paul and his writings, but my particular aim is to orientate them to the scholarly discussion of the Pauline literature, and thus to equip them to begin their studies with some critical awareness of the differing perspectives they will encounter. It is fundamentally, as the title conveys, an introduction to the *study* of Paul.

In revising the book, I have sought to update the discussion and to add some of the important recent literature, not least in the suggestions for further reading at the end of each chapter. These suggested readings are not included in the final bibliography, which compiles only those items cited in my own footnotes. There have been many small alterations throughout, but the most significant additions are in Chapters 5–7. Chapter 7 has been somewhat restructured as well as updated – partly because, as Peter Oakes helpfully reminded me, it is hardly appropriate any longer to refer to social-scientific and feminist perspectives as 'new'. Nonetheless, the book is not radically different from the previous editions, and I have deliberately limited the amount of discussion of recent literature. Unlike some disciplines, especially in the sciences, where new knowledge can rapidly render older literature entirely out of date, the field of New Testament studies is one in which the scholarship of former decades continues to establish the key contours for much ongoing debate. It is, I think, more helpful for students beginning their studies to encounter the main influential perspectives than to be overwhelmed with the full range of current debate. Once they have begun to see how and why the different perspectives emerge, they should be better placed to begin to engage critically with the more recent discussion.

As in earlier editions, the footnotes and suggestions for further reading contain only works available in English (though many of these are translations, most often from German). This seems to me appropriate in a book published in English for undergraduates, ordinands and others beginning their studies of Paul. As Stephen Westerholm commented in a generous review of the second edition, however, it would be unfortunate and misleading to give the impression that the important and relevant research on Paul is all published (or made available) in English. Let me stress, therefore, that scholarly studies of Paul are published in many languages, are not always translated, and that German scholarship in particular is highly important and influential in the field – as those who progress to more advanced levels of study will quickly discover. Westerholm also comments in that review, with typical dry wit, that students may come away from this book with the impression that scholars disagree about almost everything. While this impression (as Westerholm indicates) is not exactly false, I also hope readers will be able to see that there is a reasonable amount of agreement and clarity, at least at the level of broad-brush outlines.

Finally, some words of thanks: I would like to express my continuing gratitude to the successive generations of students at Exeter who have taken my course 'Introducing Paul'. The course is compulsory, so they have no choice about taking it, which makes me appreciate all the more their interest and enthusiasm. I am very grateful to Peter Oakes and Mark Reasoner for suggestions as to how this new edition might best be updated, though they bear no responsibility for what I have actually done. I am grateful to David M. Shaw for producing from my various files a single document of the second edition, ready for editing, and for compiling the indexes. I am also grateful to my father-in-law, Mike Round, for pointing out that the phrase 'he has taught Paul for the last nine years' – used on the back of the first edition – sounded rather odd, if not presumptuous, hence the change in the second edition to 'Pauline studies'! Most of all, however, I reiterate my profound sense of gratitude to Caroline, Emily and Cate; one of the privileges of producing subsequent editions of this book is the opportunity to repeat my appreciation for them and all the happiness they bring me.

Preface to the Second Edition

I am naturally pleased that this volume, and the series of which it is a part, has proven useful enough to warrant a second edition. In the time since this book was first published further introductory works on Paul have of course appeared. Some, like Morna Hooker's, are brief studies comparable in length to this one; others, like Michael Gorman's, are big books, covering all of the letters in some detail. Nonetheless, as far as I am aware, it is still the case that these works, hugely valuable though they are, present a view, an interpretation, of Paul and his letters. They do not take as their main aim what I seek to do here: to introduce students to the range of approaches, perspectives, issues and debates in the scholarly study of Paul. Rather than get one portrait of Paul, students who study this book will get some insight into the different views that various scholars argue for and the evidence on which these views depend, and will thus, I hope, be equipped to begin their own critical evaluation of the material they encounter in the world of contemporary Pauline studies.

It will no doubt be useful for readers to know how this edition differs from the first. In revising the material, I have updated the bibliographical references and suggestions for further reading; amended phrases and added sentences here and there; added, at the series editor's suggestion, three questions for further study at the end of each chapter; and, most importantly, added or expanded a number of sections, generally to bring the discussion up to date. The questions for further study may be used as points around which to focus class or group discussion, areas for wider reading and research, or perhaps the basis for essay assignments. The most significant additions or expansions are as follows: in Chapter 1, a section on the 'world(s)' in which Paul lived (pp. 6–7); in Chapter 5, some additional material on the narrative basis of Paul's theology and his use of scripture (pp. 80–83), on the *pistis Christou* debate (pp. 107–10) and on Paul's ethics (pp. 110–15); in

Chapter 6, some additional material on the debate between 'old' and 'new' perspectives on Paul (pp. 130–36); in Chapter 7, on the social level of the early Christians (pp. 154–56), and on Paul, the Roman Empire and the imperial cult (pp. 169–72).

It remains for me to thank Eddie Adams, Bruce Longenecker and Barry Matlock for their suggestions on what might valuably be added to this new edition (though they should not be held responsible for my decisions!), my colleagues and students in the Department of Theology at Exeter, for providing such a happy and congenial setting in which to work, and Caroline, Emily and Catharine, for far more than words and books can say.

Preface to the First Edition

'Test everything; hold on to what is good' (1 Thess 5.21)

There is already a small mountain of books about Paul, including a number of short introductory works published within the last ten years. Even those whose research specialism is Paul despair of reading all that is being published about him. Why then another introductory book, and what can this book hope to achieve which has not already been achieved before? All of the introductions published in English in recent years, enormously valuable though they are, share one thing in common: they are attempts to introduce Paul and his thought. That is to say, they present a brief interpretation of major themes in his writing, an overview of the main thrust of his gospel, or a resumé of his life and work. With the exception of the first chapter of Tom Wright's recent short book, they do not spend much time outlining the various views of Paul which have been proposed by a range of writers, nor do they help the student to understand why a range of views exists. Instead, they try to present 'what Paul really said' – to paraphrase slightly the title of Wright's book – which means, of course, what each particular writer *thinks* Paul said, one particular *interpretation* of Paul. The new student, or the interested enquirer, innocent of the diversity of views in scholarship on Paul, may take as plain truth the words of their expert guide to Paul and only much later discover how tendentious or disputable those words are. Even those who are aware of the diversity of views, or who are rightly suspicious of every author, are given little insight into the range of contemporary Pauline studies, little insight into the various interests and perspectives that motivate a wide range of approaches.

The title of this book, then, is significant: it is not an introduction to Paul, but rather an introduction to the *study* of Paul. Naturally, such an introduction will include an encounter with the apostle and his writings – it would be an empty and meaningless book without that. And, of course, while I have tried to present a range of viewpoints and show how and why they differ, my own views are an influence throughout, even if I could not say precisely where. But the main aim of this book is to introduce people to the various areas of discussion in the contemporary study of Paul, through an examination of different aspects of Paul's life, writings, theology, practice, and so on. Unlike most previous introductions to Paul, then, I have given attention, among other things, to recent social-scientific studies of Paul and his churches and to feminist perspectives on Paul. Both of these areas have been fruitful and important in recent years. While I am conscious that there is much more that could have been covered, I hope that this work will give students and others interested in Paul some insight into the range of perspectives currently promoted and the issues that underlie contemporary debate.

Because of its aims, this book essentially opens up questions rather than offering answers; it is intended not to provide a particular perspective on Paul, but to give students of Paul some tools with which they can begin to evaluate the interpretations others propose and develop a perspective of their own. It will, I hope, enable them to 'test everything' – everything scholars say, and everything that Paul says – in order to 'hold on to what is good'. Thus I hope that this book will prepare its readers to study Paul with critical awareness as well as enthusiastic interest. Most of all, I hope it will encourage people to read Paul's letters and to ponder what he says, asking questions which arise from their own contexts and experiences, and reacting with both appreciation and criticism to what they find the apostle saying.

A bibliography for the study of Paul could be enormous. On the whole I have kept references to a minimum and listed only recent or important works available in English. The suggestions for further reading at the end of each chapter will give the interested reader some indication as to where further detailed information on a particular topic can be found. Unless otherwise stated, biblical quotations are taken from the New Revised Standard Version (NRSV). Quotations marked DGH are my own translations.

Finally, I would like to record my gratitude to Fern Clarke, Carrie Horrell, Elizabeth Teague and Steve Moyise, the series editor, for their most helpful comments on a draft of this *Introduction*; to Bruce Longenecker for suggestions on my initial outline; to the University of Exeter and especially my colleagues in the Department of Theology for a period of study leave during which I wrote most of the book; to the staff of Ormond College and of the Joint Theological Library in Melbourne for making their facilities available to me during my stay there; and to Geoff, Linda, Stephen and Jamie Thompson, for their hospitality during our visit to Australia.

Introduction: Paul the Man-Mountain

. . . you are the mountain
the teaching of the carpenter of Nazareth
congealed into. The theologians
have walked round you for centuries
and none of them scaled you. Your letters remain
unanswered, but survive the recipients
of them . . .

(R.S. Thomas, 'Paul')[1]

Paul is a man of enormous influence, a religious genius whose capacity for creative thought and original writing has made him a mountain on the landscape of Christian history. During his lifetime he was a leading figure in a wide circle of fellow missionaries, some of whom co-wrote letters with him. His fellow missionaries are largely forgotten, while Paul's name is widely known. There were other leaders within earliest Christianity, Peter, James and John, with whom Paul sometimes came into conflict, and who probably at the time enjoyed more authority and influence than Paul. Yet the level of Paul's enduring influence far outweighs his influence during his lifetime, largely because of his weighty theological letters that are preserved in the New Testament. The New Testament contains just one letter ascribed to James, two attributed to Peter, and three short ones attributed to John; but even taken all together their influence is far outweighed by just one of Paul's letters, written to the Christians in Rome. The New Testament is dominated by the four Gospels – Matthew, Mark, Luke and John – and the thirteen letters attributed to Paul. Paul's continuing influence was made possible by his writing, and his influence makes him important to study.

To say that Paul is a man of enormous influence, however, is not to say that everyone regards his influence positively. For some, Paul is indeed the great hero of the Christian Church, the one who most clearly perceived the meaning of the death and resurrection of Christ and most energetically presented the message of the gospel. For others, however, Paul was largely responsible for taking the Jewish message of Jesus and corrupting it, turning it into a Greek ('Hellenistic') type of religion which Jesus would hardly have recognized, let alone approved. For some, Paul is a social and political radical who announced a message of liberation and equality for women and slaves, a feminist before his time. For others, Paul is responsible for keeping women and slaves in their place, and for fostering attitudes of misogyny and anti-Semitism.

This sample of somewhat extreme opposing views about Paul reveals not least how much assessments of Paul are based on issues arising from our contemporary context. Even when studies are conducted from a historical perspective, which may depict itself as objective and dispassionate, it is important to be aware of the contemporary factors, as well as the ideological and religious commitments, that shape the way interpreters approach their reading of Paul. For example, in Western Europe and the USA in particular, the post-World War II period has been one in which we have been forced to come to terms with the horrors of anti-Semitism; we have had to ask what factors led to Hitler's systematic attempt to annihilate the Jewish people. In the light of that modern concern, it is important to ask what Paul's attitudes were to his own people, the Jews, and to consider the influence of his writings on the history of anti-Judaism (see Chapter 6). In recent decades, many societies in the world have become concerned about the inequalities between women and men, and have debated and changed the position of women in society: in the home, the workplace, the Church, and so on.[2] Because of Paul's influence on what may broadly be called Christian (or post-Christian) societies, and especially because of his influence in the Church, where his letters are part of the canon of scripture, it becomes important to explore what Paul's attitudes to women were, or, indeed, his attitudes to other issues in sexual ethics and gender politics, such as gay relationships. That is obviously only a part of the picture for the contemporary debate, but it is an important part, and helps us to understand why a lot of scholarly energy has been invested in this particular area (see Chapter 7). A final example concerns the relation between Paul and politics. For those, especially Christians, influenced by the Bible, by Christian morality, and specifically by Paul, it is important to ask what Paul's political attitudes were, even though Paul's social, political and economic context is quite different from that faced by the entire human population at the beginning of the third millennium. Do Paul's writings teach that the correct Christian attitude is one of respect and obedience towards law and order and a happy acceptance of one's position in society? Or do they present a vision of counter-cultural communities, social groups in which power and position are abandoned in favour of love and equality? Again scholars have argued for both positions, and for others in between (see Chapter 7).

Of course, Paul's importance and influence stems primarily from his *theology*, rather than directly from his political or social attitudes. His attempts to understand and articulate the meaning of what God had done in Jesus Christ (which is basically what I take Christian theology to be) have been an essential foundation for Christian theology ever since he wrote his letters. Contemporary theologians come to Paul with questions arising from the contexts they have to address, just as Paul's theology arose because of the particular questions he faced. But different theologians interpret Paul quite differently, and there are major disagreements between various traditions of theology in terms of their understanding of Paul's gospel (see Chapter 5).

The great diversity of attitudes to Paul and his letters should also alert us to the fact that he is not an easy person to understand. While even his opponents acknowledged that his letters were weighty and impressive (2 Cor 10.10), Paul himself had to counter false and dangerous opinions about his message (see Rom 3.8). Even in New Testament times, it was recognized that his letters were difficult to understand and were subject to different interpretations and 'distortions' (see 2 Pet 3.15–16). Recognizing the complexity and variety of Paul's writing will help us to understand why such a range of different interpretations of his thought have been presented, both then and now. The purpose of this book is to serve as an introduction both to Paul's life and work and to the varied interpretations of Paul that are proposed and defended in modern scholarship. It is obviously important to try to understand Paul himself, as far as we are able, but it is also important to try to understand how and why scholars come to such different views of Paul. Part of the explanation for their different views will generally be that biblical scholars have honestly sought to interpret the complex historical evidence and present their findings without prejudice. But part of the explanation may also lie in the context and commitments which scholars bring with them to their study of Paul. It is important to consider how much a writer's context or commitments may have influenced their interpretation, and such consideration can help us not to be naive about the agenda underlying their work. But we should also be willing always to ask the same questions of ourselves: Where and how do my particular beliefs, culture, upbringing, commitments, and so on, influence my interpretation of Paul? And how much am I willing to change in the course of an encounter with Paul and his writings? As the great biblical scholar Rudolf Bultmann argued many years ago, it is impossible to come to any text, including, of course, Paul's letters, without presuppositions; but it is vital that we come without prejudging the results of our reading of the texts, that we remain *open* to what an encounter with Paul's writings may reveal to us.[3]

The cultural and chronological gap

Because Paul's letters are important and familiar to Christians today and because the questions addressed to those letters often arise from our own contemporary context, it is sometimes easy to lose sight of the fact that Paul lived and wrote in a society far removed from ours in terms of both time and culture. Some contemporary societies may share more in common culturally or economically with Paul's society than do others, but given the vast changes that have taken place in the world since Paul's time, everywhere things are now very different.

Some of Paul's writings appear to transcend the boundaries of time and culture, such as the famous passage about love in 1 Corinthians 13 (though that impression may be based on the fact that such passages are so familiar to many of us). Other parts of Paul's letters more clearly reflect views of space, the world, disease, death and so on, that seem quite different from our own and are often puzzling to us. For example, Paul suggests that sickness and death among the Corinthian congregation are a direct result of their misbehaviour at the Lord's Supper (1 Cor 11.29–30); he insists that an immoral Christian must be 'handed over to Satan' (1 Cor 5.5) and records that some believers are 'baptised on behalf of the dead' (1 Cor 15.29). He has ancient views on the kinds of bodies which living creatures, planets and stars, possess (1 Cor 15.39–41). He lives in a culture in which curses are pronounced and is prepared to pronounce them himself (1 Cor 12.3; 16.22; Gal 1.8–9). We should not let our familiarity with Paul's letters blind us to the extent to which his 'world' is different from ours. That is not to deny that Paul may speak powerfully to our own context, whatever that context may be, but it is to suggest that we should try to avoid 'making Paul in our own image', rather than letting him be himself.

Among the scholars who have done most to try to understand the social and cultural differences between the New Testament world and the contemporary one are those who belong to the 'Context Group', a group which 'is dedicated to understanding and interpreting the Biblical text within the context of the social and cultural world of traditional Mediterranean society'.[4] Scholars such as Bruce Malina and Jerome Neyrey, drawing on anthropological studies of Mediterranean societies, have sought to model the social and cultural values which were taken for granted in Paul's context, but which are very different from those of most modern citizens of the USA.[5] For example, they suggest that Paul's culture was a collectivist, group-orientated one, whereas US-culture is highly individualistic; that the dominant cultural values of Paul's context were those of honour and shame and that people competed with one another in public encounters in order to increase their honour and shame their opponents. Paul's worldview, values, psychology and so on, belonged within that ancient Mediterranean context. Although it may be argued that Malina and Neyrey paint too generalized a picture of culture at the time of Paul, and assume too much similarity between modern and ancient *Mediterranean* societies (and too much contrast between the 'Mediterranean' and America), their work has certainly helped to remind us that Paul was not a modern American, nor any other kind of modern person, but lived and thought within a very different cultural, social, economic and political context. Whoever we are, and whichever continent we live on, we should – if we heed Malina and Neyrey's warnings – seek to avoid the ethnocentric and anachronistic assumption that Paul and his contemporaries were pretty much like us. We should seek instead to listen sympathetically to a voice from a different time and a different culture, aware that, in the words of the novelist L.P. Hartley, 'the past is a foreign country; they do things differently there'.[6]

The world(s) in which Paul lived

Paul was a Jew who wrote in Greek and lived in the Roman Empire. That simple sentence indicates something about the various 'worlds' that shaped Paul's identity. But these influences cannot be neatly separated.

Judaism at the time of Paul was highly diverse, with differences not only between Palestinian and Diaspora Jews (that is, those living in the 'dispersion', in lands other than their ancestral homeland) but also between different groups: Pharisees, Sadducees, Essenes, Zealots. Though these groups – along with many 'ordinary' Jews, who were probably not aligned with any one or other group – shared some basic beliefs in common, they understood very differently what it meant to follow God's call to be a holy people. Paul, he tells us himself, was a Pharisee (Phil 3.5; see below pp. 37–38). Jews also differed widely in terms of their response to the 'Hellenistic' (Greek) culture that had influenced them since Alexander the Great brought Palestine under his control in 333 BCE. Some embraced the new culture enthusiastically; others fought hard to resist it; but its widespread influence is undeniable.

There has been a long scholarly tradition of drawing a distinction between Judaism and Hellenism, and seeking to distinguish whether this or that feature of Paul's theology is 'Jewish' or 'Hellenistic'. More recent work has, however, increasingly questioned whether such a clear distinction can be made, given the extent to which Jews, in Palestine as well as the Diaspora, had been influenced by Greek language and culture for centuries prior to Paul.[7] Contemporary scholarship has also raised questions about the very term 'Jew' and its appropriateness to the period we are studying. Some have argued that it is anachronistic, like the term 'Christian' (Greek *Christianos*), which appears only rarely in the New Testament (and never in Paul's letters). Such terms, it is argued, imply a kind of religious identity that only becomes apposite later, when (rabbinic) 'Judaism' and 'Christianity' (a term that first appears in the second century, and nowhere in the New Testament) take form as distinct religions. Those who accept this view tend to use the word 'Judean' to translate the Greek *Ioudaios*, more traditionally rendered 'Jew', and find other terms, such as 'Christ-follower', to replace 'Christian'.[8]

Well before Paul was born, the Mediterranean basin had come under the control of Rome, now the dominant imperial power and the central focus for governance, administration, taxation, systems of justice, and so on. The dominance of Rome did not, however, mean the end of Hellenistic influence; Greek remained the primary language of communication in the Eastern Mediterranean, as we see, of course, in Paul's letter-writing (see further Chapter 4). Indeed, rather than attempt to eradicate the influence of Greek literature, customs and religion, the Romans tended to promote and even assimilate them. Nonetheless, though its centre was far from Paul's place of origin, the dominant political power in his world was that of Rome, as we see from Paul's letters and from Acts (see below). This complex mix of influences, then, Jewish, Greek and Roman, shaped the world in which Paul lived, and shaped Paul himself.

Resources for the study of Paul

It will be clear from what has been said above that the most important and obvious resource for the study of Paul is the collection of Paul's letters preserved in the New Testament. Some of the letters attributed to Paul in the New Testament, however, are widely thought not to have been written by the apostle himself, but to have been written in his name, some time after his death. There are no absolutely objective or indisputable criteria on which to make such judgements, but on the basis of differences in vocabulary and style, theology and ethics, and the level of Church order and organization which is presupposed, most scholars conclude that the Pastoral Epistles (1 Timothy, 2 Timothy, Titus) were written in Paul's name some decades after his death. If this opinion is right, then these letters reveal not the thinking of Paul himself but the teaching of a leader or leaders in the Church some years later, claiming Paul's authority and attempting to bring Paul's teaching to bear on a new generation of believers (see Chapter 8).

While the Pastoral Epistles are widely believed to have been written after Paul's death, other letters are subject to more disagreement. Most scholars think that Ephesians was also written by a follower or followers of Paul after his death, and many think the same about Colossians, although the debate in this case is more finely balanced. Indeed, some of those who think that Paul did not write Colossians nevertheless consider that it was written in his lifetime, perhaps with his explicit approval. 2 Thessalonians is also debated, some regarding it as authentic, others as 'pseudonymous' (literally: written under a false name, see further Chapter 8).

There are seven letters ascribed to Paul in the New Testament whose genuineness is never seriously questioned (although certain passages within them are certainly debated as to their authenticity). These are: Romans, 1 Corinthians, 2 Corinthians, Galatians, Philippians, 1 Thessalonians and Philemon. These seven undisputed letters will form the primary evidence for our examination of Paul. The first four of these epistles have often been referred to as the *Hauptbriefe* – a German word meaning the 'major letters'. These four main epistles are, rightly or wrongly, the most influential in forming views of Paul and his theology, at least in scholarly circles. But Philippians, 1 Thessalonians and Philemon also have very important things to contribute to the picture and will feature in chapters to follow. It is difficult to date Paul's letters with precision, but they were all written within a period of no more than ten to fifteen years, during the 40s and 50s CE (see further Chapters 3 and 4).

Also important as a source for the study of Paul is the book of Acts, the first narrative history of the earliest Church, almost certainly written by the same author who wrote the Gospel of Luke (cf. Luke 1.1–4; Acts 1.1–2). (The author is therefore conventionally referred to as Luke.) Acts is important for the information it gives about the earliest Christian groups in Jerusalem and about the ways in which the Christian message spread from that place to other cities in the Roman Empire (see Chapter 2). It is also important for its portrait of Paul's pre-Christian activity, his 'conversion' and subsequent missionary activity. Indeed, the best known information about Paul's conversion and missionary travels is derived from Acts (see Chapter 3). However, the evidence of Acts is clearly secondary, compared with the material in the letters Paul wrote, though that does not necessarily mean it is unreliable. What Paul himself says, while it may at times be one-sided, emotional, polemical, and so on, is at least, as we would say, 'from the horse's mouth'. Acts, on the other hand, is the work of another author, telling the story of the early Church and making Paul a central character in that story. Scholars differ in their assessment of the date and historical trustworthiness of Acts. There is disagreement over the extent to which the author of Acts, whoever he or she was, had access to sources about the life and activity of Paul, and over the extent to which the author's theological interests have influenced the shaping (and creating?) of material. Some defend the view that the author was a companion of Paul's (perhaps the Luke mentioned in Col 4.14; Phlmn 24; 2 Tim 4.11), knew Paul's letters, and was an eye-witness of some of the events described in Acts. Others are convinced that the author of Acts had less direct knowledge of Paul. Some scholars have argued that Acts was written in the period before 70 CE, i.e., before, or shortly after, Paul's death. Others – in the majority – date Acts two or three decades later, in the 80s or 90s or perhaps later still. The material from Acts, then, must be used with caution. It should not be naively accepted as some kind of pure and unbiased history (is there any such thing?) but neither should its evidence be rejected or ignored. It remains an essential source for the study of Paul.

Less directly related to Paul (since they do not mention him), though still extremely important, are the numerous sources which can help us to construct a picture of the social, cultural and religious context in which Paul worked. Perhaps most obviously relevant are the Jewish sources, essential for helping us to understand Paul's theology, which is, after all, fundamentally rooted in Judaism (see Chapter 6). Specifically, the Jewish scriptures – the Old Testament, or Hebrew Bible – are essential for understanding Paul, since these were Paul's scriptures, from which he frequently quotes (though the 'canon' of the Hebrew Bible may not have been entirely fixed or settled in Paul's time). Other Jewish texts, such as the variety of writings discovered at the caves of Qumran, the so-called Dead Sea Scrolls, give us insight into the forms of Jewish belief and practice around the time of Paul. Particularly significant among Paul's Jewish contemporaries are the philosopher Philo of Alexandria and the historian Josephus, both of whom have left extensive writings, crucial for understanding the varieties of Judaism that existed at the time of Paul and the particular sect of Judaism to which Paul belonged (see Chapter 3).

A wide range of sources, ranging from literary texts to inscriptions, coins, graffiti, buildings, and so on, enable us to understand something of the wider social, political and philosophical context in which Paul lived and worked. Like other Jews of his day, Paul was influenced by the wider world in which he lived, and scholars have proposed various specific ways in which Paul's thought was shaped not only by Jewish traditions but by Cynic or Stoic philosophy, Greco-Roman rhetorical training, and so on (see Chapter 4). A central, though for a long time somewhat neglected, feature of this wider context, is of course the Roman Empire itself, which in its structures of occupation, governance, law, trade, and so on, shaped the conditions in which Paul and his contemporaries operated (see Chapter 7, pp. 169–72). Texts from Roman authors, along with other artefacts, can inform us about many things relevant to understanding Paul and his letters – such as, to give just one example, the institution of slavery and the conventions by which it operated.

Conclusion

In this introductory chapter, we have seen something of both *why* and *how* we should study Paul. His enormous influence within Christian history and the importance of his writings in the Church's debates both past and present, make him a figure we should certainly seek to know and understand. In this quest for knowledge and understanding, our primary resource will be Paul's own letters, written in the midst of his missionary activity and often in the heat of debate and disagreement. The book of Acts will also be an important source, invaluable as an account of the earliest years of Christian origins and of Paul's activity as a Christian missionary, even though it needs to be used with some caution and care. In the chapters that follow we shall use these and a range of other sources to build up a picture of Paul and his major ideas. We shall seek to understand Paul better. But we shall also examine some of the main views of Paul presented in recent scholarship and consider how and why these views vary. All of this, I hope, will enable you to work towards your own understanding of Paul and your own interpretation of his complex and profound writings.

Further reading

As mentioned in the Prefaces above, there are many short introductions to Paul, published in English. A recent volume that gives a very clear and up-to-date overview is T.G. Gombis, *Paul: A Guide for the Perplexed*

(London & New York: T&T Clark, 2010). Others that may be recommended include J. Ziesler, *Pauline Christianity* (revised edn, Oxford: OUP, 1990), E.P. Sanders, *Paul* (Oxford: OUP, 1991), C.K. Barrett, *Paul: An Introduction to His Thought* (London: Geoffrey Chapman, 1994), M.D. Hooker, *Paul: A Short Introduction* (Oxford: Oneworld, 2001), J.A. Harrill, *Paul the Apostle: His Life and Legacy in their Roman Context* (Cambridge & New York: Cambridge University Press, 2012), and S. Westerholm, *Preface to a Study of Paul* (Grand Rapids: Eerdmans, 1997), now published in a second edition as *Understanding Paul: The Early Christian Worldview of the Letter to the Romans* (Grand Rapids: Baker Academic, 2004), which introduces major areas of Paul's theology through an encounter with the letter to the Romans. N.T. Wright, *What Saint Paul Really Said* (Oxford: Lion, 1997), presents a particular argument as to how Paul's gospel should be understood and a response to A.N. Wilson's controversial book *Paul: The Mind of the Apostle* (London: Sinclair-Stevenson, 1997). Wright's book also contains a useful annotated bibliography. For an accessible, evangelical Christian perspective on Paul, see M.F. Bird, *A Bird's Eye View of Paul* (Nottingham/Downers Grove: IVP, 2008) – the US title is the more modest *Introducing Paul*. Readers may be drawn to those which fit their particular positions and convictions, such as the more evangelical perspectives in Bird and Wright, or the more critical stance in Harrill. Needless to say, serious study of Paul requires grappling with views you may not find congenial, and trying to assess which are most cogent, whether from historical or theological perspectives.

A much larger, thorough introduction to Paul and his letters, which includes a valuable chapter on Paul's world(s) (pp. 1–39), is provided by M.J. Gorman, *Apostle of the Crucified Lord: A Theological Introduction to Paul and His Letters* (Grand Rapids: Eerdmans, 2004). Among other extensive introductions, see U. Schnelle, *Apostle Paul: His Life and Theology* (Grand Rapids: Baker, 2005), which, originally published in German, gives a perspective strongly rooted in German (as well as other) scholarship; and B.W. Longenecker and T.D. Still, *Thinking Through Paul: An Introduction to His Life, Letters, and Theology* (Grand

Rapids: Zondervan, 2014), which offers associated study materials. Also valuable are the following edited handbooks: J.D.G. Dunn (ed.), *The Cambridge Companion to St Paul* (Cambridge: CUP, 2003); S. Westerholm (ed.), *The Blackwell Companion to Paul* (Oxford: Wiley-Blackwell, 2011); R.B. Matlock (ed.), *The Oxford Handbook of Pauline Studies* (Oxford: OUP, forthcoming); O. Wischmeyer (ed.), *Paul: Life, Setting, Work, Letters* (London & New York: T&T Clark, 2012), which, as a translation from a German original, presents perspectives from German scholars.

Introductions to each of Paul's letters (and to the other writings in the New Testament) can also be found in various commentaries and Bible dictionaries, such as the broadly evangelical *Dictionary of Paul and His Letters,* edited by G.F. Hawthorne, R.P. Martin and D.G. Reid (Leicester: IVP, 1993). Other valuable reference works include P.J. Achtemeier, J.B. Green and M.M. Thompson, *Introducing the New Testament: Its Literature and Theology* (Grand Rapids, MI: Eerdmans, 2001); L.T. Johnson, *The Writings of the New Testament* (3rd edn, Minneapolis: Fortress, 2010), R.E. Brown, *An Introduction to the New Testament* (New York: Doubleday, 1997) and U. Schnelle, *The History and Theology of the New Testament Writings* (London: SCM, 1998).

A readable overview of the scholarly 'quest' for Paul, with further bibliography, is provided by B. Witherington III, *The Paul Quest* (Leicester: IVP, 1998). A thorough overview of recent Pauline studies is provided by N.T. Wright, *Paul and His Recent Interpreters* (London/Minneapolis: SPCK/Fortress, forthcoming 2014). Attempts to set Paul in his ancient Mediterranean context (and thus to stress his difference from his modern readers) include J.H. Neyrey, *Paul in Other Words: A Cultural Reading of his Letters* (Louisville: Westminster John Knox, 1990) and B.J. Malina and J.H. Neyrey, *Portraits of Paul: An Archaeology of Ancient Personality* (Louisville: Westminster John Knox, 1996).

For further information on the 'worlds' which shaped Paul, see R. Wallace and W. Williams, *The Three Worlds of Paul of Tarsus* (London and New York: Routledge, 1998), and on Judaism in this period H. Jagersma, *A History of Israel from Alexander the Great to Bar Kochba*

(London: SCM, 1985). Harrill's introduction to Paul, mentioned above, is particularly concerned to locate Paul in his ancient Jewish and Roman context. The diverse ways in which Diaspora Jews responded to Hellenism are explored and analysed by J.M.G. Barclay, *Jews in the Mediterranean Diaspora* (Edinburgh: T&T Clark, 1996). An extensive collection of ancient sources important for understanding Paul is provided in N. Elliott and M. Reasoner, *Documents and Images for the Study of Paul* (Minneapolis: Fortress, 2011).

Questions for further study

- How do Jewish, Greek, and Roman influences shape Paul's environment and identity? To what extent are these influences separable, or intertwined?
- In what specific ways might it be important to appreciate the chronological and cultural distance between us and Paul?
- What issues from the contemporary agenda would you see as shaping the questions we ask about Paul? Or in what areas of contemporary life would you see Paul's letters as having some influence, for good or ill?

Notes

1 From R.S. Thomas, 'Covenanters', in *Later Poems: A Selection 1972–1982* (London: Macmillan, Papermac, 1984), pp. 170–73. Reprinted here by permission of Macmillan Publishers.

2 I recognize that I write as a British scholar living in Britain, and thus that my viewpoint is particularly informed by that context. The important point, however, is that the questions we address to Paul's writings arise at least in part from our own particular context, whatever that may be.

3 R. Bultmann, 'Is Exegesis Without Presuppositions Possible?' in *New Testament and Mythology and Other Basic Writings* (trans. and ed. S.M. Ogden, London: SCM, 1985), pp. 145–53.

4 This phrase is taken from the announcement of their 1997 conference. The
   best introductions to the approach taken by members of the group are B.J.
   Malina, *The New Testament World: Insights from Cultural Anthropology*
   (3rd edn; Louisville: Westminster John Knox, 2001) and R.L. Rohrbaugh
   (ed.) *The Social Sciences and New Testament Interpretation* (Peabody:
   Hendrickson, 1996). See also suggestions for further reading on pp. 10–14.
5 Malina and Neyrey are both based in the USA, and generally draw
   contrasts between Mediterranean and US society.
6 These are the opening words of Hartley's novel, *The Go-Between*.
7 A now classic study that challenged the sharp distinction between Judaism
   and Hellenism is M. Hengel, *Judaism and Hellenism* (2 vols; London: SCM,
   1974); see also, more briefly, M. Hengel, *The 'Hellenization' of Judaea in the
   First Century after Christ* (London: SCM, 1989). The distinction is even
   more radically questioned in T. Engberg-Pedersen (ed.), *Paul Beyond the
   Judaism/Hellenism Divide* (Louisville: Westminster John Knox, 2001).
8 See, for example, P.F. Esler, *Conflict and Identity in Romans* (Minneapolis:
   Fortress, 2003), pp. 63–74; J.H. Elliott, 'Jesus the Israelite was Neither a
   "Jew," nor a "Christian": On Correcting Misleading Nomenclature', *Journal
   for the Study of the Historical Jesus* 5 (2007), pp. 119–54.

2

From Jesus to Paul: Pre-Pauline Christianity

Introduction

There are some fairly obvious differences between the message announced by Jesus of Nazareth and the gospel proclaimed by the earliest Christians including Paul. As Alfred Loisy famously put it: 'Jesus proclaimed the kingdom of God, and what happened was the church'.[1] Reconstructing the mission and self-understanding of the historical Jesus is a complex matter, dependent on a careful and critical evaluation of the Gospels; and the extent of similarity and continuity between Jesus and the post-Easter Christians is open to debate. But there is a clear difference at least in language and terminology between Jesus' announcement of the kingdom of God and Paul's gospel, focused on the death and resurrection of Christ. The phrases 'son of man' and 'kingdom of God', for example, occur frequently in the Synoptic Gospels on the lips of Jesus but rarely appear in the epistles ('son of man' never in the New Testament epistles; 'kingdom of God' only eight times in the Pauline epistles).[2] Conversely, the title 'Christ' is never found directly on the lips of Jesus in the Synoptic Gospels, but appears frequently throughout Paul's letters.[3] Most scholars would agree that the early Church developed (how quickly is open to debate) an increasingly high 'Christology' – that is, its view of the person of Christ – which may have been an appropriate reflection of who Jesus was, seen in the light of his resurrection, but can hardly have been a reflection of how Jesus himself understood his identity. We also need to remember that the early 'Christian' movement, in which Paul played such a significant part, was not a distinct, defined or institutionalized religion but rather a fledgling movement, enmeshed in its Jewish matrix; as we noted above (p. 7), the terms 'Christian' and 'Christianity' are apparently unknown to Paul, and when used in this context can easily imply an anachronistic picture of what we are dealing with at this point in history.

Because of the gap between the message of Jesus and the gospel of Paul, and because of Paul's enormous influence within Christian history, some critics of Christianity have claimed that Paul was 'the real founder of Christianity' (Friedrich Nietzsche).[4] Some today propound the view that Paul was largely responsible for creating a Hellenistic salvation-religion focused on the death and resurrection of Christ, whereas Jesus himself, as a Jewish prophet, had called for the renewal of Israel under the rule of God.[5] Others, similarly emphasizing the contribution of Paul, have labelled him 'the second founder of Christianity'.[6]

Our task in this chapter is to examine briefly the evidence concerning the development of Christianity from its earliest post-Easter beginnings to the time when Paul became an active and prominent apostle. This examination will help us to assess whether there is any justification in calling Paul the real founder, or the second founder, of Christianity. I shall not here consider the important questions concerning the historical Jesus, his self-understanding, teaching and mission, as these would take us beyond the scope of this book.[7] I shall, however, briefly consider the appearance of Jesus' teachings in Paul's letters (see pp. 28–30).

Using the evidence of Acts

Our only substantial source for the very earliest months and years of the Christian movement after the death and resurrection of Jesus is Acts. Unfortunately, unlike the case of the Synoptic Gospels, we have no other accounts of the earliest churches with which to compare Acts, except where there are overlaps with Paul's letters, so it is hard to judge how accurate Luke's picture is (on the authorship of Acts, see above

p. 9). Scholars have long differed widely in their assessment of Acts' historicity. For example, some, like Ernst Haenchen, emphasize how Luke's theological agenda has led him to shape and even create material. Thus, the portrait of Paul in Acts is, according to Haenchen, quite different from that which emerges from Paul's letters: 'the real Paul, as known to his followers and opponents alike, has been replaced by a Paul seen through the eyes of a later age'.[8] Similarly, Albert Harrill insists that Acts should be treated as 'one of the first interpretations of Paul, rather than as a primary source providing independent information about his life'; great caution is needed in using it to make historical claims about Paul.[9]

Others, such as Howard Marshall and Rainer Riesner, while acknowledging that Luke has shaped his material according to his theological interests, insist that Luke is a more careful and accurate historian than critical scholars like Haenchen and Harrill allow. Marshall writes:

it is unfair to suggest that he is a thoroughly tendentious and unreliable writer, freely rewriting the history of the early church in the interests of his own theology ... there is in our judgment sufficient evidence in his favour to demand a more positive evaluation of his historical ability.[10]

Marshall accepts, however, that we cannot expect Luke to be a historian in exactly the modern sense of the word: that would be both anachronistic and unrealistic, since Luke did not have access to the same kinds of documentation and resources as are available today, and the cultural expectations of written history then were somewhat different. Martin Hengel, a prominent defender of the historical value of Acts, also stresses this point: 'Luke is no less trustworthy than other historians of antiquity ... His account always remains within the limits of what was considered reliable by the standards of antiquity'.[11] For example, we cannot expect the speeches in Acts to be verbatim accounts of what was actually said on that occasion by Stephen, Peter, Paul or whoever. There were no dictaphones or voice recorders then. Luke may well have had access to sources when writing Acts, and may possibly have been a companion of Paul's (though his lack of reference to Paul's letters is then something of a puzzle). But his attitude to writing speeches may have been broadly similar to that expressed by the ancient historian Thucydides, who described his own approach as follows:

> As to the speeches that were made by different men ... it has been difficult to recall with strict accuracy the words actually spoken, both for me as regards that which I myself heard, and for those who from various other sources have brought me reports. Therefore the speeches are given in the language in which, as it seemed to me, the several speakers would express, on the subjects under consideration, the sentiments most befitting the occasion, though at the same time I have adhered as closely as possible to the general sense of what was actually said.[12]

So Luke has probably written the speeches in Acts himself, expressing in them what he thought appropriate to their speakers. Questions still remain, of course, about how accurately Luke has summarized the theology of Stephen, Peter, Paul and others, in the speeches he put into their mouths; questions remain about how much Luke's own theological interests have shaped the picture he presents. But just as theological convictions and priorities appear to have shaped the distinctive presentations of Jesus in the Gospels of Matthew, Mark, Luke and John, so too it seems most likely that Luke's theological agenda has in some ways influenced the presentation of the material in Acts. This issue will reappear when we consider Paul's biography in Chapter 3.

The earliest house-churches in Jerusalem

One of the puzzles in the Synoptic Gospels is that Matthew and Mark have the disciples instructed to return to Galilee to meet the risen Jesus (Matt 28.10; Mark 16.7), whereas in Luke they are told to remain in Jerusalem (Luke 24.47–52; Acts 1.4). Luke certainly shows an interest in ordering his material into a geographical scheme and this may well account for his emphasis on Jerusalem. In Luke's Gospel, Jesus' 'journey' from Galilee to Jerusalem underpins the narrative from 9.51 onwards, and in Acts the gospel is shown to spread from Jerusalem to Rome. But Paul's letters confirm Luke's information that the earliest Christian assembly was centred in Jerusalem, with Peter, James and John as its leaders (Gal 1.18, 2.1–2, 2.9). Disciples of Jesus may well have returned to Galilee, and some groups of Christians may have met there, but we know virtually nothing about them if they did.

From Luke's portrait of the earliest Christians in Jerusalem we may distil the following basic information:

- Jesus' followers continued to meet together after his death, though initially disappointed, and convinced that their hopes had not been realized (cf. Luke 24.21).
- Some of them had experiences in which they saw the risen Lord and which convinced them that Jesus was alive and was indeed the Messiah (Luke 24; Acts 1.3–11). (Whether one actually believes in the resurrection or not, this much can hardly be denied, even by the most sceptical historian.)
- These early Christians received an experience which they understood as the Holy Spirit. (Again, whatever actually happened, the *belief* that the Spirit of God had been poured out upon them is clear – though differently presented – in both Acts and Paul's letters: Acts 2.1ff.; Rom 8.9; 1 Cor 12.3; Gal 3.2).
- The members of the early Jerusalem Church met in fellowship, in people's homes, led by the apostles (especially Peter, James and John), and remembered Jesus in the 'breaking of bread' (Acts 2.42, 46; presumably equivalent to what Paul calls 'the Lord's Supper': 1 Cor 11.20). They also shared their property with one another (Acts 2.42–47; 4.32–37). Even if Luke has painted a somewhat idealized portrait of this earliest Christian community, these basic features seem essentially authentic. (We need of course to remember that 'church' in this period refers to a gathering or assembly of Christ-followers – not yet known as 'Christians' –

generally described in the New Testament using the Greek word
ekklēsia, which essentially means 'assembly'; it does not denote a
special building, nor does the word *ekklēsia* imply a specifically
Christian gathering; see further pp. 157–59 below).

- At this point in time the Church was comprised entirely of Jews
  who believed in Jesus as Messiah, but who in all other respects
  continued to live and worship as loyal Jews (Acts 2.46–3.1). This is
  an important point to note.

Division and the spread of the gospel

The somewhat rosy picture of the infant Church presented in Acts 1–4
is first spoilt by the incident involving Ananias and Sapphira, who are
struck down dead for their deception concerning the proceeds received
from the sale of some of their property (Acts 5.1–11). Shortly afterwards,
Luke gives a brief but important piece of information about division
and disagreement in the Jerusalem churches: 'Now during those days . . .
the Hellenists complained against the Hebrews because their widows
were being neglected in the daily distribution of food' (Acts 6.1). Who
were the 'Hebrews' and the 'Hellenists'? One thing we should note is that
they were almost certainly all Jews. It is widely agreed that the terms
refer to a primarily linguistic division: the Hebrews were those
(Christian) Jews, probably of Palestinian origin, whose first language
was Aramaic (though they may well have known Greek as well), who
understood Hebrew and used the Hebrew scriptures in their worship
together. The Hellenists, on the other hand, probably originated in the
Diaspora and spoke Greek as their main language. They may have been
unable to understand the scripture readings and synagogue worship in
Aramaic/Hebrew, and used the Greek translation of the Hebrew
scriptures known (to us) as the Septuagint (LXX).

According to a prominent theory, this division between Hebrews
and Hellenists was profoundly significant for the spread of Christianity
from Jerusalem and for the development of the mission to the Gentiles.

Martin Hengel's influential reconstruction may be summarized as follows[13]:

1. The seven who were appointed, according to Luke, to oversee the distribution of food and thus resolve the cause of complaints (Acts 6.2–5), were actually the leaders of the Hellenist group among the Jerusalem Christians. Stephen, for example, was a leading Hellenist, who caused controversy in the synagogue he attended (note that it was a synagogue of *diaspora* Jews – Acts 6.9).

2. The Hellenists, who worshipped separately from the Hebrews (because of the language barrier) and attended different synagogues, developed a theology which was distinctive, more critical of the temple cult and Jewish law than that held by the 'Hebrew' Christians, who maintained their loyalty to Jewish law and cult. For example, Hengel sees Stephen's speech in Acts 7 as 'the remnants of a Jewish-Christian Hellenistic sermon from an earlier period which has been stylistically improved by Luke . . . its tendency to be critical of the cult is unmistakable. With this attitude, the "Hellenists" were evidently more radical than the "Hebrews" . . .'[14] This attitude of criticism of law and temple had roots in the teaching of Jesus, but was developed by the Hellenists and became the cause of hostility towards them in Jerusalem.

3. Persecution broke out in Jerusalem against the Hellenists (see Acts 8.1–3). It is hardly likely that the central circle of 'apostles' would alone have been left untouched by persecution, as Luke reports (Acts 8.1). Rather, it was the Aramaic-speaking Jewish Christians, including 'the apostles', who were more or less unaffected directly by this persecution. The persecution was directed against the Hellenists, at least some of whom were driven from the city.

4. As they fled from Jerusalem, the Hellenists took the gospel with them, and shared it with those they met (Acts 8.4). Luke records Philip, for example, announcing the gospel in the city of Samaria (Acts 8.5–8), to a person he meets on his travels (Acts 8.26–39) and in various towns and cities (Acts 8.40).

5. Some of the Hellenists shared the gospel with non-Jews, a radical step of enormous significance for the history of Christianity (Acts 11.19–20). Moreover, in at least some places, these Gentile converts were not expected to become Jewish (to be circumcised, etc.) in order to be welcomed into the Christian fellowship. While the details and ordering of Luke's accounts can certainly be doubted, in reporting this development in places like Antioch and Caesarea, he seems essentially accurate. Thus, through 'the pioneers here, the "Hellenists", . . . the earliest church was led step by step to a mission to the Gentiles without the law'.[15]

6. The Hellenists therefore were of decisive significance for the spread of Christianity, both because they first formulated the gospel message in Greek, the common language of the eastern Roman Empire, and because they took their gospel from Jerusalem to other cities, and shared it with non-Jews.

This view of the history of earliest Christianity is not, however, without its critics, notably Craig Hill.[16] Hill relates this view of the Hebrew and Hellenist parties in the Jerusalem churches to the influential theory of Ferdinand Christian Baur (1792–1860), a German historian of early Christianity. Starting with the divisions between those who followed Paul and those who followed Peter in the church at Corinth (1 Cor 1.12), Baur developed a theory of early Christianity which revolved around the conflict between a Jewish, law-observant form of Christianity associated with Peter and a Gentile-welcoming, law-rejecting form associated with Paul. Using terminology derived from the philosopher G.W.F. Hegel, Baur saw the dialectical opposition between these two wings of early Christianity overcome in the synthesis of Christianity in Rome, where towards the end of the first century the Petrine and Pauline groups were brought together. On this view, then, the basic division between Jewish (Petrine) and Gentile (Pauline) Christianity was already present, in undeveloped and embryonic form, in the division between the Hebrews and the Hellenists in Jerusalem. Hill's basic objection is that the evidence is too slender to allow the reconstruction of a distinctively 'Hellenist' theology, versus that of the

Hebrews; there were certainly divisions and diversity, but to present a picture of two distinct groups with distinctive theological positions is, according to Hill, both to go beyond and to contradict the available evidence. Can we really deduce the theology of a whole *group* from the speech of Stephen written by Luke? And what about the diversity of positions represented in the supposedly 'conservative' Hebrew wing? Not all of these 'Hebrew' Jewish Christians took the same stance with regard to what the Gentiles should be required to do; they were prepared to welcome Gentile converts into the Church (just as Jews welcomed proselytes) but disagreed as to the level of law-observance required of them. Some thought that circumcision was obligatory, others that only a minimum of law-observance, such as that encapsulated in the 'apostolic decree' (see Acts 15.20, 29), was necessary.

Hill raises some important questions, highlighting not least the degree of diversity among what can too easily be portrayed as more or less monolithic groups in the earliest churches, and warning against an oversimplified reconstruction. However, it has been suggested that he fails to deal adequately with the central piece of evidence, Acts 6.1, and a widespread view of the significance of the Hellenists remains.[17] A vital question concerns how much can legitimately be deduced from Luke's brief reports, which really supply all the information we have about this very earliest period of Christian history.

What seems clear, and what is of greatest importance, is that, for whatever reasons and through whichever people, the gospel message did spread from Jerusalem, taken by those leaving, or driven from, that city. After a short time, a few years at most, the Christian message began to be shared with non-Jews.[18] Moreover, at some point, in at least some places, notably Antioch in Syria, non-Jewish converts were accepted into the fellowship without them having to become Jewish (be circumcised, follow Jewish food-laws, etc.) – though this was to be a cause of heated debate, involving Paul, for years to come. Exactly when and where these developments took place is impossible to say, but they are of profound importance because they mark the beginnings of the process whereby Christianity developed a distinct identity – a process which, during the century or so thereafter, would lead eventually to the separation of Christianity from its Jewish parent.

These developments are also important because they raise a distinct question-mark over the idea that Paul was the founder of Christianity, or even the second founder of Christianity. Paul, who understood himself called to be 'Apostle to the Gentiles' certainly did come to be extremely influential in the debates which took place concerning what demands should be placed upon the Gentile converts, and crucial in establishing and justifying theologically the Gentile mission, but he did not single-handedly or uniquely start a Christian mission to Gentiles, nor dream up on his own the gospel which we later find in his letters.

Paul and pre-Pauline Christianity

How, if at all, does Paul feature in this crucial period of early Christian history? In the next chapter we shall consider Paul's biography in more detail; here I want to try to relate Paul to the developments sketched above. His first appearance in the book of Acts comes in 7.58–8.1, where he sees and approves the killing of Stephen (and where he is called by his Jewish name, Saul – see below, p. 38). He becomes an active persecutor of the Christians (Acts 8.3), setting off to Damascus to seek out believers there, in order to bring them to Jerusalem for punishment (Acts 9.1–2). Paul's own testimony confirms that he was indeed a persecutor of the Church prior to his conversion (1 Cor 15.9; Gal 1.13, 23; Phil 3.6), though some have doubted whether it took place in *Jerusalem*, because of Paul's comment in Gal 1.22 that he was 'unknown by face to the churches in Judea' prior to his first visit there after his conversion. However, it is by no means certain that this reference excludes the possibility of persecution by Paul in Jerusalem. Riesner suggests that: 'The statement concerning the lack of familiarity with the churches of Judea is referring to Paul as a Christian, and stems from his intention of proving his independence from the apostolic authorities in the holy city'[19] – though this argument may itself be motivated by a desire to defend Luke's historical accuracy. It may have been specifically the Hellenists whom Paul persecuted and drove from Jerusalem and whom he pursued to Damascus; it may have been their theology and mission in particular which Paul the Pharisee found so objectionable (though Hill may be right to suggest that the evidence does not allow us to be so sure about any distinctively 'Hellenist' views). What is certain, again from Paul's own testimony, is that the persecutor experienced a dramatic change, and became an ardent believer in that which he had sought to stamp out. Paul's so-called conversion (on which see below, pp. 40–43) probably took place around three years after the crucifixion of Jesus. For some of the years that followed we know very little: from Paul's own account, for example, we know that he spent the three years after his conversion in Arabia and Damascus, but we know nothing definite about what exactly he did there – though he may have independently begun missionary activity there among the Gentiles, at around the same time as, or even earlier than, the Hellenists or others did elsewhere (see Chapter 3). We do know, however, that Paul then visited Jerusalem for fifteen days (Gal 1.18), and that he was later based in the church at Antioch, acting for some years as a missionary under the commission of that church, in partnership with Barnabas (Acts 11.26–15.40).

The significance of these biographical details is that, in these various contexts, Paul encountered and thus learnt about the Christian message. Even as an ardent persecutor, Paul must have learnt about this new movement, or else he would not have become convinced of the need to stamp it out. Once converted, Paul learnt from and shared with others through his visit to Jerusalem, and especially through his extended relationship with the church at Antioch. What then can we see of Paul's contact with, and learning from, these other early Christians in his letters?

1. The shared apostolic gospel

In 1 Cor 15.1–11 Paul reminds the Corinthians of the gospel which he announced to them; the gospel which he himself received and which is also proclaimed by the other apostles: 'For I handed on to you as of first importance what I in turn had received: that Christ died for our sins in accordance with the scriptures, and that he was buried, and that he was raised on the third day in accordance with the scriptures' (1 Cor 15.3–4). After listing the appearances of the risen Christ to Cephas (Peter), to 500 of the brothers and sisters at once, to James and lastly to himself, Paul claims that he has worked harder than any of the other apostles. Nevertheless, he concludes, concerning the basic message of the gospel: 'Whether then it was I or they, so we proclaim and so you have come to believe' (1 Cor 15.11). When facing opposition and defending his own authority, as in Galatians, Paul can strongly stress his independence from others, insisting that he did not receive his gospel via any other human being (Gal 1.11–20). Here, by contrast, though he does not state where or how he 'received' what he proclaimed to the Corinthians, Paul stresses that the message is one shared in common with the other apostles.

2. Jesus' words and teachings

Paul makes very few explicit references to words or teachings of Jesus in his letters; the few instances generally agreed upon are 1 Cor 7.10–11, 1 Cor 9.14, 1 Cor 11.23–25, and (with somewhat more doubt about whether these are explicit references to Jesus' words) 1 Thess 4.15–17, Rom 14.14. Even in these few instances, there is hardly any direct quotation of Jesus' teaching (except in the very particular case of the narrative of the Lord's Supper, recorded in 1 Cor 11.23–25). In some ways this is puzzling: we might have expected Paul to recount some of Jesus' parables or stories (if he knew them), or to cite Jesus' teaching (if he knew it) when some matter of conduct was in dispute. There are all sorts of reasons which may help to explain why he did not do this,[20] but important for our purposes here is the fact that Paul did clearly know *some*, if only a few, of the Jesus-traditions which are recorded in the Gospels.

Paul appears to have known, for example, that Jesus had spoken against divorce and passes on the command of the Lord to the Corinthians (1 Cor 7.10–11; cf. Matt 5.31–32; Matt 19.3–9; Mark

10.2–12; Luke 16.18). The command is not presented in exactly the same wording as in the Synoptic Gospel parallels, but Paul makes the point that this teaching is not from him, but from 'the Lord' (1 Cor 7.10). It is *possible* that Paul is referring here to a word from the risen Lord, communicated through a Christian prophet or directly to Paul himself, as has occasionally been suggested, but this seems most unlikely, since the Lord's (i.e. Jesus') instruction on this matter is recorded in a number of forms in the Gospel traditions.

Paul also apparently knew of Jesus' instruction to his missionaries not to take their own means of material support on their travels, but to depend on the support of those who welcomed them wherever they went; he refers to Jesus' instruction with his phrase 'the Lord commanded' (1 Cor 9.14; cf. Matt 10.1–15; Mark 6.7–11; Luke 9.1–5; 10.1–12). Paul knew quite precisely the tradition of Jesus' words at the Last Supper, probably because these words were recited regularly at Christian meetings to celebrate the Lord's Supper, and so Paul learnt them from his participation in such fellowship meals. Since Paul states that he received these words 'from the Lord' (1 Cor 11.23; cf. 15.3; Gal 1.12) one could conceivably argue that he came to this knowledge by direct divine revelation. However, when we see how closely Paul's words compare with those in the Synoptic Gospels, especially in Luke, yet with significant differences, it seems much more plausible that Paul learnt these words (*indirectly* 'from the Lord', perhaps) because they were being remembered and used in the meal-celebrations in the Christian communities where Paul was based; he may have learnt them in Antioch:

1 Cor 11.23–25 (DGH)	Luke 22.19–20 (DGH)
the Lord Jesus, on the night in which he was betrayed, took bread, gave thanks and broke it, and said, 'This is my body which is for you. Do this in remembrance of me.'	he took bread, gave thanks, broke it and gave it to them saying, 'This is my body which is given for you. Do this in remembrance of me.'

In the same way also [he took] the cup after supper, saying, 'This cup is the new covenant in my blood. Do this, whenever you drink it, in remembrance of me.'	And [he took] the cup in the same way after supper, saying, 'This cup is the new covenant in my blood, poured out for you.'

It is clear, then, that Paul knew more about Jesus than that he had lived, died on the cross, and been raised from the dead by God. He also knew some of the teachings and words of Jesus. He presumably learnt about Jesus on his visit to Jerusalem, when he spent time getting to know Peter (Gal 1.18), who, unlike Paul, had been a disciple of Jesus. He also learnt some of the words and teachings which were being used in Christian worship and fellowship, and in turn passed them on to the communities which he founded.

3. Pre-Pauline formulae: creeds, poems, hymns

Somewhat more debated and uncertain are what some scholars call 'pre-Pauline formulae' in the Pauline letters. This term refers to phrases, statements of faith, poems or hymns, and so on, which may have originated with Paul's predecessors, been adopted by Paul and later woven into one of his letters. What may indicate the presence of one of these pre-Pauline traditions is the use of language or terminology otherwise unusual in Paul, concise or rhythmic phrases which suggest a regular and established form, content which goes beyond what is specifically relevant to the matter in hand in the letter, and literary indicators suggesting that a short section stands out from its context.

One example of such a formula may be found in Rom 1.3-4, which describes the 'gospel of God' (v.1): 'concerning his Son, who was born from the seed of David according to the flesh, and was declared to be Son of God in power according to the Spirit of holiness by resurrection from the dead, Jesus Christ our Lord' (Rom 1.3-4; DGH). Not only do these verses contain a concise and balanced confession of Christian faith, but they also contain phrases which are highly unusual for Paul ('seed of David' occurs elsewhere only in 2 Tim 2.8, 'Spirit of holiness' is found nowhere else in the Pauline letters). Moreover, they may represent an early 'adoptionist' Christology – the view that Jesus, the faithful and obedient human servant of God who was crucified, was appointed, or became, Messiah when God raised him from the dead and thus 'adopted' Jesus as his Son (cf. Acts 2.36). This is, however, debated, and depends largely on the translation of the Greek verb *horizō*, which may mean to 'appoint', 'declare', or 'designate' (it is translated above 'declared to be'). Indeed, whether these verses are a pre-Pauline formulation or not is also debated, with some arguing that they are simply Paul's own introductory composition, leading into the major themes of the letter. Another example in Romans, with similar debates for similar reasons, is Rom 3.24–25, while important passages in other letters include the so-called Christological hymns in Phil 2.5–11 (which we shall consider below, pp. 89–90) and Col 1.15–20. Another well-known instance is the baptismal teaching found in Gal 3.26–29:

> For you are all sons of God, through faith, in Christ Jesus. For as many of you as were baptized into Christ have put on Christ. There is no longer Jew or Greek, no longer slave or free, no longer male and female; for you are all one in Christ Jesus. And if you are Christ's, then you are Abraham's seed, heirs according to the promise.
>
> (DGH)

Again there are good reasons for suggesting that this may be a traditional formulation learnt by Paul, perhaps at Antioch – might it even have been a declaration which was formulated by those first (Hellenist?) missionaries who arrived in Antioch and shared the gospel with non-Jews? The passage is marked off from its context by the change from 'we' forms, used by Paul before and after this section, to 'you' (plural) forms in these verses; the phrase 'no longer slave or free, no longer male and female' has no particular relevance to Paul's argument in Galatians (though 'no longer Jew or Greek' certainly does) and thus suggests the quotation of an already established creed. Furthermore, a very similar tradition appears in 1 Cor 12.13 and Col 3.11, showing at least that Paul used this tradition on more than one occasion (Colossians may have been written by a follower of Paul).

However, there are also reasons why some doubt that such 'pre-Pauline' formulae can really be identified as such. First, it is only by somewhat subjective judgements that we can claim that a passage does not represent Paul's own words but those he has received from others, not least because Paul's own vocabulary and phrasing vary so widely from letter to letter. Second, it is important to remember that Paul was converted only a few years after the crucifixion of Jesus, so the period of time in which there was a strictly *pre*-Pauline Christianity was very short. Paul was active as a Christian missionary for some years before he wrote his first letter, so even if Paul cites what seem to be established traditions in his letters, they may be 'traditions' that he himself has formulated, or at least had a hand in formulating. For this reason, some scholars are wary of identifying 'pre-Pauline' traditions in the Pauline letters.

Conclusion

In this chapter we have seen something of the earliest Church in Jerusalem, and how, through division and persecution, the gospel spread from Jerusalem and came to be shared with non-Jews. At some point in time, and in some places, the view developed that these Gentile converts did not have to become Jewish or adopt all the marks of Jewish identity (such as circumcision) in order to be members of this community of God's people, built on faith in Jesus as Messiah. It is important to note that this crucial development in early Christianity first took place independently of Paul, even if he was engaged in missionary activity on a similar basis during his 'unknown years' in Arabia and Damascus.

However, we have also seen that there is debate concerning this earliest period of Christian history. To some extent the debate hinges on using the evidence of Acts, our only source for this period: how much, if anything, can we reconstruct from the few hints Luke gives us in the opening chapters of Acts? Can we be confident that the Hebrews and Hellenists, as groups, held distinctive theological views? Can we see the Hellenists as both a theological and historical 'bridge' between Jesus and Paul? Or does this reconstruction build too much on too slender a foundation?

We have also briefly mentioned Paul's contact with the early Christian movement, both as persecutor and as convert and missionary. There is sufficient evidence, I think, to show that Paul learnt, in various ways and places, something of the teaching of Jesus, and to reveal something of the ways in which the gospel message was understood and expressed by other early Christians. However, determining the extent of 'pre-Pauline' influence in the letters of Paul is an uncertain and subjective exercise. Scholars differ as to which, if any, traditions they identify as pre-Pauline. Can we glimpse the theology and faith of pre-Pauline Christians in Paul's letters? Can we see the influence of the Antioch community? Whether or not it is possible to do this, I think it can be said that Paul owed a good deal to his predecessors. Furthermore, though it is often forgotten, throughout his missionary activity Paul worked with a wide circle of co-workers and fellow missionaries, some of whom are named as co-authors in some of the letters we tend to think of as Paul's alone (see 1 Cor 1.1; 2 Cor 1.1; Gal 1.2; Phil 1.1; 1 Thess 1.1; Phlmn 1). Although we shall be focusing almost entirely on Paul, his letters and his churches, in the chapters that follow, we do well to remember these many other characters – some almost completely forgotten, or never mentioned by name – who also played their part in the growth and spread of early Christianity.

Further reading

As well as the many commentaries on Acts, valuable introductions to Acts are provided by D. Juel, *Luke-Acts* (London: SCM, 1984), I.H. Marshall, *The Acts of the Apostles* (NT Guides; Sheffield: JSOT, 1992), and V.G. Shillington, *An Introduction to the Study of Luke-Acts* (London and New York: T&T Clark, 2007), which particularly sets out a range of approaches to reading and interpreting Luke-Acts. Supporting Luke's value as an ancient historian is M. Hengel, *Acts and the History of Earliest Christianity* (London: SCM, 1979). One may contrast the commentary by G. Lüdemann, *Early Christianity According to the Traditions in Acts* (London: SCM, 1989) which, while seeking to identify historical traditions in Acts, assigns a good deal to the editorial activity of Luke.

Hengel's detailed and influential essay on the Hellenists can be found in his book *Between Jesus and Paul: Studies in the History of Earliest Christianity* (London: SCM, 1983). For other arguments for seeing the Hellenists as a bridge between Jesus and Paul see A.J.M. Wedderburn, 'Paul and Jesus: Similarly and Continuity', in A.J.M. Wedderburn (ed.) *Paul and Jesus: Collected Essays* (Sheffield: JSOT, 1989), pp. 117–43. Criticisms of this dominant theory are mounted by C.C. Hill in his book *Hellenists and Hebrews: Reappraising Division within the Earliest Church* (Minneapolis: Fortress, 1992).

Valuable studies of the use of Jesus-tradition in Paul, along with the book edited by Wedderburn and listed above, are M.B. Thompson, *Clothed with Christ: The Example and Teaching of Jesus in Romans 12.1–15.13* (Sheffield: JSOT, 1991); D. Wenham, *Paul: Follower of Jesus or Founder of Christianity?* (Grand Rapids/Cambridge: Eerdmans, 1995) and the short introduction by V.P. Furnish, *Jesus According to Paul* (Cambridge: CUP, 1993). On Paul's indebtedness to his predecessors the old book by A.M. Hunter, *Paul and his Predecessors* (2nd edn, London: SCM, 1961) is still worth reading, though readers should be aware that the discussion has since moved on in various directions.

Questions for further study

* How do you weigh the evidence for or against the historical accuracy of the information about Paul contained in Acts? How far has Luke's theological agenda shaped or influenced his writing?

- How much can we know about the process by which Christianity spread from Jerusalem and to non-Jews? Do you find Hengel's theory about the Hellenists' role convincing?
- To what extent can we glimpse the influence of Paul's predecessors and collaborators in his letters? Do we tend to place too much emphasis on the single figure of Paul?

Notes

1 Quoted by G. Theissen, *Social Reality and the Early Christians* (Edinburgh: T&T Clark, 1993), p. 45.

2 See e.g. 'son of man': Mark 2.10, 28; 8.38, 9.31; 'kingdom of God': Mark 1.15; 4.11; 9.1. In the Pauline letters (including those which may be pseudonymous) 'kingdom of God' is found at Rom, 14.17; 1 Cor 4.20; 6.9–10; 15.50; Gal 5.21; Col 4.11; 2 Thess 1.5.

3 For places where Jesus comes closest to accepting and acknowledging the title see Mark 8.29–30; 9.41; 13.21; 14.61–62 (and parallels).

4 Cited by J.C. Beker, *The Triumph of God: The Essence of Paul's Thought* (Minneapolis: Fortress, 1990), p. 62.

5 A well-known proponent of this view is H. Maccoby, *The Mythmaker: Paul and the Invention of Christianity* (London: Weidenfeld & Nicolson, 1986); *Paul and Hellenism* (London: SCM, 1991).

6 A description accepted with approval by M. Hengel and A.M. Schwemer, *Paul Between Damascus and Antioch* (London: SCM, 1997), p. 309.

7 On this subject, see the companion volume in this series: C. Marsh and S. Moyise, *Jesus and the Gospels* (2nd edn, London & New York: T&T Clark, 2006). For a larger textbook on this subject, see G. Theissen and A. Merz, *The Historical Jesus: A Comprehensive Guide* (London: SCM, 1998).

8 E. Haenchen, *The Acts of the Apostles* (Oxford: Blackwell, 1971), p. 116. On 'Luke and Paul' see pp. 112–16.

9 J.A. Harrill, *Paul the Apostle: His Life and Legacy in their Roman Context* (Cambridge & New York: Cambridge University Press, 2012), pp. 97–98 and p. 8.

10 I.H. Marshall, *Luke: Historian and Theologian* (Exeter: Paternoster, 1970), p. 75. Cf. also I.H. Marshall, *The Acts of the Apostles* (New Testament

Guides, Sheffield: Sheffield Academic Press, 1992), pp. 83–99; R. Riesner, *Paul's Early Period: Chronology, Mission Strategy, Theology* (Grand Rapids/ Cambridge: Eerdmans, 1998), pp. 318–33.

11 M. Hengel, *Acts and the History of Earliest Christianity* (in *Earliest Christianity*, London: SCM, 1986), pp. 60–61.

12 Thucydides, *History of the Peloponnesian War* 1.22.1 (trans. C.F. Smith, Loeb Classical Library; London: Heinemann, 1928).

13 See M. Hengel, *Between Jesus and Paul* (London: SCM, 1983), pp. 1–29.

14 M. Hengel, *The Pre-Christian Paul* (London: SCM, 1991), p. 83.

15 Hengel, *The Pre-Christian Paul*, p. 82.

16 C.C. Hill, *Hellenists and Hebrews: Reappraising Division within the Earliest Church* (Minneapolis: Fortress, 1992).

17 See the criticisms in the lengthy review by P.F. Esler. 'Review of C.C. Hill, *Hellenists and Hebrews*', *Biblical Interpretation* 3 (1995), pp. 119–23.

18 Hengel and Schwemer suggest a date of c. 36/37 CE for the beginning of the Hellenists' mission in Antioch (*Paul Between Damascus and Antioch*, p. xi).

19 Riesner, *Paul's Early Period*, p. 72.

20 See M.B. Thompson, *Clothed with Christ: The Example and Teaching of Jesus in Romans 12.1–15.13* (Sheffield: JSOT, 1991), pp. 37–76.

3

Paul's Life: Before and After his Encounter with Christ

Introduction

Ask anyone what they know about Paul and, assuming they know which Paul you mean, their answer might include some of the following: came from Tarsus, changed his name from Saul to Paul, converted on the road to Damascus when he saw a blinding light, went on three missionary journeys, taken to Rome as a prisoner. All of these well-known 'facts' about Paul, however, are known to us only from Acts – though some of them can be confirmed to some degree by inference from Paul's letters. Just because Paul does not mention something that is recorded in Acts, does not of course mean that it is necessarily untrue! Nevertheless, there is obviously scope for questioning Luke's information, since it does not come 'from the horse's mouth'. We have already seen something of the diversity of scholarly opinion regarding Acts and its reliability, and this area of debate will feature again in this chapter.

The pre-Christian Paul

Paul tells us little about his life prior to his conversion, but he does give us some important information. He tells us of his identity as a Jew: 'of the people of Israel, of the tribe of Benjamin, a Hebrew of Hebrews' (Phil 3.5; cf. Rom 11.1; 2 Cor 11.22). More specifically, Paul informs us that he was a Pharisee (Phil 3.5), a member of a grouping within first-century Judaism which sought to practise holiness by careful adherence both to written *Torah* (the Jewish law) and to the traditions of its interpretation and application – what came to be known as the oral *Torah*. Paul's 'zeal' for God's law and for Israel's holiness was such that, by his own admission, he persecuted the Church (Phil 3.6; Gal 1.13, 23; 1 Cor 15.9). Paul was not a 'zealot' in the sense of belonging to the Zealot movement in Judea, a movement which involved armed rebellion against Roman rule. But his zeal for God did lead him to violent activity against the earliest Christians, whom he saw as a dangerous threat to the holiness of Israel.[1]

Luke corroborates the information Paul himself provides and also supplies further details. Only from Luke do we hear of Paul's Jewish name 'Saul' (Hebrew: *Sha'ul*; Greek: *Saoul/Saulos*). The popular notion that Paul changed his name from Saul to Paul on his conversion is not exactly an accurate reflection of Luke's usage. It is indeed the case that the name Saul appears mainly in the first half of Acts (up to 13.9) and elsewhere only when Paul's conversion story is retold (Acts 9.1–30; 22.3–21; 26.9–23), while 'Paul' appears consistently from 13.9 onwards. Acts 13.9 – 'Saul, also known as Paul' – seems to mark for Luke a point of transition to Paul's Gentile mission, whereafter he uses his Roman rather than Semitic name. Acts 13.9 also conveys the most likely picture concerning Paul's names: rather than *changing* his name at any point, he had two names, one Jewish and biblical, the other Latin/Roman, as was common among Jews of his time. One alternative suggestion is that he adopted the name 'Paulus' after receiving the support of the Roman proconsul Sergius Paulus, who, according to Luke, was converted by Paul and Barnabas in Cyprus (Acts 13.4–13).[2] Although Paul does not confirm it, then, Luke's information about his Jewish name is most likely to be correct.

Luke also tells us that Paul was originally from Tarsus (Acts 9.11; 21.39; 22.3) and this information is hardly ever doubted, though there is some debate as to whether Paul was a citizen both of Tarsus and of Rome, as Luke reports (Acts 21.39; 22.25–29). Paul himself never mentions the subject. Those who doubt that Paul was a Roman citizen and/or a citizen of Tarsus point not only to Paul's silence on the matter, but also to his having suffered punishments which were not supposed to be inflicted on Roman citizens (2 Cor 11.25; cf. Acts 22.25). Moreover, they argue that to accept Roman or Tarsan citizenship involved a level of involvement in civic religion which would have compromised the stance of loyal Jews and thus seems unlikely for Paul, given his own testimony about his zeal for his ancestral faith.[3] Others, however, maintain that these points can be answered and that on balance the evidence favours the conclusion that Paul was indeed a Roman and a Tarsan citizen.[4]

Luke informs us that Paul was educated in Jerusalem at the feet of the famous teacher Gamaliel (Acts 22.3). Although there is some debate as to when Paul went to Jerusalem – whether as a young child, an adolescent, or a young adult – few doubt that he did indeed receive education in that city (whether from Gamaliel or not), since Pharisaic training seems to have taken place only in Jerusalem. The longer Paul spent in Tarsus, the more influenced he would have been by that diaspora context, where, for example, it was the Greek translation of the Jewish scriptures (the Septuagint, or LXX) that was used in the synagogue. However, in the light of Martin Hengel's work, it is no longer possible to maintain any sharp distinction between a supposedly 'Hellenized' diaspora Judaism and a non-Hellenized Judaism in Palestine: Hellenistic culture and language had influenced the whole region.[5]

Neither Paul nor Luke tells us explicitly whether or not Paul had been married. It is clear that he was 'unattached' when he wrote his letters (1 Cor 7.7–8; 9.5) but whether he was widowed, divorced or had always remained single is uncertain. On the basis of Jewish texts showing marriage as the norm at a relatively young age (eighteen to twenty for men) and as a requirement for those ordained to the rabbinate, some have argued that Paul is most likely to have married young.[6] Some of the evidence is rather too late to be convincing in the case of Paul, but it is nonetheless quite likely that he had been married. Certainty, however, is impossible.

Paul's call/conversion and its effect

The most memorable and well-known accounts of Paul's conversion are recorded by Luke, who has Paul tell his story three times during the narrative of Acts (9.1–30; 22.3–21; 26.9–23). Paul's own references to this dramatic experience are much more concise and allusive. We cannot confirm from Paul's own testimony whether or not he actually heard the risen Jesus say to him 'Saul, Saul, why are you persecuting me?' (Acts 9.4). We do not know from Paul whether or not he was actually struck blind (Acts 9.8–9; though cf. Gal 4.15), nor does Paul ever mention Ananias (Acts 9.10–17). We do know from Paul, however, that he 'saw' the risen Jesus and that it was this revelation which was the foundation of his call to be an apostle of Christ to the Gentiles (1 Cor 9.1; 15.8; Gal 1.12–16). Paul also confirms that this experience took place near Damascus, as Luke more famously reports (Gal 1.17; cf. 2 Cor 11.32). An 'apostle' (Greek: *apostolos*) is someone who is sent as a messenger, though in the New Testament the word most often has a somewhat more specialized meaning, referring to a special circle of leaders in the earliest Church. Luke generally restricts this title to 'the twelve', only rarely applying it to Paul and Barnabas (Acts 14.14). Paul, however, insists that he is an apostle, on the basis of his having seen the risen Lord and having been commissioned by him to proclaim the gospel among the Gentiles (1 Cor 9.1–2; 15.8; Gal 1.1).

Paul's encounter with the risen Christ was no doubt a dramatic and life-changing experience, which led him completely to revalue everything he had previously thought and done (Phil 3.4–14). However, there has been some scholarly discussion about whether or not this experience can appropriately be labelled a 'conversion'. In an influential book published in 1976, Krister Stendahl argued that we should speak not of Paul's conversion, but rather of his 'call':

> Here is not that change of 'religion' that we commonly associate with the word *conversion*. Serving the one and the same God, Paul receives a new and special calling in God's service ... Rather than being 'converted', Paul was called to the specific task – made clear to

him by his experience of the risen Lord – of apostleship to the Gentiles ...[7]

Paul does indeed speak of God 'calling' him (Gal 1.15), and uses language highly reminiscent of the calling of Jeremiah and of the 'servant' of deutero-Isaiah (Jer 1.5; Isa 49.1–6; cf. Gal 1.15 16). In this sense Stendahl is right that Paul was not 'converted' at all, but rather commissioned to a new task by the God whom he had served all his life. Moreover, in terms of the change that takes place, this may be seen more as a shift within a Jewish matrix rather than a departure from it. As Albert Harrill puts it, 'Paul ... did not "convert" in the sense of changing from one religion to another, but rather moved from Pharisaic Judaism to join a rival Jewish sect that had already deeply engrossed his emotional and religious attention, albeit hostily'.[8]

However, the Jewish scholar Alan Segal, while finding much to commend in Stendahl's essay, nevertheless insists that 'Paul is a convert in the modern sense of the word ... Paul was both converted and called'. Segal continues:

> By using the term *conversion* I wish to stress the wrenching and decisive change of Paul's entrance to Christianity, thereby linking Paul with many modern accounts of conversion ... conversion does involve a radical change in a person's experience ... From the viewpoint of mission Paul is commissioned, but from the viewpoint of religious experience Paul is a convert.[9]

While his whole outlook and theological perspective remains profoundly Jewish (see further Chapters 5–6), Paul does also describe his life 'in Christ' as radically distinct from his former life 'in Judaism' (Gal 1.13; cf. Phil 3.5–8). Whatever we label it, Paul certainly saw his call/conversion, at least in retrospect, as the moment when he was commissioned by God to the task of being Apostle to the Gentiles (Gal 1.15–16; 2.7–8). But here there are grounds for further debate – as I have indicated with the cautious phrase 'at least in retrospect'. Did Paul, from the moment of his conversion, understand himself as commissioned to take the gospel to the Gentiles? And was his distinctive theology – his message of salvation through faith in Christ, apart from works of the law – formed straightaway as the consequence of this life-changing experience? Various views on this matter have been proposed.

Seyoon Kim, for example, has vigorously argued that Paul's conversion experience was the foundation for practically every aspect of his theology, including his 'law-free' gospel for the Gentiles.[10] Rainer Riesner suggests that Paul's first visit to Jerusalem, three years after his conversion, may have been the occasion for the beginning of his Gentile mission.[11] James Dunn argues that Paul's views on the justification of the Gentiles 'apart from the works of the law' were forged in the context of later conflict, notably at Antioch.[12] Francis Watson maintains that Paul at first engaged in a mission to Jews, only later turning to the Gentiles and dropping the demands of circumcision etc., so as to increase the success of the gospel.[13]

Each of these arguments draws on and interprets the evidence from Paul's letters in various ways. One of the factors which enables such a wide range of views to be maintained is that we have so little information about Paul's early missionary activity (see next section). The kinds of questions and judgements involved may be illustrated with a few examples from Paul's letters (though more evidence is involved in each of the arguments mentioned above, and each of the texts below is subject to various interpretations, as the commentaries will show):

> To the Jews I became as a Jew, in order to win Jews ... To those outside the law I became as one outside the law ... so that I might win those outside the law.
>
> (1 Cor 9.20–21)

> Why am I still being persecuted if I am still preaching circumcision?
>
> (Gal 5.11)

Do these texts imply an initial mission to Jews, or a mission which at first demanded from Gentile converts full adherence to Jewish law (circumcision etc.)?

> From Jerusalem and as far round as Illyricum I have fully
> proclaimed the good news of Christ.
>
> (Rom 15.19)

Does this text imply that Paul's evangelistic mission began in Jerusalem?

> We know that a person is justified not by the works of the law but
> through faith in Jesus Christ.
>
> (Gal 2.16)

Did Paul come to this realization at his conversion, when all his zeal to serve God seemed to have been in vain and when he was set right purely through the grace of God, or is it an argument which originated in Paul's attempt to defend the Gentiles' membership of the Christian community without their having to become Jewish? (See further Chapters 5 and 6).

Because of the lack of evidence it is difficult to say much for certain about the origins of Paul's gospel and the impact of his conversion experience. Even Paul may have seen things differently with the benefit of hindsight! However, it is clear that, by the time he wrote his letters, he was convinced of his call to be apostle to the Gentiles, his commission to take the good news of God's saving grace in Christ to all the nations. In the following section we shall look briefly at the progress of Paul's missionary career.

Paul's missionary career

Reconstructing the course of Paul's life as an apostle is complex and difficult, not least due to the lack of clear evidence, particularly from Paul himself. Here especially the problems involved in using Acts along with the epistles become obvious. There is clearly a sense in which Paul's letters form the primary data, though we should not make the mistake of simply assuming that the letters give us straightforward information; Paul is often involved in heated argument, and presumably says things in the way best suited to his argument.

Among those who have sought to reconstruct the chronology of Paul's missionary career there is considerable variation with regard to using the evidence of the letters and of Acts. Some, like Gerd Lüdemann, emphasize the value of the letters as primary data, and attempt to build their chronologies in the first place upon the evidence of the epistles alone.[14] Others, such as Rainer Riesner (often in criticism of Lüdemann) argue that Luke is generally a reliable source (he may, Riesner suggests, have been an eye-witness and sometime companion of Paul) and insist that the evidence of Acts is essential to the reconstruction of Paul's career.[15]

Decisions on the chronology of Paul's life are important for a number of reasons. Firstly, they are crucial in order for us to place Paul's letters into their original sequence and thus to consider, for example, whether there is any pattern of development, or any significant change, in Paul's theology over time. How much difference is there between Paul's earliest and his latest letter? Clearly, such a consideration requires a knowledge not only of the sequence of letters, but also of the length of the time gaps between them. Secondly, decisions on chronology are important in order to relate Paul's activity to important events narrated both in the letters and in Acts. For example, is the conference in Jerusalem described in Galatians 2 the same as that described in Acts 15 or not? Might the meeting described in Galatians actually have taken place during the visit to Jerusalem mentioned in Acts 11.29–30? If the same meeting is described in Galatians 2 and Acts 15, then it is possible to compare and contrast the different perceptions of that meeting recounted by Paul and by Luke. Deciding when the crucial meeting in Jerusalem did take place is also important for the interpretation of some of Paul's letters. Was the Apostolic Decree agreed at the meeting in Jerusalem (see Acts 15.20, 29) – if it was ever accepted by Paul – in force before Paul visited Corinth? Or was it formulated after Paul's first visit there, but before he wrote 1 Corinthians? In that case, as John Hurd has argued, the Apostolic Decree might be a decisive influence on the shape of Paul's instruction in 1 Corinthians.[16]

Two aspects of the reconstruction of Pauline chronology may be distinguished. Firstly there is what we may term the relative chronology, that is, the relative sequence of visits and letters. Secondly there is the absolute chronology, that is, the actual dates on which visits took place and letters were written. In both cases agreement on a number of significant points is currently lacking.

1. Relative chronology

As an illustration of some of the problems involved in using both Acts and the epistles to determine the course of Paul's activity, we may focus on his visits to Jerusalem. Paul's most important autobiographical narrative, at least for chronological purposes, is found in Gal 1.13–2.14. From that text, the following sequence emerges:

i.   activity as a persecutor of the Church
ii. call/conversion
iii. three years in Arabia and Damascus
iv. first visit to Jerusalem ('to get to know Peter')
v.   fourteen years (activity in 'the regions of Syria and Cilicia')
vi. second visit to Jerusalem (meeting about Paul's gospel for the Gentiles and whether circumcision is necessary for Gentile converts)
vii. disagreement at Antioch

Even here, we should note, there are some ambiguities: Paul's three years and fourteen years may be meant consecutively, i.e., a total period of seventeen years (although, to add further complication, that could be little more than fifteen years, if the period in question ran from the last month of the first year until the first month of the final year); or they might be meant concurrently, i.e., three years after his conversion, and fourteen years after his conversion. Furthermore, Lüdemann has argued that the incident at Antioch, despite its place in Paul's narrative, took place *before* the second visit to Jerusalem, though few have followed him in this.[17]

A further sequence may be derived from Paul's various references to the money he is raising for the poor in the Jerusalem church and his plans for the delivery of that money.

i.   Paul's agreement to 'remember the poor' (Gal 2.10 – assuming
     [note, since this is certainly open to serious question!] that this is
     a reference to the specific collection mentioned in the following
     references)[18]
ii. instruction to the Corinthians to set money aside for the
     collection (1 Cor 16.1–4)
iii. exhortation to the Corinthians to complete the task of getting the
     money ready (2 Cor 8–9)
iv. Paul's preparations to deliver the money to Jerusalem (Rom
     15.25–28)

These references to the collection enable a relative ordering of Paul's
Corinthian and Roman letters. They also indicate Paul's plans for a third
visit to Jerusalem, to deliver the money, though we do not know from
Paul's letters whether or not that journey was made.

Putting the two sequences together, we find that Paul mentions three
visits to Jerusalem: firstly, to get to know Peter; secondly, for a discussion
with the Jerusalem church leaders; and thirdly, to deliver the collection.
It should be noted, however, that although Paul is insistent in Galatians
that he has at that point in time, since his 'conversion', paid only two
visits to Jerusalem (Gal 1.17, 20), it is not stated in Romans that his
planned collection visit is only his third visit. In other words, it is
possible that other visits to Jerusalem were made between the writing
of Galatians and Romans, though some argue that 'three visits only' is
the most reasonable interpretation of Paul's statements.[19]

Acts mentions five visits of Paul to Jerusalem:

i.   some time relatively soon after his conversion (Acts 9.26–30)
ii. to deliver relief aid sent from Antioch to Jerusalem
     (Acts 11.29–30; 12.25[20])
iii. for a meeting to discuss the extent to which it is necessary for
     Gentile converts to obey Jewish law (circumcision etc.)
     (Acts 15.1–29)
iv. to greet the church in Jerusalem (Jerusalem is not named in the
     Greek text, but all agree that this is the implication here) (Acts 18.22)

v. the final visit to Jerusalem (note the reference to bringing 'alms' in 24.17), followed by arrest and transport under guard to Rome (Acts 21.15ff)

The problem, then, is how to correlate the visits mentioned by Paul with those listed in Acts. Here scholars diverge widely in their solutions. Some, especially those concerned to defend the historicity and reliability of Acts, solve the problem by equating the second visit mentioned by Paul in Gal 2.1ff. with the visit recorded in Acts 11.29–30.[21] One implication of this view is a relatively early date for Galatians (one can see how the chronological issues start to interrelate ...). Since Paul declares only in Galatians that he has made just two visits to Jerusalem, visits mentioned in Acts that are *subsequent* to the writing of Galatians are not a problem – as long as they can be fitted in with the overall picture of Paul's travels and the time necessary for such travel. However, Robert Jewett argues that this 'solution' does not allow sufficient time for the activities of Paul we know about to take place *prior* to Galatians and the second meeting in Jerusalem.[22]

Others therefore favour a more radical solution. Jewett follows John Knox in his influential proposal for a three-visit framework (thus giving priority to the evidence of the epistles over that of Acts). Knox noted how the three 'reasons' given by Paul for visits to Jerusalem were also found in Acts[23]:

'acquaintance'	Gal 1.18	Acts 9.26–27
'conference'	Gal 2.1–10	Acts 15.1–29
'offering'	Rom 15.25–28	Acts 11.29–30 (cf. 24.17)

But Knox argued that Luke had reordered the chronology of these visits to Jerusalem. The visit for the purpose of discussing the mission to the Gentiles actually took place, Knox proposed, at the time of the visit mentioned (but with no reason or activity given) in Acts 18.22, and the visit to deliver aid (Acts 11.29–30) is actually a misplaced reference to what took place during the final visit mentioned in Acts 21.15ff. Thus the evidence of the epistles and of Acts could be correlated in the following way, reducing the five visits mentioned in Acts to the three found in the epistles:

'acquaintance'	Gal 1.18	Acts 9.26–27
'conference'	Gal 2.1–10	time = Acts 18.22
		description = Acts 15.1–29
'offering'	Rom 15.25–28	time = Acts 21.17ff
		description = Acts 11.29–30

Whether or not either of these solutions works is not to be decided here, though I think there is a good deal to be said for Knox's three-visit framework; the purpose has been to illustrate the issues and the complexity involved. Paul's letters provide only minimal information about the course of his missionary activity and the writing of his letters; Acts provides rather more information, but assessing how reliable it is and correlating it with the information in the letters is difficult. Most scholars – even those who give the letters clear priority – agree that Acts cannot simply be dismissed out of hand. But beyond that, agreement on the details of Paul's activity is elusive.

2. Absolute chronology

Correlating the sequence of Paul's travels and letters with external historical dates is even more difficult and uncertain than ascertaining their relative order. There are not many pieces of externally-relatable evidence, and most of them are in Acts. The three most important are as follows:

(i) Paul's escape from Damascus (2 Cor 11.32–33)

Practically the only information Paul gives in his letters that might allow us to correlate his activities with a historical date is found in the account of his escape from Damascus, where he refers to the 'governor of King Aretas'. While some (e.g., Lüdemann) do not regard this reference as supplying a secure chronological datum, others maintain that it can provide a solid date (e.g., Jewett). Basically the matter hinges on the dates of the reign of King Aretas IV (an Arabian king, ruler over the Nabateans from 9 BCE to 38–40 CE, when he died) and more specifically on the date when the Nabateans acquired control over Damascus (Jewett argues for c. 37 CE). If these dates are secure then Paul's escape from Damascus can be dated to around 37–39 CE.[24]

(ii) *The edict of Claudius (Acts 18.2)*

Luke mentions an edict of the emperor Claudius compelling Jews to leave Rome and thus gives the reason why Priscilla and Aquila have come to Corinth. This edict is also mentioned by the Roman historian Suetonius (*Claudius* 25) and is dated by the fifth-century Church historian Orosius to 49 CE. Thus Paul's arrival in Corinth appears to be datable to some time shortly after this date, around 49–50 CE (see also (iii) below). However, this date has also been challenged by Lüdemann, who argues that Orosius' date is inaccurate, and that other earlier evidence (notably from Dio Cassius) suggests that the edict was issued in 41 CE.[25] If Lüdemann is right, then Paul's arrival in Corinth may – but *need* not – be dated to the early 40s. A decision on this matter affects not only the dating of Paul's arrival in Corinth, but also the dating of 1 Thessalonians, generally agreed to have been written from Corinth during Paul's first visit there. Most scholars date 1 Thessalonians to around 50–51 CE; but if Lüdemann is correct, it may have been written up to ten years earlier.

(iii) *The proconsulship of Gallio (Acts 18.12)*

Luke also reports that Paul was publicly accused by Jews in Corinth during the time when Gallio was proconsul of Achaia (the Roman province in which Corinth was located). Fragments of an inscription found at Delphi mention Gallio as proconsul of the province and enable his proconsulship to be dated to 50–51 or 51–52 CE (probably the latter).[26] On the traditional dating of Claudius' edict this fits in rather well with Luke's description of Paul's eighteen-month stay in Corinth (Acts 18.1–18). Paul would have arrived shortly after the edict – say, around 50 CE – and left during Gallio's proconsulship, sometime, probably, in 51–52. Lüdemann, as we have already seen, argues for a different reconstruction. He proposes that in Acts 18 Luke has woven together accounts of *two* visits of Paul to Corinth (the other of which is hinted at in Acts 20.2). According to Lüdemann, Paul's *first* visit took place soon after the edict in 41 CE, the second took place when Gallio was proconsul, in 51–52.[27]

Even with these externally-verifiable dates, then, there is no consensus as to how exactly they fit with the details of Paul's life. That is not to say that there is no agreement at all, but that detailed reconstructions of Pauline chronology vary considerably. The following broad-brush sketch presents the general picture, important for appreciating the range of Paul's activity, but is subject to debate over many points of detail and order.

3. A sketch of Paul's Christian career

No one doubts that Paul's conversion took place after the crucifixion of Jesus, the exact date of which is however disputed. The suggested dates range between 26–36 CE, with 30 or 33 as probably the most likely. Paul's conversion took place shortly after this, though again various dates have been proposed. Somewhere around the year 33 is probably not too far from the truth. Paul himself tells us that he spent the three years after his conversion in Arabia and Damascus, so if his escape from Damascus can be dated to 37 CE, that would put his conversion in 33/34. Unfortunately, Paul does not tell us what he did during those first three years as a follower of Christ. Some argue that he was already engaged in spreading the gospel – why else, they argue, would he have attracted the criticism of the governing authorities in Damascus? – whereas others support the idea of a 'reclusive' period. We know from Paul that after this three-year period he went up to Jerusalem and spent fifteen days with Peter, and also met James the brother of Jesus (Gal 1.18). Then, Paul tells us, he spent time in Syria and Cilicia (Gal 1.21), presumably engaged in missionary activity, about which only Acts gives details. Hints in the letters seem to confirm, and certainly do not contradict,

Luke's picture here: soon after his first visit to Jerusalem as a Christian convert Paul joined the church at Antioch (in Syria) and acted as a missionary alongside Barnabas, or possibly as a junior partner to Barnabas (see Acts 11.26–15.40; cf. Gal 2 1, 9, 11–13; 1 Cor 9.6). Barnabas and Paul travelled together, commissioned by their church community in Antioch. This was Paul's so-called 'first missionary journey' – though it should be stressed that the organization of Paul's activities and travels into three missionary journeys is a construction that owes much more to Acts than to the information in Paul's letters.

From about 46 CE, on Robert Jewett and Jerome Murphy-O'Connor's reckoning, Paul began an extensive independent journey (the so-called 'second missionary journey') which took him through Galatia, Macedonia and Achaia, where he founded churches (see map on p. 52).[28] Not all would agree with this dating: as we have seen, integrating the evidence of the letters and Acts, and relating both to absolute dates, has been done in various ways. Lüdemann places Paul's mission to Corinth (in Achaia) significantly earlier; others place it later, after the apostolic conference, thus retaining the order in Acts, where the mission to Corinth (Acts 18) comes after the conference described in Acts 15.

Fourteen years after his first visit to Jerusalem (or, possibly, fourteen years after his conversion) Paul returned there again, this time for the 'conference' – sometimes referred to as the first Apostolic Council – called to discuss the issue of Gentile converts and the requirements to be placed upon them (see above; Gal 2.1–10). Jewett and Murphy-O'Connor date the conference to 51 CE; some place it somewhat earlier (this depends, of course, on when Paul's conversion is dated, and how the periods of three and fourteen years are reckoned). After this conference Paul undertook another extensive tour, his so-called 'third missionary journey', returning first to Antioch (Gal 2.11–14), then moving on to Ephesus (1 Cor 16.8), Macedonia (2 Cor 1.16; 2.13), Illyricum (cf. Rom 15.19) and Corinth (2 Cor 13.1; Rom 15.26), finally preparing once more to return to Jerusalem, with the proceeds of his long-standing collection project – money raised from the Pauline congregations for the 'poor among the saints in Jerusalem' (Rom 15.25–26).[29] It is from

Figure 1 Significant places in the activity and travels of Paul

this period of missionary activity that almost all of Paul's letters come. The exceptions are Paul's earliest letter, 1 Thessalonians, widely agreed to have been written from Corinth during Paul's founding visit there (prior to the Apostolic Council?), and possibly Philippians and Philemon, which may have been written during Paul's Roman imprisonment (see below p. 65).[30]

We do not know from Paul whether or not he actually made that planned visit to Jerusalem to deliver his collection. It is only from Acts that we hear of his final visit there, although Luke is strangely quiet about the collection into which Paul invested so much time and energy (see only Acts 24.17; cf. 24.26; 11.27–30). Various explanations for this have been put forward: perhaps the collection was refused by the Jerusalem church, which was suspicious and critical of Paul's 'law-free' Gentile mission; perhaps it was an insubstantial amount of money.[31] Only from Acts do we learn of Paul's arrest in Jerusalem and his subsequent transfer to Rome, to face trial there (Acts 21.17ff.), though most accept the validity of Luke's account concerning these key points. What finally became of Paul is not recounted, either in Acts or in Paul's authentic letters. Acts ends its story with Paul under house arrest in Rome, free to proclaim the gospel there (Acts 28.16–31). Whether he was released for a time and made his hoped-for visit to Spain (Rom 15.24) is possible but seems unlikely, for there is no direct evidence of such a visit – unless we count the reference in the early Christian epistle, *1 Clement* (c. 96 CE), to Paul as a herald of the gospel in both the east *and west (1 Clement* 5.6–7). If the Pastoral Epistles (1–2 Timothy, Titus) are authentic, then they probably indicate a further period of missionary activity, after the accounts of Acts, since they do not fit into the itinerary known from Luke (and from Paul's other letters). A large majority of scholars, however, regard these epistles as pseudonymous (see above p. 8 and below pp. 191–94). In 2 Timothy in particular, Paul – or the later author writing in his name – speaks of being at the point of death, about to be sacrificed (2 Tim 4.6–8). Such references, written perhaps with the benefit of hindsight, support what early Church tradition records as the fate of Paul: he and Peter were executed in Rome under the emperor Nero, sometime in the 60s CE (*1 Clement* 5.2–7; Eusebius, *Ecclesiastical History* 2.25.5).

Whatever the details of Paul's travels and their dates – and the conventional picture of Paul's 'three missionary journeys' is, as John Knox has pointed out, based upon the evidence of Acts much more than on that of the epistles[32] – Paul travelled many thousands of miles, enduring all the dangers of travel: shipwreck, robbery, lack of sleep, hunger and thirst, not to mention punishments by both Roman and Jewish authorities (2 Cor 11.24–29). He did so because he believed he had a crucial role to play – and one he was divinely compelled to play (1 Cor 9.16–17) – in making the gospel known among the Gentiles (Rom 15.18–24), so fulfilling his part in the divinely orchestrated drama which was reaching its final culmination. And his claim, somewhat exaggerated perhaps, was that he had worked harder than any of the other apostles in doing this (1 Cor 15.10). In Chapter 5 we shall examine in depth these theological convictions that drove Paul onwards in his work, and consider how scholars have sought to understand and interpret them.

Conclusion

We can reconstruct from Paul's letters a broad but incomplete outline of his activity before and after his call/conversion. Luke's information is also important, though as we have seen there are great differences among scholars as to how to use the information in Acts and how reliable it is. A concern to defend Acts and to harmonize its evidence with that of Paul's letters sometimes reflects particular theological commitments and a concern to defend the accuracy of the Bible. Sometimes, perhaps, on the other hand, a radical persuasion inclines scholars to doubt Luke almost as a matter of course! However, serious and careful arguments are mounted on both sides, and it is widely agreed that the evidence of Acts cannot simply be dismissed. The task of reconstructing the course of Paul's missionary career is complex, and consensus on the details seems unlikely – though we should not lose sight of the extent to which a broad picture can be known. Chronology can have important implications for our understanding of Paul's letters, of their relationship to one another and to various periods in Paul's life. It is to those letters that we turn in the following chapter.

Further reading

The best study of Paul's pre-Christian life is M. Hengel's book, *The Pre-Christian Paul* (London: SCM, 1991). Hengel followed this book with a massive co-authored study of Paul's early period, *Paul Between Damascus and Antioch* (M. Hengel and A.M. Schwemer, London: SCM, 1997). Hengel's defence of the historical value of Acts is a prominent theme throughout.

On Paul's call/conversion, see the studies of K. Stendahl, *Paul Among Jews and Gentiles* (Philadelphia: Fortress, 1976), esp. pp. 7–23; A.F. Segal, *Paul the Convert* (New Haven and London: Yale University Press, 1990); B.R. Gaventa, *From Darkness to Light: Aspects of Conversion in the New Testament* (Philadelphia: Fortress, 1986), esp. pp. 17–51; and S.J. Chester, *Conversion at Corinth* (London: T&T Clark, 2003), esp. pp. 149–204. For an overview of the debate, see L.W. Hurtado, 'Convert, Apostate, or Apostle to the Nations: the "Conversion" of Paul in Recent Scholarship', *Studies in Religion/Sciences Religieuses* 22 (1993), pp. 273–84.

Among many studies of Pauline chronology, J. Knox's short book, *Chapters in a Life of Paul* (first published in 1950, revised edition London: SCM, 1989) provides a reasonably accessible way into the issues, offering one particular solution to the problem of reconciling Acts with the evidence of the letters. Other important subsequent studies include R. Jewett, *Dating Paul's Life* (London: SCM, 1979) and G. Lüdemann, *Paul, Apostle to the Gentiles: Studies in Chronology* (London: SCM, 1984), both of which, in different ways, prioritize the evidence from the letters. R. Riesner, *Paul's Early Period* (Grand Rapids/Cambridge: Eerdmans, 1998) defends Luke's accuracy (often in criticism of Lüdemann) and uses the evidence of Acts along with that from the epistles.

For a stimulating biography of Paul see J. Murphy-O'Connor's *Paul: A Critical Life* (Oxford: OUP, 1996), and also his *Paul: His Story* (Oxford: OUP, 2004). Also valuable is the volume in a series on personalities of the New Testament by C.J. Roetzel, *Paul: The Man and the Myth* (Columbia: University of South Carolina Press, 1998).

Questions for further study

- Is it better to speak of Paul as having been 'called' or 'converted'? How do we best assess both the continuity and change between the 'pre-Christian' and the 'Christian' Paul?
- Do you think Knox's 'three-visit framework' provides a convincing way to align the evidence of Acts with that of Paul's letters?
- What is your assessment of Lüdemann's argument for the early dating of Paul's first visit to Corinth and of 1 Thessalonians? What are the implications of a decision on this matter?

Notes

1   See further Hengel, *The Pre-Christian Paul*, pp. 63–86; Wright, *What Saint Paul Really Said*, pp. 25–37.

2   S. Mitchell, *Anatolia: Land, Men, and Gods in Asia Minor. Vol. II: The Rise of the Church* (Oxford: Clarendon Press, 1993), p. 7. Mitchell suggests that the reason Paul then travelled on to Pisidian Antioch is because this was Sergius Paulus' homeland, and he provided Paul 'with letters of introduction to aid his passage and his stay' (p. 7). It should be noted, however, that these details of Paul's travel itinerary and personal contacts are only recorded in Acts, so one may doubt whether they are historically accurate.

3   See the various points presented by C.J. Roetzel, *Paul: The Man and the Myth* (Columbia: University of South Carolina Press, 1998), pp. 19–22.

4   See for example Riesner, *Paul's Early Period*, pp. 147–56.

5   M. Hengel, *Judaism and Hellenism* (2 vols, London: SCM, 1974); *The 'Hellenization' of Judaea in the First Century after Christ* (London: SCM, 1989).

6   J. Murphy-O'Connor, *Paul: A Critical Life* (Oxford: OUP, 1996), pp. 62–65.

7   K. Stendahl, *Paul Among Jews and Gentiles* (Philadelphia: Fortress, 1976), p. 7; see further pp. 7–23.

8   Harrill, *Paul the Apostle*, p. 35.

9   A.F. Segal, *Paul the Convert* (New Haven and London: Yale University Press, 1990), p. 6. For an overview of the considerable discussion on this subject, see L.W. Hurtado, 'Convert, Apostate, or Apostle to the Nations: the "Conversion" of Paul in Recent Scholarship', *Studies in Religion/Sciences Religieuses* 22 (1993), pp. 273–84.

10 S. Kim, *The Origin of Paul's Gospel* (Grand Rapids: Eerdmans, 1982), pp. 56–66, 269–311 etc. Kim responds to criticism of his work in *Paul and the New Perspective* (Grand Rapids: Eerdmans, 2002).

11 Riesner, *Paul's Early Period*, pp. 263–64.

12 J.D.G. Dunn, *Jesus, Paul and the Law* (London: SPCK, 1990) pp. 129–82.

13 F. Watson, *Paul, Judaism and the Gentiles* (Cambridge: CUP, 1986) pp. 28–38, heavily revised in the new edition (Grand Rapids, MI: Eerdmans, 2007), pp. 69–86.

14 G. Lüdemann, *Paul, Apostle to the Gentiles: Studies in Chronology* (London: SCM, 1984).

15 Riesner, *Paul's Early Period*.

16 J.C. Hurd, *The Origin of 1 Corinthians* (London: SPCK, 1965).

17 Lüdemann, *Paul, Apostle to the Gentiles*, pp. 75–77.

18 Scholars have long assumed that this text does refer to the collection, though this has been questioned by F.K.T. Clarke, 'God's Concern for the Poor in the New Testament. A Discussion of the Role of the Poor in the Foundation of Christian Belief (Early to Mid First Century CE)' (PhD thesis, University of Exeter, 2000), pp. 188–93 and B.W. Longenecker, *Remember the Poor: Paul, Poverty, and the Greco-Roman World* (Grand Rapids: Eerdmans, 2010), pp. 157–219.

19 See J. Knox, *Chapters in a Life of Paul* (revised edn, London: SCM, 1989), pp. 35–36.

20 There are text-critical and other problems affecting the interpretation of 12.25, which, in the NRSV's translation, looks like another visit of Paul and Barnabas to Jerusalem. Most commentators agree, however, that it must refer to their return to Antioch after completing their work in Jerusalem. See, e.g., C.K. Barrett, *A Critical and Exegetical Commentary on the Acts of the Apostles* (Vol. 1, Edinburgh: T&T Clark, 1994), pp. 595–96. Haenchen translates: 'And Barnabas and Saul returned, when they had fulfilled their relief mission in Jerusalem, taking with them John whose surname was Mark' (Haenchen, *The Acts of the Apostles*, p. 381).

21 E.g. Witherington, *The Paul Quest,* pp. 314–18, 328; I.H. Marshall, *Acts* (Leicester: IVP, 1980), pp. 204–205.

22 R. Jewett, *Dating Paul's Life* (London: SCM, 1979) pp. 69–75, 86.

23 See Knox, *Chapters in a Life of Paul,* pp. 34–35, 43–52.

24 See Jewett, *Dating Paul's Life,* pp. 30–33.

25 Lüdemann, *Paul, Apostle to the Gentiles,* pp. 164–70.

26 See J. Murphy-O'Connor, *St Paul's Corinth: Texts and Archaeology* (Wilmington, Delaware: Michael Glazier, 1983), pp. 141–52, 173–76; *Paul: A Critical Life,* pp. 15–22.

27 Lüdemann, *Paul, Apostle to the Gentiles,* pp. 157–77, 262–63.

28 Jewett, *Dating Paul's Life,* p. 164; Murphy-O'Connor, *Paul: A Critical Life,* pp. 24–28.

29 For the details of this itinerary see Murphy-O'Connor, *Paul: A Critical Life,* pp. 24–31; Jewett, *Dating Paul's Life,* pp. 162–65.

30 Philippians (if it is a single letter – and that is debated) was certainly written from prison (see Phil 1.7, 13–17), as was Philemon (see Phlmn 1, 9–13, 23), but where is less certain. Rome, Ephesus and Caesarea have all been suggested as possibilities. While Rome seems a likely location for the writing of Philippians, Philemon was more likely written from a prison in Ephesus, somewhat earlier. The commentaries on Philippians and Philemon discuss these issues.

31 On Paul's collection see D.G. Horrell, *Solidarity and Difference: A Contemporary Reading of Paul's Ethics* (London & New York: T&T Clark, 2005), pp. 231–41, and other literature mentioned there. Major works on the collection include K.F. Nickle, *The Collection* (London: SCM, 1966), D. Georgi *Remembering the Poor* (Nashville: Abingdon, 1992), S. Joubert, *Paul*

as *Benefactor: Reciprocity, Strategy and Theological Reflection in Paul's Collection* (Tübingen: Mohr Siebeck, 2000); D.J. Downs, *The Offering of the Gentiles: Paul's Collection for Jerusalem in its Chronological, Cultural, and Cultic Contexts* (Tübingen: Mohr Siebeck, 2008).

32 Knox, *Chapters in a Life of Paul*, pp. 25–26.

4

Paul the Letter-Writer

Introduction

Paul is known to us primarily through the letters that he wrote; it is these weighty theological texts that are responsible for his enduring influence within the Church. In his lifetime Paul and his co-workers must have been successful missionaries before they were letter-writers, for they founded a number of Christian communities which were later recipients of Paul's letters. Even while Paul was alive, however, at least one of his opponents suggested that his letters were much more powerful and impressive than his personal presence (2 Cor 10.10).

One thing that should be clear even to a casual reader of Paul's letters is that they are enormously varied. Because Paul deals with particular problems and issues facing particular communities, and because the situations he addresses vary greatly, the content of each of his letters is distinctive. Certainly there are themes, convictions, ideas, phrases, and so on which appear in more than one letter, but the unique character of each letter should be appreciated. For this reason, some scholars are wary of 'overall' discussions of Paul's theology or gospel, wary of an over-hasty harmonizing of the varied letters into an amalgamated whole. A group studying the theology of the Pauline epistles under the auspices of the USA-based Society of Biblical Literature, for example, published a series of studies of Pauline theology focusing on particular letters in turn, seeking to highlight the distinctive contribution and characteristics of each before moving towards any overall synthesis.[1]

Since the following chapters all examine various areas in the study of Paul, and draw evidence from all of his letters, it is important that we gain some appreciation of the distinctive character of each individual letter. In this chapter we shall also consider some of the methods used in recent years to study the individual letters and to highlight their structure and argument, particularly the methods which come under the heading of 'rhetorical criticism'.

The letters and their circumstances

1. 1 Thessalonians

It is widely agreed that 1 Thessalonians is Paul's earliest letter, written to the Christians in Thessalonica from Corinth, during Paul's mission to found the church there. Its date could be anywhere between 41 CE (Lüdemann) and 50–51 CE (the more commonly accepted date). One of the striking things about 1 Thessalonians is that some of what are often thought to be Paul's central themes (see Chapter 5) – being made righteous, or 'justified', through faith in Christ and not through the works of the law, for example – do not feature in 1 Thessalonians at all. It is a letter apparently free of anger, or criticism of the Thessalonians. (2 Thessalonians, often taken to be inauthentic, is discussed in Chapter 8, p. 184). Paul and his co-authors, Silvanus and Timothy, recall their exemplary conduct whilst with the Thessalonians, give thanks for the Thessalonians' response to the gospel, and mention their hope to revisit Thessalonica. The Thessalonian converts are urged to live holy lives and to love one another, just as they are already doing. The specific issue about which Paul gives detailed teaching concerns the return of the Lord and the fate of those who have died before this expected '*parousia*' (the Greek word meaning 'arrival' or 'coming'). Paul's assurance to the Thessalonians that those who have died are not lost seems to be a response to their worries about this very matter (1 Thess 4.13–18). Were they surprised and troubled when some of their number died before the Lord had returned? Had Paul's gospel led them to expect only a very short wait before this great and final event? Note how in 1.10 Paul speaks of their response to the gospel as 'waiting for God's Son from heaven'. Paul reminds them that the 'day of the Lord' will come suddenly, 'like a thief in the night' (5.2), and that no one knows the time; therefore they must be ready!

2. Galatians

In stark contrast to 1 Thessalonians, Galatians is a letter in which Paul's anger is obvious. Here there is no opening 'thanksgiving', as is usual in Paul's letters; instead Paul expresses his astonishment that the Galatians are so quickly turning to 'another gospel' (Gal 1.6) and curses those who proclaim this other gospel (1.8–9). This is strong language indeed! Scholars disagree about whether Galatians is relatively early or late in the sequence of Pauline letters, a disagreement linked in part with debate as to whether the 'Galatians' Paul addresses are in the southern part of the Roman province of Galatia (thus in that sense 'Galatians', but not the people traditionally known as Galatians; see map on p. 52) or in the more northern parts (where the people's tribal/ethnic origin was known as Galatian). What is clear is that the Galatian converts, having heard and accepted Paul's gospel, have since been informed that this gospel is really incomplete. Missionaries announcing a more 'Jewish' version of the gospel have told them that if they truly want to be children of Abraham, to belong to God's people, then they must obey the law set out in scripture and be circumcised (Gal 5.2). Paul is vehemently opposed to such a message, and deeply angered and distressed by his converts' attraction to it. He recounts the story of previous occasions when this issue was discussed and when he stood up for the gospel as he sees it, and he urges the Galatians not to nullify their faith in Christ by submitting to the demands of the law. This is not to say, however, that they should be lawless – their Christian freedom does not imply the freedom to be immoral – but they live in the Spirit and not under law (5.13–18). (We should note here that Paul's post-conversion view of the Jewish law is the subject of considerable debate and is discussed in Chapter 6.)

3. 1–2 Corinthians

The two letters in the New Testament addressed to the Corinthians are clearly only part of a more extensive correspondence between Paul and the church in Corinth. In 1 Corinthians Paul refers both to an earlier letter he had sent (1 Cor 5.9, a letter now almost certainly lost) and to a letter he has received from the Corinthians (7.1). In 2 Corinthians Paul refers to a letter written 'with tears', in much distress and anguish (2 Cor 2.4), which he wrote prior to writing 2 Corinthians 2 and 7. Paul also visited Corinth at least three times: once when he founded the church there, once on a painful visit (2 Cor 2.1), and again when the collection was ready to be taken to Jerusalem (2 Cor 8–9; Rom 15.25–26).

The letter known to us as 1 Corinthians deals with a number of issues that have come to Paul's attention, some through oral reports (see 1 Cor 1.11; 5.1; 11.18) and some from the Corinthians' letter to Paul (7.1). Paul's first concern is with the divisions among the community in Corinth (1.10ff.), though he goes on to deal with a whole range of issues, some of which may be connected with these divisions: sexual immorality, taking disputes to court, marriage and divorce, food that has been offered to idols, the appearance of women and men at worship, the Lord's Supper, the use of spiritual gifts in worship, the resurrection, the collection for Jerusalem, and future visits by Timothy and Apollos.

After the writing of 1 Corinthians relations between Paul and the Corinthians worsened. Apparently Paul paid a second visit to Corinth which turned out to be somewhat disastrous (2 Cor 1.23–2.11): it seems most likely that he was confronted by a particular opponent, probably a prominent member of the church at Corinth (though possibly an outsider or missionary from elsewhere), and withdrew, probably to Ephesus. Paul then wrote his 'painful letter' to Corinth, a letter which may be lost, or which may be largely identical with 2 Corinthians 10–13. That statement implies, of course, that 2 Corinthians may contain what was originally more than one letter. Indeed, while so-called 'partition' theories have been proposed for a number of Paul's letters, including 1 Corinthians and Philippians, 2 Corinthians is the Pauline letter whose unity is most often questioned, with various partition hypotheses competing for acceptance. Certainly, whether it was originally part of the same letter as 2 Corinthians 1–9, or came earlier or later, 2 Corinthians 10–13 is angry and confrontational, full of Paul's reluctant 'boasting', comparing himself with his opponents; 2 Corinthians 1–7, on the other hand, is dominated by Paul's thankfulness for an apparent reconciliation with the Corinthians and his bold comparisons of his own ministry with that of Moses (2 Cor 3). Chapters 8–9 deal with the collection for Jerusalem, and express Paul's hopes that the Corinthians' contribution will soon be ready. It may be that 2 Corinthians 10–13 originally came some time before 1–9 (i.e., as the painful letter), or that it was written later, due to fresh opposition to Paul arriving in Corinth. Whatever was the original order of events and letters, the letter to the Romans indicates that the Corinthians did get their money ready, and that Paul went there along with others to receive it and take it to Jerusalem (Rom 15.25–26).

4. Philemon and Philippians

At least two of Paul's letters were written from prison: Philemon and Philippians. The same situation is also apparent in Colossians and Ephesians, though there is considerable doubt as to whether these are genuinely letters from Paul's own hand (see pp. 8, 189–91). Where Philemon and Philippians fit into Paul's life depends on whether they were written from prison in Ephesus (thus around the time of the Corinthian letters), or from Caesarea or Rome (thus towards the end of Paul's life, and after all his other letters; see Acts 23.31ff.).

The letter to Philemon is a short and basically personal letter, appealing to Philemon, a householder and slave-owner, on behalf of one of his slaves called Onesimus, who had either run away or gone away temporarily to seek Paul's help in mediating a difficult relationship with his owner (cf. Phlmn 18). Paul had met Onesimus in prison, perhaps converted him, and would have liked to have kept him as a companion. But he sent him back to Philemon, perhaps bearing the letter. It is not entirely clear whether Paul wanted Philemon to manumit (i.e., set free) Onesimus or not, but it is certainly clear that he expected him to welcome him back without punishment and indeed as a beloved brother, to be received as if he were Paul himself (Phlmn 16–17). The letter to Philemon, being so short and lacking in explicit theology, has understandably been given little attention in studies of Paul's theology. However, as a personal window onto social relationships in the early churches, churches in an empire where slavery was an everyday reality, Philemon is a fascinating and valuable document. Its focus on the subject of slavery has also made it an important point of reference for writers grappling with more modern forms of slavery.

The impact of Paul's imprisonment is clear in Philippians, where Paul refers a number of times to his suffering and to the possibility of his death. However, Philippians is also a letter marked by the theme of rejoicing: Paul expresses his thanks to God for the Philippians' partnership with him in the gospel, a partnership expressed in practical as well as spiritual ways. He also rejoices that the gospel is being spread, even if not always from the best motives, and encourages the Philippians to rejoice too. He urges the Christians in Philippi to treat one another with selfless love, following the example of Christ, whose 'story' is told in the beautiful and famous poetic passage – often seen as a kind of early Christian 'hymn' – in Phil 2.5–11 (see below, pp. 89–90). Some argue that Philippians was originally two separate letters, mainly due to the abrupt change of tone and theme at 3.2, where Paul suddenly launches into a theme familiar from Galatians: an attack on those Jewish-Christian missionaries who preach circumcision. Paul's Jewish pedigree, he asserts, is all 'crap'[2] compared to knowing Christ (3.7–11) and he wants the Philippians also to stand firm in their commitment to Christ. After appealing to two prominent women in the congregation who have had a disagreement (4.2–3), Paul returns to the themes of rejoicing and thanksgiving to close the letter.

5. Romans

Paul's most influential letter is undoubtedly Romans, one of his last letters to be written and dating from around 55–58 CE. All of the letters, then, were probably written within a period of less than ten years (or perhaps around fifteen, if Lüdemann is right about an early date for 1 Thessalonians). Unlike Paul's other letters, Romans is addressed to a church Paul had not founded or previously visited. Moreover, Romans presents an extended and intricate theological argument which runs throughout the first eleven chapters and which forms the basis for the ethical instruction given from chapter 12 onwards. For centuries, Romans has been regarded as a systematic compendium of Paul's theology, or as his last will and testament, setting out the main elements of his gospel.[3] Today, however, there is widespread agreement that the argument of Romans reflects the particular circumstances of both Paul's life and the Roman churches.[4] Paul was preparing to go to Jerusalem with the collection for the Jerusalem church and wanted the support of the Roman churches in this venture (Rom 15.25–27). More significantly in terms of the letter, Paul's next plan was to undertake a mission to Spain which would involve stopping off in Rome and for which Paul would need the practical and spiritual support of the Roman Christians (Rom 15.24, 28). This meant that Paul needed to set out his gospel in a way that would commend him to the Roman Christians and at the same time counter any malicious rumours about him and his message (see Rom 3.8). It is also likely that Paul's letter was intended to confront particular problems in the churches at Rome, caused by tensions between Jewish and Gentile Christians, or, more specifically, between those (whether Jew or Gentile) who followed Jewish regulations concerning food, sabbath observance and so on, and those who did not (see Rom 14–15). That is perhaps in part why Paul emphasizes in Romans that *both* Jew and Gentile are alike under sin, and that God's salvation is available to both through faith in Christ. Both Jew and Gentile are justified, or 'righteoused' (see Chapter 5), by faith, and released from sin by dying with Christ, beginning a new life lived in the power of the Spirit. Presented in those terms, Paul's gospel raises questions about what has become of Israel, and of God's covenant promises to her, issues Paul addresses in Romans 9–11, where he seeks to make sense of God's saving purposes and to demonstrate that God has not been unfaithful (see Chapter 6). After the lengthy theological argument of chapters 1–11, Paul turns to more practical and ethical instruction, concluding his letter with a lengthy list of greetings (Rom 16; though some have suggested that chapter 16 was not originally a part of the letter to the Romans).

Paul's letters and other ancient Greek letters

Paul's letters are probably known to us, if at all, as part of the Bible, encountered perhaps in church services or study groups and read in our own language. They were originally written, of course, in Greek, and sent as communications between the apostle and his churches. Just as letters written today follow various customs and conventions, so did Paul's letters, and it can help us to understand their form and structure if we compare them with other letters written at that time.

Some of the letters of the period were preserved because they were part of the correspondence between high-ranking administrators and rulers in the Roman Empire, such as the letters (in Latin) sent by Pliny to the emperor Trajan when Pliny was governor of the province of Bithynia early in the second century CE.[5] Thankfully, we also have many pieces of correspondence exchanged between not-so-prominent inhabitants of the Empire, mostly written on pieces of papyrus and later discarded, only to be uncovered in recent archaeological digs. (For example, thousands of papyri have been recovered from a former rubbish dump at Oxyrhynchus in Egypt, including a number of fragments with biblical texts written on them.) The typical form of such letters can be seen from the following examples, where I have set out the structure on the right.

The structure of ancient Greek letters

Theon to the most honoured Tyrannus very many greetings.	Horus to the most honoured Apion greeting.	Sender and recipient named Greetings to the recipient(s)
Heraclides, the bearer of this letter, is my brother, wherefore I entreat you with all my power to take him under your protection. I have also asked your brother Hermias by letter to inform you about him. You will do me the greatest favour if you let him win your approval.	Regarding Lampon the mouse-catcher, I paid him on your account 8 drachmae as earnest money to catch mice in Toka. You will kindly send me this sum. I have also lent 8 drachmae to Dionysius, president of Nemerae, and he has not sent them back; this is to inform you.	Main body of the letter
Before all else I pray that you may have health and the best of success, unharmed by the evil eye.		Prayer for the recipient's health (often found immediately after the opening greeting)
Goodbye	Goodbye Pauni 24	Closing greeting
(Addressed: To Tyrannus the dioecetes) (*P.Oxy.* 292; c. 25 CE; trans. Hunt and Edgar)[6]	(*P.Oxy.* 299; late first century CE; trans. Hunt and Edgar)	

Although the precise form is much adapted and developed by Paul, his letters follow a broadly comparable pattern; indeed, they are often seen to fall somewhere between the short and everyday letters preserved in the papyri and the more formal and rhetorically polished official letters. For example, Paul's letters begin with the conventional naming of the sender and the recipients, but in a much expanded form. Paul not only gives his name (and the names of any co-authors) but usually also describes his identity as servant or apostle of Jesus Christ. He also describes the recipients of the letter in Christian terms. Paul's standard greeting is longer than the traditional one word 'greetings' (*chairein*) and takes a clearly Christian form: 'grace to you and peace from God our Father and the Lord Jesus Christ' (e.g. Rom 1.7; 1 Cor 1.3; 2 Cor 1.2; Gal 1.3). This greeting also reflects the influence of the Jewish greeting of 'peace' (Hebrew: *shalōm*). Just as standard Greek letters often included wishes or thanksgiving for the health and welfare of sender or recipient, so Paul generally opens his letters with a thanksgiving for the recipients and their faith (e.g. Rom 1.8; 1 Cor 1.4–9; 1 Thess 1.2ff.). The main body of Paul's letters is far longer, of course, than the short notes quoted above; his shortest letter in the New Testament is the personal one written to Philemon, his longest is Romans (hence the order in which they were placed, from longest to shortest). At the close of his letters, Paul sends greetings, again more extended than the concise 'goodbye' or 'farewell' which was customary, sometimes including a 'doxology' of some sort – words in praise of God's glory – and generally ending with a form of what has come to be known as 'the grace' (e.g., Rom 16.21–27; 1 Cor 16.19–24; Phil 4.20–23).

Rhetorical criticism of the Pauline letters

The private letters preserved in the papyri and other manuscript forms may not, however, be the best – and are certainly not the only – means of comparison for understanding the literary structure and aims of Paul's letters. In recent decades, some scholars have sought to understand and illuminate the form of the New Testament epistles by comparing them with the conventions established in Greco-Roman rhetoric.

Rhetoric was essentially the art of public speaking, originally in the public gatherings of the ancient city-states and later especially in trials before magistrates and jury, where both prosecutors and defenders made lengthy speeches intended to persuade the listeners one way or the other. Many ancient authors wrote about the construction and characteristics of such rhetoric, from Aristotle (fourth century BCE) onwards, classifying and explaining the types of speech which could be used and the various sections which made up an ideal speech. The art of rhetoric was thus codified in handbooks and taught by teachers to pupils. The Roman orator and famous teacher Quintilian, for example, taught for twenty years and published towards the end of his life (near the end of the first century CE) a large work entitled *Institutio Oratoria (Education in Oratory)*. This work covers the education of an orator from their very earliest childhood years, and describes in detail the various parts of a speech and the ways in which it may be most powerfully and artistically presented.

In 1975 Hans Dieter Betz published an article outlining how Paul's letter to the Galatians could be analysed in the light of ancient rhetoric, a proposal fully developed in his 1979 commentary on the letter.[7] Betz outlined the structure of Galatians as follows (I have summarized the character of each of the sections on the right):

The rhetorical structure of Galatians (following Betz)

The epistolary prescript (1.1–5)	The letter opening, naming the sender, addressees, etc.
The *exordium* (1.6–11)	The opening section of the speech, intended 'to prepare our audience in such a way that they will be disposed to lend a ready ear to the rest of our speech' (Quintilian 4.1.5).[8]
The *narratio* (1.12–2.14)	A 'statement of facts': the events and facts leading up to and bearing upon the case.
The *propositio* (2.15–21)	A summary of what is to be drawn from the *narratio*, any points of disagreement, and the main theses to be proven.

The *probatio* (3.1–4.31)	The 'proof' (often in various parts) which is essential to establish the case.
The *exhortatio* or *paraenesis* (5.1–6.10)	Exhortation and instruction.
The epistolary postscript or *conclusio* (6.11–18)	Written in Paul's own hand (see 6.11), authenticating the letter, summing it up, and adding any final concerns.

Betz thus sees Paul's letter as an 'apologetic letter' in which Paul sets out to defend the truth and validity of his gospel, against the rather different version which his rivals have introduced to the Galatians. As well as highlighting the fact that the Pauline letters are written with the aim of *persuasion*, rhetorical analysis can help in understanding the letter itself. For example, the section 2.15–21 can be seen as a key summary of the essential argument Paul seeks to prove, with the following sections (3.1–4.31) as the various proofs intended to uphold this case.

Using similar methods, Margaret Mitchell, in a doctoral dissertation written under the supervision of Betz, presented a detailed and careful rhetorical analysis of 1 Corinthians.[9] Mitchell is particularly concerned to identify the precise type, or *genre*, of rhetorical writing that 1 Corinthians represents. There are three types of rhetoric identified in the ancient sources: forensic (or judicial), deliberative and epideictic. George Kennedy distinguishes the three species as follows:

> The species is judicial when the author is seeking to persuade the audience to make a judgment about events occurring in the past; it is deliberative when he seeks to persuade them to take some action in the future; it is epideictic when he seeks to persuade them to hold or reaffirm some point of view in the present.[10]

Mitchell argues that 1 Corinthians should be identified as *deliberative* rhetoric; that is to say, it seeks to persuade the Corinthians to act in a particular way in the future. Specifically, she argues, Paul's central exhortation or 'thesis' is found at the beginning of the main letter-body: 'Now I appeal to you, brothers and sisters, by the name of our Lord Jesus

Christ, that all of you be in agreement and that there be no divisions among you, but that you be united in the same mind and the same purpose' (1 Cor 1.10). The whole of the letter serves as an appeal for unity. Thus, for Mitchell, the various sections from 1.18–15.58 comprise a series of 'proofs' contributing to this overall aim: the building up of a united Church.

These two early examples of rhetorical criticism only begin to illustrate the diverse work that has been done in this area. Rhetorical analysis is, for example, central to the socio-rhetorical approach applied to Paul's letters in a series of commentaries by Ben Witherington III.[11] While Betz and Mitchell have drawn upon ancient Greco-Roman sources for their understanding of rhetoric, other scholars have used the modern tools of the so-called 'new rhetoric', which focuses less on form and genre and more on analysing 'techniques of argumentation and their effectiveness'.[12]

Rhetorical criticism can certainly claim to help us to understand better both the structure and the aims of Paul's letters. By comparing Paul's writings with examples of rhetoric from Paul's own time, we can examine Paul's style of communication in the light of the techniques current at that time; we can perhaps see more clearly what is the central thesis or argument that Paul wants to prove in each letter, and we can certainly appreciate better how Paul's letters are artfully shaped attempts at persuasion as well as communication.

But there are also questions to be raised about the enterprise. How appropriate are the categories used to designate sections of a speech for the analysis of Paul's written communications? Is there perhaps more to be gained from comparison with various epistolary (letter-writing) forms and techniques in the ancient world? One of the most fundamental questions concerns Paul's level of education: was he really of a high enough social level to have been educated in the sophisticated techniques of rhetoric? How seriously should we take Paul's own claim to be 'untrained in speech' (2 Cor 11.6; but contrast 2 Cor 10.10)? When rhetorical critics discern a rhetorical arrangement in Paul's letters which corresponds to the structure outlined in the rhetorical handbooks and found in other ancient speeches and letters, does that necessarily mean that Paul is educated and conscious in his use of such forms, or is the artistic structure to some extent 'in the eye of the beholder'? Is Paul's undoubtedly skilful and persuasive writing a reflection rather of a somewhat more elementary level of education and an encounter with rhetoric at a more 'popular' level? Martin Hengel and Anna Maria Schwemer, for example, argue that:

> Paul's language and 'elements of education' do not go beyond what he could have learned within the Greek-speaking synagogues and in conversation with learned non-Jews, whom he did not avoid . . . The significance of the rhetoric of the schools on [sic] Paul is much exaggerated today, following a fashionable trend.[13]

Dean Anderson similarly concludes that 'Paul probably had no knowledge of rhetorical theory, nor was directly influenced by the more specific methods of school rhetoric'; at most, he might have known some of the basic rhetorical exercises.[14] However, Anderson maintains that the study of ancient rhetoric can still be valuable in appreciating and understanding Paul's letters in their ancient context. While rhetorical criticism can lead us to a clearer understanding of the aim of Paul's letters, it is also possible that it sometimes distorts or misinterprets that aim. For example, Mitchell may well be right to draw our attention to the importance of Paul's call for unity among the Corinthians, but it is arguable that she does not perhaps do justice to the issues raised elsewhere in the letter by reducing them to a series of 'proofs' in relation to this single overriding aim.

Conclusion

In one sense it must be true to say that letters were only a secondary part of Paul's activity as an apostle: his main task in response to God's commission was to spread the gospel among the Gentiles, something which he did with unquenchable energy. He wrote letters only to already established communities of converts, encouraging and instructing them in their faith, confronting problems and disputes. Nevertheless, even in his lifetime Paul's letters were recognized as a powerful means of communication and persuasion. For us, of course, it is really only through the letters that we can encounter Paul's thought directly at all. It is important to appreciate the distinctive character of each letter Paul wrote, and not to proceed too hastily to a synthesis of Pauline theology. While there are questions and debates about how best to do this, with varied methods adopted by different scholars, comparing Paul's letters with other forms of written and oral communication roughly contemporary with Paul can help us to set his letters in historical context and to appreciate better their structure and aims.

Further reading

Further information on each of Paul's letters can be found in the Introductions to the New Testament by Johnson, Brown, Schnelle and Achtemeier, Green and Thompson, and also in the larger Introductions to Paul by Gorman (*Apostle of the Crucified Lord*), Dunn (*The Cambridge Companion*) and Longenecker and Still (*Thinking Through Paul*), all of which are listed at the end of Chapter 1. Commentaries are also invaluable resources for studying the letters, providing both a general introduction to questions of date, circumstances of writing, major themes etc., and detailed verse-by-verse comment. There are many commentary series available, ranging in scope from short and accessible to huge and comprehensive. Needless to say, students beginning to study the letters of Paul are best advised to start with the shorter-length and recent commentaries, though the more detailed works may be particularly valuable for insight on specific and puzzling verses. Also worth mentioning are the series of *New Testament Guides* published originally by Sheffield Academic Press and now by Bloomsbury T&T Clark, and the series *New Testament Theology* published by Cambridge University Press. The former provide a brief introduction to scholarly treatment of individual books, while the latter focus specifically on the theology of each New Testament book. Valuable discussions of the theologies of the various letters are also found in the series on Pauline theology listed in footnote 1 of this chapter.

Books which set the early Christian letters in the context of ancient letter-writing include W.G. Doty, *Letters in Primitive Christianity* (Philadelphia: Fortress, 1973); S.K. Stowers, *Letter Writing in Greco-Roman Antiquity* (Philadelphia: Westminster, 1986); and D.E. Aune, *The New Testament in Its Literary Environment* (Cambridge: Clarke, 1988), pp. 158–225. For recent discussion of Paul's letters as ancient letters, see S.E. Porter and S.A. Adams (eds), *Paul and the Ancient Letter Form* (Pauline Studies 6, Leiden & Boston: Brill, 2010). See also M.L. Stirewalt Jr, *Paul the Letter Writer* (Grand Rapids: Eerdmans, 2003), who argues that Paul adapted the official form of ancient letter-writing to his own purposes. An important study, setting early Christian letters into the (neglected) context of ancient Jewish letters, is L. Doering, *Ancient Jewish Letters and the Beginnings of Christian Epistolography* (Tübingen: Mohr Siebeck, 2012); on Paul's letters specifically, see pp. 377–428.

For introductions to rhetorical criticism see G.A. Kennedy, *New Testament Interpretation through Rhetorical Criticism* (Chapel Hill: University of North Carolina Press, 1984) and B.L. Mack, *Rhetoric and the New Testament* (Minneapolis: Fortress, 1990). A valuable survey related specifically to Paul's letters is D.F. Watson, 'Rhetorical Criticism of the Pauline Epistles since 1975', *Currents in Research: Biblical Studies* 3 (1995), pp. 219–48. See also P. Lampe and J.P. Sampley (eds), *Paul and Rhetoric* (London & New York: Bloomsbury T&T Clark, 2010).

Questions for further study

- How distinctive do you find each individual letter of Paul's? How difficult, and how important, is it to try to read one letter without interpreting it through the lens of the other letters?
- In what particular ways do Paul's letters follow conventions of letter-writing in the ancient world? Why is it important to appreciate these conventions?

- To what extent does rhetorical analysis help us to understand the structure and aim of Paul's letters? What would you see as the strengths and weaknesses of this approach?

Notes

1 See J.M. Bassler (ed.), *Pauline Theology. Vol. 1: Thessalonians, Philippians, Galatians, Philemon* (Minneapolis: Fortress, 1991); D.M. Hay (ed.), *Pauline Theology. Vol. 2: 1 and 2 Corinthians* (Minneapolis: Fortress, 1993); D.M. Hay and E.E. Johnson (eds.) *Pauline Theology. Vol. 3: Romans* (Minneapolis: Fortress, 1995); D.M. Hay and E.E. Johnson (eds.) *Pauline Theology. Vol. 4: Looking Back, Pressing On* (Atlanta: Scholars, 1997).

2 This is the translation of the Greek word *skubala*, which Paul uses in Phil 3.8, suggested by R.B. Hays, *Echoes of Scripture in the Letters of Paul* (London and New Haven: Yale University Press, 1989), p. 122. Whether this is the best rendering has been disputed but the word is certainly a vulgarity referring to filth, dirt, excrement etc. (cf. KJV: 'dung'). Hays' translation seems to me a good one to convey the colloquial and vulgar term which Paul uses.

3 Philip Melanchthon (1497–1560), for example, famously referred to Romans as a 'compendium of Christian doctrine'.

4 See further A.J.M. Wedderburn, *The Reasons for Romans* (Edinburgh: T&T Clark, 1988); K.P. Donfried, *The Romans Debate: Revised and Expanded Edition* (Edinburgh: T&T Clark, 1991); A.A. Das, *Solving the Romans Debate* (Minneapolis: Fortress, 2007).

5 See Pliny, *Letters and Panegyricus* (2 vols, trans. B. Radice, Loeb Classical Library, London: Heinemann, 1969). Two letters of particular significance for the study of early Christian history are 10.96–97.

6 See A.S. Hunt and C.C. Edgar, *Select Papyri I* (Loeb Classical Library, London: Heinemann, 1932).

7 H.D. Betz, 'The Literary Composition and Function of Paul's Letter to the Galatians', *New Testament Studies* 21 (1975), pp. 353–79; *Galatians* (Philadelphia: Fortress, 1979).

8 H.E. Butler, *The Institutio Oratoria of Quintilian* (4 vols, Loeb Classical Library, London: Heinemann, 1920–22).

9 M.M. Mitchell, *Paul and the Rhetoric of Reconciliation* (Tübingen: Mohr, 1991).

10 G.A. Kennedy, *New Testament Interpretation through Rhetorical Criticism* (Chapel Hill: University of North Carolina Press, 1984), p. 19.

11 E.g., B. Witherington III, *Conflict and Community in Corinth: A Socio-Rhetorical Commentary on 1 and 2 Corinthians* (Grand Rapids: Eerdmans, 1995); *Paul's Letter to the Romans: A Socio-Rhetorical Commentary* (Grand Rapids: Eerdmans, 2004).

12 R.D. Anderson, Jr., *Ancient Rhetorical Theory and Paul* (Kampen: Kok Pharos, 1996), p. 21; see further pp. 19–28.

13 M. Hengel and A.M. Schwemer, *Paul Between Damascus and Antioch* (London: SCM, 1997), pp. 170–71.

14 Anderson, *Ancient Rhetorical Theory and Paul*, pp. 255, 249.

5

Paul the Theologian: The Central Elements of Paul's Gospel

Introduction

As we saw in the first chapter of this book, Paul is a figure of enormous influence in the history of Christianity. With remarkable energy and conviction, he spent the years after his 'conversion' travelling around the cities of the Roman Empire, sharing his message, visiting and encouraging the churches he had founded, and writing letters. Along with others, Paul was among the pioneering Christian theologians – not that he would have used or recognized that label – and because he wrote a number of comparatively lengthy letters (and these letters were preserved and treasured by the Church after his death) he has left us more record of his theology than did any of his Christian contemporaries.

Given then that Paul was such an early and influential Christian theologian it is important to ask what exactly his message was. How did Paul understand and express what he believed God had done in Jesus Christ? In this chapter we shall consider the major elements of Paul's theology and the different ways in which scholars have sought to express what lies at its heart. As soon as we begin to do this, all sorts of important questions arise: To what extent did Paul's theology change from the Jewish theology which he had ardently espoused as a Pharisee? What changed and what remained unchanged? In the next chapter we shall look specifically at Paul's views of the Jewish Law and of the Jewish people, since these have been major and important areas in modern discussion of Paul. Another question is whether it is legitimate to try to abstract Paul's 'theology' from his varied letters, all of which were addressed to particular situations and none of which therefore represents a systematic summary of Paul's beliefs (see Chapter 4). Some scholars have argued that Paul's theology changed during the years when he wrote his letters; others maintain that Paul's statements are not always consistent and so cannot be harmonized into a coherent whole.

Certainly the variations between Paul's letters should not be ignored. Nevertheless, in this and the following chapters we shall try to consider Paul's ideas as a whole, drawing evidence from various letters where it is relevant. I think it is possible to say something about the theology which Paul held, on the basis of his varied letters. But throughout the following discussion you should always be ready to question whether a particular idea is characteristic only of a particular letter, or arose only because of a specific argument in a particular place. You should also be aware that the relative length of each of the following sections is not a direct indication of the relative importance of their subject, but rather an indication of where there are areas of significant debate and disagreement which need to be discussed.

The basic story

Before we look in detail at specific elements of Paul's theology it may be helpful to gain some sense of its overall shape. Influenced in particular by ground-breaking work by Richard Hays, a number of scholars have come to the view that this overall shape is best grasped not in terms of a number of concepts or ideas, but as a story or narrative.[1] This story is not one which Paul sets out as such, but is rather the narrative which appears to underpin his varied statements and arguments on specific topics. N.T. Wright, for example, argues 'that Paul's worldview had a strongly implicit and frequently explicit narrative . . . a set of underlying stories'.[2]

To claim that Paul's gospel has, to use Hays' term, a 'narrative substructure', is not, however, uncontroversial. Indeed, the value of a 'narrative' approach to Paul has been subjected to critical assessment by a team of (at the time of its production) UK-based Pauline scholars, in a volume entitled *Narrative Dynamics in Paul*.[3] Most of the contributors find a narrative approach, conceived in various ways, valid and useful as a way to understand Paul's theology. For some, however, the idea that Paul's gospel is based on a story, even the story of God's saving act in Christ, looks too much like the idea that Paul tells a story of salvation, or presents a salvation history, and does not do justice to the way Paul depicts the Christ-event as an invasive, punctiliar, 'vertical' event that interrupts all human and historical stories. In a review essay, Hays has responded to *Narrative Dynamics*, and insists, against Francis Watson in particular, that Paul's gospel is, and must be, narratable – that it has a 'story' at its foundations.[4]

If, then, we do set Paul's theology in the context of a wider story, what does that story look like? At its heart is clearly Christ and the story of his coming, dying and rising. More broadly, Paul's 'story' begins, as the Jewish scriptures begin, with God's act of creation, closely followed by the fall of Adam (Eve is mentioned only rarely in the Pauline letters: 2 Cor 11.3; 1 Tim 5.13). Paul sees Adam as the one through whom sin came into the world (Rom 5.12–14), and sin, as that which corrupts and enslaves humanity, setting people in opposition to God and to one another, is what Paul sees as the root problem from which humanity needs deliverance (Rom 1.18–3.20 etc.). Of particular significance in Paul's story of God's dealings with the world is the figure of Abraham. Abraham is important both because he is a model, for Paul, of the faith that leads to righteousness (Rom 4) and also because Paul sees the promise God made to Abraham – to bless all the nations of the earth through him (Gen 12.3) – fulfilled in Jesus Christ, whom he describes as the 'seed' of Abraham (Gal 3.16). In the time between the promise made to Abraham and the coming of Jesus Christ, God gave the law, the Jewish *Torah*, through Moses (see 2 Cor 3.7–16; Gal 3.17–25). How Paul understands the purpose of this law and its continuing status after the coming of Christ is a matter of great discussion among scholars (see Chapter 6). But what is clear is that, for Paul, God's action in the death and resurrection of Christ marks the decisive moment in the fulfilment of God's promises, though the final completion of this saving work of God is still awaited (and is expected very soon). Jesus

Christ was sent by God as a human being, and died on the cross for the sins of humanity. God raised him from death and exalted him as Lord, the firstborn of a new redeemed family (Rom 8.29), so that, in him, all who have faith might also die to sin, to their former lives, and live as holy people in the power of God's Spirit, which is given to all who believe. It is through Jesus Christ, Paul insists, and not through the works of the law, that people can stand as members of the righteous covenant people of God (see Rom 3.21–28; Gal 2.16). And as members of God's holy people, people endowed with God's Spirit, living new lives 'in Christ', believers are expected to live upright lives, in accordance with what God desires (1 Thess 4.1–12), as they await the Lord's return. The completion of the process of salvation is near, when the mysterious plan of God to show mercy to all and to liberate the whole of creation will finally come to fruition (see Rom 8.21; 11.32), and when believers will live with the Lord forever (1 Thess 4.17).

It is clear from this brief summary that the key concepts and characters with which Paul thinks and does his theology come from the Jewish scriptures, the Christian Old Testament; we can hardly make sense of Paul's references to Adam and Abraham, to Moses and the law, nor even of terms like Christ ('Messiah'), 'the day of the Lord', and so on, without knowing something of their use in scripture and Jewish tradition. There are, of course, many quotations of Old Testament texts, along with echoes and allusions, in Paul's writings.[5] Another of Richard Hays' books, *Echoes of Scripture in the Letters of Paul*, has been influential in drawing attention to Paul's use of scripture, specifically in arguing that Paul's citations and allusions establish an 'intertextual' relationship between his letters and the Jewish scriptures, such that the 'echoes' of scripture in the letters call to the readers' mind the wider context and message of the texts from which they are drawn.[6] Indeed, a major book by Francis Watson develops at length the idea that Paul is fundamentally to be seen as a reader of scripture, whose theology is, in large part, a product of that reading.[7] On the other hand, questions have also been raised, for example by Christopher Tuckett and Christopher Stanley.[8] One question is whether, in fact, Paul's citations of scripture do indeed depend on, and point to, the wider scriptural contexts from which they were drawn. Tuckett and Stanley argue that they often do not, but may simply serve as isolated texts to illustrate or support Paul's point. Stanley also addresses a key question: would Paul's Gentile readers have known the scriptures well enough to have appreciated the allusions and their wider contexts? Because of both the low levels of literacy in the ancient world, and the lack of direct access to the Jewish scriptures, especially on the part of Gentiles, Stanley argues that often the answer to this question would be 'no'. Moreover, Stanley suggests that Paul's arguments in many cases would have worked best if there were only a limited knowledge of the scriptures on the part of his readers; he stresses the way in which the quotations function as part of Paul's rhetoric, part of his strategy to persuade. There is no serious doubt that Paul's thought is shaped by the Jewish scriptures, nor that understanding these scriptures is vital to understanding Paul. But there is more room for debate as to how far Paul's theology is shaped by, and deliberately echoes, broader scriptural texts and themes, and how far Paul simply uses scripture to back up his own points, even where the scripture cited (and its wider context) hardly supports what Paul makes of it (e.g. Gal 3.16).[9]

Even when we attempt a broad-brush summary of Paul's theology, then, there are questions and disagreements about precisely how we should conceive of that theology, and how we should understand its relationship to Jewish scripture and tradition (see further Chapter 6). I hope, nonetheless, that the central aspects of the 'story' set out above represent the key elements in Paul's message and theology, assuming one may represent it as a 'story'. Yet when we probe these aspects in more detail, again we find that different interpretations are proposed, and that scholars disagree as to how we should make sense of Paul. The following sections outline some of the most significant areas of debate.

Christ

There can be little doubt that Jesus Christ, and specifically his death and resurrection, lies at the heart of Paul's Christian message. In Phil 3.8

Paul writes, 'I regard everything as loss because of the surpassing value
of knowing Christ Jesus my Lord' (see further vv. 7–12). Christ's death
and resurrection are both equally important for Paul, and both are
central to the early Christian confession of faith (1 Cor 15.3–5;
see above, pp. 27–28). Paul's belief that Jesus of Nazareth had been
raised from death by God and exalted to the position of Lord
distinguished him (and the other early Christians) from most of his
fellow Jews, who did not accept that the crucified Galilean had been
raised, nor that he was the promised Messiah. Nevertheless, it is
important to keep in mind that Paul's language about Christ is essentially
Jewish: the name Christ is a transliteration of the Greek word *Christos*,
which translates the Hebrew *Mashiah*, Messiah, meaning anointed
one. Paul thus proclaims Jesus as the Christ, the anointed one of
God, the one through whom God has fulfilled his promises to Israel and
(through Israel) to the world.[10] The other term Paul most frequently
applies to Jesus is 'Lord', *kurios* in Greek. Indeed, the affirmation
'Jesus is Lord' is seen by Paul as the most fundamental Christian
confession (Rom 10.9; 1 Cor 12.3). Although the word *kurios* is used in
the Greek translation of the Hebrew scriptures to render the sacred
(Hebrew) name of God, *Yhwh*, the naming of Christ as *kurios* does not
necessarily indicate that he is being acclaimed as God, though some
argue that this is its implication. Masters, husbands, landowners, and
so on, as well as the Roman emperor, were all addressed as *kurios*
in Greek, and the term indicates essentially a position of authority.
Similarly, Paul's description of Jesus as 'son of God' (Rom 1.4; 2 Cor
1.19; Gal 2.20 etc.) is based on the language of the Hebrew scriptures,
where Israel (Exod 4.22), and Israel's king (Psa 2.7) are described as
God's son. So again the term does not necessarily imply that Jesus is
divine, nor that he is 'God the Son' in the sense of the later trinitarian
creed. As we shall see below, there is considerable debate concerning
Paul's view of Jesus. Indeed, while it is relatively clear that Jesus – Christ,
Lord, Son of God, crucified and risen – is central to Paul's gospel, many
questions of interpretation arise when we start to examine these ideas
in more detail.

1. The death of Christ

Paul clearly shares and repeats the early Christian confession, 'Christ died for us' (cf. Rom 5.8; 1 Cor 15.3; 2 Cor 5.14; 1 Thess 5.10). But what exactly does that mean, and how does Christ's death 'for us', or more specifically, 'for our sins' (1 Cor 15.3), enable people to be 'saved'? Broadly speaking there have been two main schools of thought concerning Paul's understanding of the death of Christ, though there are many nuanced variations and debates, within as well as between these two perspectives. One line of thought emphasizes the notion of Christ's death as a *sacrifice* offered in atonement for sin; the other argues that more important to Paul is the idea of Christ's death as something in which the believer *participates*. The sacrificial understanding would run something like this: human beings are guilty of sin, the consequence of which is death. But instead of condemning human beings to death, God presented Christ, the sinless one, as a sacrifice to die in their place, that through the shedding of his blood they might be forgiven and freed from condemnation. The participationist understanding, on the other hand, would go something like this: human beings live 'in Adam', that is, in the sphere of sinful humanity, under the reign of sin and death. The only escape from this realm is death. Christ became a human being, sharing the fate of those in Adam, dying on the cross, but, having been faithful and obedient to God, was raised from death by God, to become the first-born son of a new, redeemed humanity. In baptism, believers die *with* Christ; they too die to sin and to their old life in Adam. In Christ they become part of the new creation, freed from the power of sin. In short, then, the two interpretations offer different answers to the question of how (in Paul's view) Christ's death deals with sin. From a sacrificial perspective, Christ's death provides atonement for the transgressions of humanity and opens the possibility of forgiveness and justification; from a participationist perspective, people are freed from sin by *sharing* in the death of Christ, by dying to sin and its power.

How are both of these views possible? The simple answer is that there are texts in Paul's letters that support both schools of thought. Consider the following examples:

> Since all have sinned and fall short of the glory of God; they are now justified by his grace as a gift, through the redemption that is in Christ Jesus, whom God put forward as a sacrifice of atonement by his blood, effective through faith.
>
> (Rom 3.24–25)

> Should we continue in sin in order that grace may abound? By no means! How can we who died to sin go on living in it? Do you not know that all of us who have been baptized into Christ Jesus were baptized into his death? Therefore we have been buried with him by baptism into death, so that, just as Christ was raised from the dead by the glory of the Father, so we too might walk in newness of life.
>
> (Rom 6.1–4)

The first of these texts clearly represents a sacrificial interpretation of the death of Christ, the second a participationist one. Other texts are probably open to either interpretation:

> we entreat you on behalf of Christ, be reconciled to God. For our sake he made him to be sin who knew no sin, so that in him we might become the righteousness of God.
>
> (2 Cor 5.20–21)

The debate, then, hinges in part on how to interpret certain texts in Paul's letters (there is much discussion, for example, about the precise meaning of the words in Rom 3.24–25), and also on which of Paul's lines of thought is felt to be most central to his understanding of the death of Christ. E.P. Sanders, for example, is among those who argue that the participatory idea of dying *with* Christ is where the focus of Paul's thought lies:

> The prime significance which the death of Christ has for Paul is not that it provides atonement for past transgressions (although he holds the common Christian view that it does so), but that, by *sharing* in Christ's death, one dies to the *power* of sin or to the old aeon, with the result that one *belongs to God* ... The transfer takes place by *participation* in Christ's death.[11]

Sanders suggests that the passages where Paul expresses the 'sacrificial' view are generally ones where he is citing established Christian tradition (see Chapter 3). Rom 3.24–25, a key passage for the sacrificial interpretation, is often suggested to be a pre-Pauline tradition (cf. also Rom 4.25, where Paul seems to use a concise and well-known formula). Thus, on Sanders' interpretation, while Paul accepts this established Christian view, it is not one on which his own thought focuses. Rather, Paul spends more time developing the ideas of dying *with* Christ and beginning a new life 'in Christ' (e.g. Rom 6.3–11; 1 Cor 15.22; 2 Cor 5.14–17; Gal 2.19–20).

This phrase 'in Christ' (or near equivalents, such as 'in the Lord') has long been recognized as significant and distinctive to Paul (the phrase occurs very frequently in Paul's letters, but elsewhere in the New Testament only in 1 Peter 3.16, 5.10 and 5.14, which may be influenced by Paul's language), Albert Schweitzer proposed that this notion of 'being-in-Christ' was the heart of Pauline theology, though others question whether this is really the 'key' to Paul's thought (see below).[12] For Paul, Christians live, individually (2 Cor 5.17; 12.2) and corporately (1 Cor 12.12–27; Gal 3.26–28) 'in Christ'; indeed, they are 'the body of Christ' (1 Cor 12.27) – one of Paul's most profound and memorable descriptions of the church community.

This kind of language about Christ also appears in the way Paul speaks about Adam. Indeed, one of the figures from the Jewish scriptures with which Paul most often compares Christ is Adam. Paul refers to Adam as a 'type' of Christ (Rom 5.14; see vv. 12–21), that is, someone who shares the same essential shape or form, as if made from the same mould. Indeed, he explicitly speaks of 'the first Adam' (= Adam) and 'the last Adam' (= Christ), contrasting their identities and roles (1 Cor 15.45–49). Both Adam and Christ as somehow persons 'in' whom people live, in ways that define and determine their identity and fate: life 'in Adam' (under the power of sin and death) is contrasted with life 'in Christ' (as children of God, freed from condemnation and the dominion of sin). The contrasting spheres of life are concisely described in 1 Cor 15.22: 'for as in Adam all die, so in Christ will all be made alive'.

The comparisons Paul draws between Adam and Christ seem to strengthen the case for a participationist reading of Paul's Christology. However, one may question whether it is necessarily right to relegate the texts which indicate a sacrificial interpretation of Christ's death to mere citations of early Christian tradition (as does Sanders). Both sacrificial and participationist ideas are present in Paul, in the same letters (so it cannot be the case that he held one view earlier, the other later). Indeed, it may be significant that the sacrificial interpretation of Christ's death appears earlier in the progressive argument of Romans (3.24–25; 4.25; 5.6–9) while the participatory ideas emerge strongly later (6.1–11; 7.4); both ideas perhaps play their part in Paul's explanation of the gospel.[13]

2. Paul's Christology: 'high' or 'low'?

Those who come to the study of Paul from a Christian perspective may come with the assumption that Paul regards Jesus as the pre-existent Son of God, who became incarnate of the virgin Mary, and who, as the second person of the Trinity, is himself God – God the Son. However, whether Paul held all or any of these views is very much open to debate: he never refers to the virgin birth of Jesus, stating only that he was 'born of a woman' (Gal 4.4) – i.e., born like everyone else – and never refers to Jesus directly either as God or as God the Son (though there are some passages, open to various interpretations, where Jesus' divinity may be implied, e.g., Rom 9.5; Phil 2.5–11; Col 1.15–20 – though Colossians may not be by Paul himself).

There has been considerable debate among New Testament scholars as to what view of Christ, what 'Christology', Paul held: was it 'high' (that is, attributing a divine status to Jesus) or 'low' (that is, regarding Jesus as a human person who was exalted to the position of Lord by God's raising him from the dead)? Did Paul regard Jesus as pre-existent and divine?

In an important but controversial book, *Christology in the Making*, James Dunn argues that Paul did *not* view Jesus as a pre-existent divine

figure who became 'incarnate' at his birth.[14] On the contrary, Dunn
argues, Paul's Jesus was a man in whom God's 'wisdom' and power were
embodied, and who, through his obedience to the call and commission
of God, was raised and exalted to *become* Lord. Others maintain that
Paul does view Jesus as someone who was with God from the beginning,
and who took on the form of a human being at his birth (what came to
be known as the 'incarnation'). A particularly crucial passage is Phil
2.5–11, often thought to be a pre-existing hymn to Christ which Paul
adapts for his purposes in that letter. It is worth quoting in full:

> Let the same mind be in you that was in Christ Jesus, who, though
> he was in the form of God, did not regard equality with God as
> something to be exploited, but emptied himself, taking the form of
> a slave, being born in human likeness. And being found in human
> form, he humbled himself and became obedient to the point of
> death – even death on a cross. Therefore God also highly exalted
> him and gave him the name that is above every name, so that at the
> name of Jesus every knee should bend, in heaven and on earth and
> under the earth, and every tongue should confess that Jesus Christ
> is Lord, to the glory of God the Father.
>
> (Phil 2.5–11)

Many of the words and phrases in this passage have been much
discussed; their interpretation is clearly crucial for an understanding of
Paul's Christology: What does it mean to be 'in the form of God'? Did
Jesus have equality with God, or did he resist the temptation to reach
out and try to obtain it? And what would equality with God mean
anyway? When God exalted Jesus and gave him the position of authority
as 'Lord', was this a case of returning Jesus to the position that was
previously and rightly his, or an appointing of Jesus to a new status,
because of his 'obedience unto death' (cf. also Rom 1.4; Acts 2.36)?

According to Dunn, this whole passage is best read in the light of its
parallels with the story of Adam in Gen 1–3: both Adam and Jesus were
made in God's image (– 'form'), yet while Adam reached out to become
like God (Gen 3.5, 22), Jesus willingly took the role of humble obedience,

even to the point of death on the cross. Because of his obedience, he accomplished the restoration of what Adam had ruined, and was exalted by God to the position of Lord, from where he will receive the acclamation due to God himself (cf. Isa 45.23).[15]

Others disagree, and argue that being 'in the form of God' and 'taking the form of a slave' refer not solely to Jesus' human existence and then his going to the cross, but rather to his pre-incarnate existence with God and his becoming human.[16] Similar debate exists over the interpretation of other passages, such as Rom 8.3, 1 Cor 8.6, 2 Cor 8.9 and Gal 4.4. Do any or all of these passages imply that Christ existed before his birth, or only that he was a person chosen and commissioned to a task by God and who obediently endured the humiliation of the cross?

If Paul did believe that Jesus had existed before his birth, is that the same thing as believing that he was divine, or even that he was God? It is notable that Paul avoids stating directly that Jesus is God (note the language used in Phil 2.6, 11; also Col 1.15–20; 2.9);[17] he generally makes a distinction between God the Father and Christ the Lord. Indeed, there are places where Paul seems to imply that Christ is subordinate to God (1 Cor 3.23; 11.3; 15.24–28). Most striking is the passage about the end of all things in 1 Cor 15.27–28:

> For 'God has put all things in subjection under his [i.e. Christ's] feet'. But when it says, 'All things are put in subjection', it is plain that this does not include the one who put all things in subjection under him. When all things are subjected to him, then the Son himself will also be subjected to the one who put all things in subjection under him, so that God may be all in all.

There are, however, also places where Paul comes close to describing, or perhaps even does describe, Jesus Christ as divine, even as God. We have already seen the relevant phrases in Phil 2.5–11, though their meaning and implications are open to debate. One short but crucial reference is found in Rom 9.5, which may (depending on how we punctuate and translate the Greek)[18] contain an acclamation of Christ as God. This, however, is much disputed, and the verse may also be taken as concluding with a typically Jewish blessing of God. The following two translations illustrate the different interpretations:

> To them belong the patriarchs, and of their race, according to the flesh, is the Christ. God who is over all be blessed for ever. Amen.
>
> (Rom 9.5, RSV)

> Theirs are the patriarchs, and from them is traced the human ancestry of Christ, who is God over all, for ever praised! Amen.
>
> (Rom 9.5, NIV)

It is therefore possible to argue for a 'high' Christology on the part of Paul. N.T. Wright, for example, while maintaining that Paul remains within the framework of Jewish monotheism, argues that Paul has in fact 'redefined' God, weaving Christ and the Spirit into the Jewish confession of the one God (Deut 6,4), moving in the direction of the Christian trinitarian confession: there is one God, known and confessed as Father, Son and Spirit.[19] Wright sees what he calls Paul's Christological monotheism, for example, in 1 Cor 8.6:

> Yet for us there is one God, the Father, from whom are all things and for whom we exist, and one Lord, Jesus Christ, through whom are all things and through whom we exist.

Richard Bauckham similarly argues that Paul's Christology is a 'Christology of divine identity', one which identifies 'Jesus directly with the one God of Israel, including Jesus in the unique identity of this one God'.[20]

It will by now be obvious that there is rather a lot that is open to debate here; there are many questions about how far Paul's Christology differs from that of orthodox trinitarian Christianity. One thing does, however, seem clear: Paul remained firmly a monotheist (Gal 3.20: 'God is one'). Unlike most of the other inhabitants of the Roman Empire, for whom, as Paul says, there were 'many gods and many lords' (1 Cor 8.5), Jews and Christians (who affirmed their Jewish roots in this regard) professed their allegiance to only one God. Moreover, many of the terms and ideas with which Christians began to acclaim and label Jesus were derived from Jewish ways of speaking about God's attributes, agents and messengers – and, as Larry Hurtado and Richard Bauckham have emphasized, the early Christian practice of worshipping Jesus may have been a crucial impetus behind its Christological formulations.[21] Without leaving the framework of Jewish monotheism at the time, Paul and the early Christians could, for example, affirm that Jesus was the embodiment of God's eternal wisdom and acclaim his exalted position as God's supreme agent, since there were parallels in Jewish scripture and tradition, notably in the personification of wisdom as God's agent in creation (see esp. Prov 8.22–31; Wisd 7.22–8.1; Sirach 24.2–22). Consider, for example, the following statements about Wisdom:

> The LORD created me at the beginning of his work, the first of his acts of long ago. Ages ago I was set up, at the first, before the beginning of the earth. When there were no depths I was brought forth, when there were no springs abounding with water. Before the mountains had been shaped, before the hills, I was brought forth – when he had not yet made earth and fields, or the world's first bits of soil. When he established the heavens, I was there . . .
>
> (Prov 8.22–27)

> Wisdom . . . is a breath of the power of God, and a pure emanation of the glory of the Almighty; therefore nothing defiled gains entrance into her. For she is a reflection of eternal light, a spotless mirror of the working of God, and an image of his goodness. Although she is but one, she can do all things.
>
> (Wisd 7.25–27)

We can begin to see from such passages the extent to which the early Christians, Paul included, adopted and adapted these various Jewish traditions for speaking about God's attributes and agents, and applied them to Christ (cf. 1 Cor 1.24, 30). *He*, they claimed, was the true representation of God, God's supreme agent in the world.

God

Although the central focus of Paul's gospel seems to be Christ, and specifically his death and resurrection, we should not ignore the evidence which indicates that Paul's theology is profoundly focused on *God*. In J.C. Beker's terms, Paul is a *theocentric* theologian whose thought is centred around the conviction that God has acted in Christ in a final and decisive manner, and that the final triumph of God is now eagerly awaited.[22] Indeed, it is clear throughout Paul's letters that his good news about Jesus Christ is the good news of what *God* has done in Christ, how God has sent his Son, raised him from death, exalted him as Lord, and so on (see e.g. Rom 3.25; 8.3; 1 Cor 15.15; Phil 2.9). All this is the work of God, and in the end, God will be all in all (1 Cor 15.28).

We also need to recognize that Paul, along with his Jewish and Christian contemporaries, when they mentioned God, meant the particular 'God' in whom *they* believed. Today we might ask people whether or not they believe in God, without specifying what God we mean, but that bare question would have been meaningless to Paul and his contemporaries. As we have already seen, most of the inhabitants of the Roman Empire believed in a number of gods, who exerted their influence over the world and humanity in various ways (cf. 1 Cor 8.5). Jews and Christians, however, worshipped only one God, creator of heaven and earth (other so-called gods were regarded by them as idols and demons). That is to say, they gave their sole allegiance to the God of Israel, the God whose acts of creation, election, redemption, and so on, are recorded in the Jewish scriptures (cf. 1 Cor 8.6, quoted above). It is this God, the God who gave the law to Moses, spoke to his people through the prophets, made covenant promises to Abraham, Moses, David, and so on, whom Paul believes has acted in Jesus Christ and raised him from the dead. Paul believes that this God, the one true God, has fulfilled his promises to Abraham in Christ; this God is the Father of Jesus Christ and of all who believe in him (Rom 8.15–17, 29; Gal 4.4–7).

The Spirit

Right at the very beginning of the biblical story, in Gen 1.2, the Spirit of God is described as active, hovering over the formless earth and the deep waters as God's work of creation begins.[23] God's Spirit continues to be active as God's power and presence in the world (Judg 15.14; Psa 139.7), inspiring prophets and visionaries (1 Sam 10.6–11; Ezek 3.12), anointing judges and kings (1 Sam 16.13; 2 Sam 23.1–2). The prophet Joel envisioned a day when God's Spirit would be poured out on all God's people (Joel 2.28–29, quoted in Acts 2.17–18). Paul and the early Christians clearly believed that they were those for whom this prophecy had come true: all who believed and were baptized received the Spirit – a clear sign that God had accepted Gentiles as well as Jews to be his people (cf. Gal 3.2). Indeed, for Paul the Spirit is the essential mark of someone's being a true Christian (Rom 8.9; 1 Cor 12.3). The Spirit affirms their adoption as one of God's children (Rom 8.14–29; Gal 3.26; 4.4–7), gives diverse gifts for the good of the whole community (1 Cor 12.4–11), produces the fruit of holy living (Gal 5.22–23), and groans and prays with the believer in their present time of suffering and yearning for redemption (Rom 8.26–27). Just as there is a basic contrast in Paul's thought between life 'in Adam' and life 'in Christ', so another clear dichotomy is between life 'according to the flesh' (Greek: *kata sarka*) and life 'according to the Spirit' (Greek: *kata pneuma*). The former produces deeds of wickedness that lead to destruction, whereas the latter produces the fruit of love, joy, peace, patience, and so on (Gal 5.16–26). Just as it is fundamental for Paul that Christian life is 'life in Christ', so also it is fundamental that this life is 'life in the Spirit'.[24]

So far, then, we have considered Paul's theology in terms of how God, the Father and Creator, has acted through his Son, Jesus Christ, and is present in power by his Spirit. To progress further in our understanding, and to begin to see how this theology fits into Paul's wider perception of what God is doing, we need to look at some further aspects of Paul's thought.

Eschatology and salvation

One of the '-ologies' most frequently mentioned by New Testament scholars is eschatology, and for good reason. The word is derived from the Greek *eschata*, meaning the last things, or end. So eschatology, literally, is talk about the end, or the final things. The prophets of the Hebrew Bible sometimes saw visions of what would happen 'in the last days' (e.g. Isa 2.1–5) and Jewish apocalyptic writers – those who saw graphic and symbolic revelations of the heavenly realm and of the events stored up for the future – similarly refer to what is to come about 'in the last days' (e.g., Daniel 7–12; 4 Ezra). Indeed, Jewish prophets and visionaries spoke in terms of a contrast between this present evil age (cf. Gal 1.4) and the age to come, an age of righteousness and peace (4 Ezra 6.9; 7.113; 8.50–52; cf. 1 Cor 1.20; 2.6; Eph 1.21). The dramatic turning point was described as 'the day of the Lord' – an awesome and terrible day of both judgement and salvation (see e.g. Isa 13.6–9; Joel 2; Mal 4.1–6; 4 Ezra 7.113; 8.52; Matt 12.32; Mark 10.30). Thus, in a somewhat oversimplified and overgeneralized way (given that Judaism at the time of Paul was very diverse), the structure of Jewish apocalyptic eschatology may be illustrated as in Figure 2.

Paul and the early Christians believed that they were living in the last days; they were the ones 'upon whom the ends of the ages had come down' (1 Cor 10.11). Christ's coming, and specifically his resurrection, marked 'the beginning of the end'. In Beker's words: 'The Christ-event is the turning point in time that announces the end of time'.[25] The long awaited intervention of God had happened, but yet, in a sense, it had not happened; it was yet to be completed. The destruction of sin and death had not yet been fully accomplished; evil powers were still apparently dominant in the world; the kingdom of God had not yet been established. The return of Christ, the day of the Lord, was still awaited, but would very soon come, and the salvation for which believers longed would be completed (1 Cor 5.5; 1 Thess 5.2). That salvation would mean inheriting the kingdom of God, living forever with the Lord, being clothed with a new and immortal body. According to Paul, those who lived in Christ had already died to sin

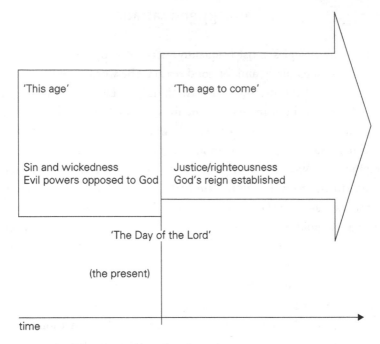

Figure 2 Jewish apocalyptic eschatology

Adapted from C.A. Davis, *The Structure of Paul's Theology* (Lampeter: Edwin Mellen, 1995), p. 18, by permission of The Edwin Mellen Press (see further pp. 16-24).

and begun a new life in the power of the Spirit; they were already part of the new creation (2 Cor 5.17), but they also groaned and suffered as they awaited the completion of this process (Rom 8.18–39). The present was therefore a time of tension, an in-between time, a time 'between the ages'. Paul's eschatology is therefore often summarized in the phrase, 'already but not yet'. Understanding this sense of eschatological tension is vital to an appreciation of Paul's theology. It may be represented in a diagram, as in Figure 3, which should be compared with Figure 2.[26]

Although there is general agreement about the importance of eschatology to Paul's theology, there has been some discussion about how much, if at all, Paul's ideas in this regard changed over time. In his earliest letter, 1 Thessalonians, Paul seems to envisage that he and many of the

Figure 3 Paul's eschatology

Adapted from C.A. Davis, *The Structure of Paul's Theology* (Lampeter: Edwin Mellen, 1995), p. 24, by permission of The Edwin Mellen Press (see further pp.16-24).

believers to whom he writes may still be alive when the Lord returns (1 Thess 4.15), whereas in later letters he seems to reckon more clearly with the possibility, or even the likelihood, of his death (e.g. 2 Cor 5.1-5; Phil 1.20–24). In a famous article on 'the mind of Paul', C.H. Dodd argued that through his experiences of near-death suffering and imprisonment (around the time of 2 Corinthians), Paul's focus shifted from the imminent return of Christ to the likelihood of his own death, and to eternal life here and now in communion with Christ.[27] It is true that the most extensive discussions of the final day of victory and resurrection are found in Paul's earlier letters (1 Thess 4.13–5.11; 1 Cor 15.12–58), whereas reflections on the prospect of death occur in later letters. The shifts may be explained in part by Paul's own experiences of suffering and imprisonment and in part by the delay of the Lord's return. However, it remains open to discussion how far these contrasts represent a significant change of outlook, as Dodd suggested, or a less dramatic shift of emphasis: to what extent does Paul's belief that the return of Christ is *imminent* fade? Is there a sense of the timetable becoming more open-ended (as clearly happens in 2 Pet 3.8–9)?

Whatever the changes in emphasis or timetable (and, after all, Paul himself declared that the day would come 'like a thief in the night', i.e., suddenly and unexpectedly: 1 Thess 5.2; cf. Matt 24.43; Luke 12.39), Paul's expectant hope for the final day of salvation is a constant feature throughout his letters (Rom 13.11–13; Phil 3.11, 20–21; 4.5). Even Paul's reflections on death are framed by his belief in the final day of judgement (2 Cor 5.10) and his hope for resurrection (2 Cor 4.14; Phil 3.11).

Paul was clearly convinced that the resurrection of Christ marked the beginning of the final act in the drama of God's saving work. According to Paul, in Christ God has now fulfilled his ancient promise to Abraham – to bless all the nations of the earth in him (Gen 12.3) – and has provided the means whereby people can be liberated from their enslavement to sin. Through the saving work of Christ, people who were previously slaves to sin have been 'redeemed', bought back, by God (cf. 1 Cor 6.20); they can now be reconciled to God, where previously they were enemies because of sin (2 Cor 5.19–20). 'In Christ', Paul proclaims, 'God was reconciling the world to himself' (2 Cor 5.19). In Rom 8.18–39, a unique passage in Paul's letters, Paul expresses his belief that the scope of this redemption encompasses much more than the relatively small number of people who, in Paul's time, had become believers. The main purpose of this passage seems to be to assure Christians that whatever the sufferings or hardships of the present, there is far greater glory to come, and that absolutely nothing can separate them from the love of God in Christ (Rom 8.35–39). Here, however, Paul also declares that the whole of creation is yearning to be set free from its bondage to decay: the result of the redemption and reconciliation of humanity will be redemption and liberation for the whole of creation (8.20–23). (This passage, unsurprisingly, has been a particular focus for those seeking a biblical perspective on contemporary questions about Christian responsibility towards the environment.)[28]

Salvation for Christians, according to Paul, means a new resurrection body, a body which is immortal and incorruptible (1 Cor 15.42–44); it means living forever with the Lord (1 Thess 4.17); it means an end to suffering, sin and death (Rom 8.18; 1 Cor 15.54–57). Facing the hardships and dangers that he did, it is not surprising that Paul yearned to see and experience the completion of this process (2 Cor 11.23–29). But what will the completion of the process of God's redeeming work mean for those who have not put their faith in Christ? Here there is something of an ambivalence in Paul's theology. On the one hand, he speaks of judgement, wrath and destruction for those who have not been obedient to God's will – although it seems that both believers and unbelievers will have to face God's judgement (cf. e.g. Rom 2.5–11; 1 Cor 3.12–15; 4.4–5; 2 Cor 5.10; 1 Thess 1.10; 5.9). On the other hand, however, he declares that God's purpose is to show mercy to *all* (Rom 11.32; cf. 1 Cor 15.22). Indeed, as we have just seen, in Romans 8 he sees the whole of creation as anticipating the prospect of redemption. Paul never set out an answer to this apparent tension in his thought; nor did he wrestle explicitly with the issue of the relationship between human decision and the sovereignty of God. For Paul, both seemed important: people were urged to respond to the gospel (e.g. 2 Cor 5.20), and yet God's saving purposes are presented as ultimately unstoppable (Rom 9.16; 11.29–36). Sanders captures the ambivalence well:

> How could Paul, on the one hand, think that it mattered desperately that people come to faith in Christ ... and predict destruction for those who rejected his message (for example, Phil. 3: 18–19), and, on the other hand, say that God would save everyone and everything? Which did he really think? Both, almost certainly ... Let us not put him entirely into the strait-jacket of logical arrangement.[29]

Paul leaves various strands and ideas in his theological legacy: we may feel that some of them are more enduring or significant than others. Paul did not expound or explain them in detail, yet they are clearly of importance in theological debates over who will be saved and on what basis (see further Chapter 6, on the question of Israel's salvation).

What remains clear is that Paul's theology is eschatologically orientated: he is constantly looking forward amidst the sufferings and pressures of the present to the completion of the process of redemption, the resurrection and immortality of God's children. These are the future visions towards which Paul's life and work as apostle of Jesus Christ were orientated; these are the goals which drove him on with resolute determination (cf. Phil 3.13–14).

Righteousness and faith

Up to this point in this chapter we have concentrated on aspects of Paul's theology; we have not thought much about how Paul describes the basis on which someone is 'saved', 'redeemed', 'rescued', or comes to belong to the people of God – all alternative perspectives on what kind of process is in view. On this crucial subject, Paul makes what most would agree to be an important statement: 'we know that a person is justified not by the works of the law but through faith in Jesus Christ' (Gal 2.16; cf. Gal 2.17; 3.11, 24; 5.4; Rom 3.20, 28; 4.2; 5.1, 9). It is obvious, however, that we need to know what Paul *means* by this statement in order to understand what he is asserting. What does he mean by 'justified', and is that the best translation of the Greek verb used here? Why does he insist that such 'justification' does not come by 'the works of the law' and in any case what are these 'works'? What exactly does the phrase 'faith in Jesus Christ' mean (in the original Greek) and is this the correct way to translate it? Is it right to say, as I did above, that here Paul is describing 'the basis on which someone . . . comes to belong to the people of God'? That is not obvious from the quotation above, and depends on how we interpret what Paul is saying. I have quoted the NRSV translation, and most other English translations give a similar rendering, but, as we shall see, there are some words and phrases which can be translated in various ways, and the different translations reflect quite different understandings of what Paul is stating.

First of all, though, we must ask how central and important this language of 'justification by faith' is to Paul's gospel. A long tradition associated especially with the name of the great reformer Martin Luther (1483–1546) regards this idea as central to the Christian gospel, and sees Paul as its first and most influential exponent. Early in the twentieth century, however, two prominent New Testament scholars, William Wrede and Albert Schweitzer, challenged this understanding of Paul's gospel, maintaining that the doctrine of justification by faith was not its central key. According to Wrede, justification by faith was a 'polemical doctrine', intended primarily to defend the place of the Gentiles within the people of God, while Schweitzer saw it as a 'subsidiary crater' alongside the real centre of Paul's theology, the mystical doctrine of 'being-in-Christ'.[30] One of the reasons why these and other scholars argue that justification by faith is not central to Paul's whole theology is that such language is virtually absent from some of Paul's letters, notably 1 Thessalonians.[31] The ideas seem to emerge most prominently in contexts where Paul is arguing with opponents over the Jewish Law, and specifically over whether Gentile converts must obey this law and be circumcised. Galatians, as we noted briefly above (p. 63), is dominated by this issue, and in Romans – the other letter where justification language is prominent – a major theme is Paul's insistence that both Jews and Gentiles stand equally in need of salvation and are 'justified' only by faith in Christ. Krister Stendahl therefore maintains that 'Paul's doctrine of justification by faith has its theological context in his reflection on the relation between Jews and Gentiles, and not within the problem of how *man* is to be saved …'[32] Schweitzer, as we have noted, followed to a considerable extent by Sanders, as well as many others, argued that 'being-in-Christ' was the more central idea in Paul's theology. Schweitzer described this as a form of 'Christ-mysticism' – mysticism denoting the idea of human union with the divine – but Sanders and others have tended to talk of '*participation* in Christ'.[33]

Other scholars, however, maintain that justification by faith is indeed a central theme of the Pauline gospel; its absence from certain letters simply reflects the fact that Paul's letters deal with the particular issues and problems facing a particular community and do not set out all of the central elements of his gospel. But at its heart, it is argued, Paul's gospel does present the message that God justifies guilty sinners by God's grace, because of what Christ has done, and not because of their own works.[34]

Discussion of these issues continues to be at the centre of much contemporary debate about Paul's theology. For example, Douglas Campbell, who proposes a broadly 'participatory' reading, launches a massive and polemical attack on what he calls 'justification theory', an approach which he finds profoundly problematic due to its inherently 'contractual' character (sinners can be acquitted in return for their response of faith).[35] By contrast, Michael Gorman has attempted to move beyond the oppositional alternatives of justification or participation: he argues for an understanding of justification as an essentially participatory notion, as 'a participatory death-and-resurrection experience'.[36] For N. T. Wright, Paul's notion of 'justification' is to be understood within his wider theological narrative about the redefinition of the covenant people of God around the crucified and risen Messiah.[37] Stephen Westerholm has rearticulated the case for a traditional understanding of Paul's doctrine of justification: salvation and righteousness cannot come by means of the Law, since humans are sinful, but only through the grace of God in Jesus Christ.[38]

Whichever side of these arguments we find convincing, it remains true that the language traditionally translated into the terminology of justification by faith plays a prominent role in some of Paul's most influential letters. We should therefore seek to understand it as accurately as possible. We first need to know what Paul means by 'justified'. How scholars interpret this depends in part on how they understand Paul's view of the Jewish law, and of how justification and works relate to this. This important subject is discussed in the next chapter. For now, we must first consider what exactly Paul means when he uses the language of justification or righteousness.

1. The language of justification/righteousness

In order to begin to understand Paul's language, we need to get back behind the English translations and consider the Greek words Paul used. This is because the words used in the English language obscure the links between a whole group of words which are central to this area of Paul's thought. These words all begin *dik-* in Greek and are to do with righteousness and justice. The problem in English translations is that some of the words in this group are usually translated with terms like 'righteousness', 'righteous', whereas others are translated 'justify', 'justified' etc. The links between this family of words in Greek may therefore be missed. Below is a list of the most important Greek words in this group along with their usual English translations[39]:

Noun: *dikaiosunē*	righteousness (or sometimes 'justification')
Adjective: *dikaios*	righteous (or sometimes 'just')
Verb: *dikaioun*	to justify

It is clear that what is missing is an English verb which could show its links with the noun 'righteousness' and the adjective 'righteous'. We might overcome this situation by translating the verb *dikaioun* 'to declare righteous' or 'to make righteous'. E.P. Sanders has suggested stretching the English language and coining the verb 'to righteous'.[40] But which of these alternatives would be preferable? For they actually convey somewhat different theological ideas, and reflect different understandings of what the verb *dikaioun* usually means in Paul's letters. Indeed the alternatives of 'declare righteous' and 'make righteous' have often stood on opposing sides of a long-standing debate on the meaning of righteousness in Paul.[41]

One understanding of righteousness language in Paul, associated again with Luther, is that to be 'justified' means to be 'declared righteous'; in other words, God pronounces the verdict 'righteous', 'in the right', acquitted and innocent, over the person who has faith in Christ. Justification by faith is seen as the central theme of Paul's gospel and is interpreted in primarily legal or forensic terms; the imagery is that of the law court. On this view the believer remains a sinner, but is declared by God to be righteous. In Luther's words, they are *simul justus et peccator* – 'at the same time justified and a sinner'. This view of the meaning of righteousness in Paul is traditionally termed 'imputed righteousness': by his pronounced decision God 'imputes', or attaches, the status 'righteous' or 'justified' to someone who is actually still a sinner. It has long been objected, however, that it is problematic, even for God, to declare something which is plainly not the case. Moreover, it may also be argued that this interpretation hardly does justice to Paul's thought, in which the believer clearly *is* changed, or at least is meant to be changed, by dying to sin and beginning a new life in Christ.

An alternative view has therefore also been argued, namely that Paul's verb *dikaioun* should be translated 'to make righteous'. This view interprets Paul's view of righteousness not as merely 'imputed' – a *legal* fiction – but as 'imparted'; God actually bestows righteousness upon the believer, who is really changed. It may again be objected that this is something of a fiction – a *moral* fiction – since Christians plainly do not become perfect or sinless through being justified (though Paul clearly expects real moral change on the part of his converts; see Rom 6.1–14; 1 Cor 6.9–11; 1 Thess 4.1–12 etc.). However, those who adopt this view of righteousness language in Paul argue that the terms do not describe the ethical or moral behaviour of the 'justified' person, but rather their relationship with God: someone who is justified is someone who has been put into a right relationship with God.[42]

Sanders argues that, while the Greek verb *dikaioun* does normally carry the legal sense 'to regard someone who is right as being in the right ... to consider or declare the guiltless to be innocent', Paul uses it in a somewhat different sense. When Paul uses the verb in its passive voice (as in the text quoted above: 'a person is justified ...') he is almost always referring, Sanders suggests, to a process of being changed, or *transferred* from one realm to another.[43] Thus the crucial thing about Paul's righteousness language, for Sanders, is that it is *transfer* terminology: it denotes not a legal verdict, but a process of incorporation or transfer into the people of God. He therefore suggests the translation 'to righteous' for the verb *dikaioun*. Sanders is thereby siding to some extent with Schweitzer in his argument that at the centre of Paul's gospel is *not* the idea of a guilty person being acquitted by God the (merciful) judge ('justification by faith'), but rather the idea that by dying with

Christ and beginning a new life, a person may be 'righteoused', or incorporated into the people of God ('participation in Christ'). (These two alternatives of course begin to link up with the two views of the death of Christ – the sacrificial and the participatory – which were outlined above.)

Further angles on the meaning of justification/righteousness in Paul have been proposed by N.T. Wright. The language of 'righteousness', Wright suggests, has 'four layers of meaning' in the Jewish scriptural sources that shape Paul's use of this terminology. Its 'primary meaning' is of 'right behaviour', not just in the sense of doing what is right and good but also of being in right relation with others. Second, it can refer to a law-court setting in which the judge who acts properly is *dikaios*, 'in the right', and where the person who is declared *dikaios* by the court is 'in the right *in terms of the court's decision*'. Third, the language is used to refer to the covenant relationship between God and Israel, and, finally, it has an eschatological focus when it refers to the final 'righteous' judgement of God. It thus concerns the declaration of who is included in the people of God who will be vindicated and declared 'righteous' by God on the final judgement day: 'God's eschatological judgment will be the ultimate cosmic law court, but it will also be the moment of ultimate covenant vindication'.[44] In Paul's theology, the future eschatological verdict – God's vindication of the covenant people – is brought forward into the present: 'God declares "in the right", "within the covenant", all those who hear, believe and obey "the gospel" of Jesus the Messiah'.[45]

Wright's interpretation of Paul's gospel centres around the idea that Israel's vocation and hope has been realized in and through Jesus Christ. Israel's calling as the covenant people of God was to serve as the means of salvation for the world, yet this covenant calling has been focused onto one person, Christ, in whom God has dealt with the sin of the world and fulfilled his promise to bless all the nations. Now, in Christ, by faith, people can belong to the covenant people of God, the people who will be declared righteous on the last day. Justification is essentially about the declaration of membership of the covenant people of God: those who are 'justified' are those who can be sure that, through their faith in Christ – the 'badge' of covenant membership – they are members now of the eschatological covenant people who will be vindicated on the day of judgement.[46]

As the brief survey above will already have made clear, there are other perspectives – and many intricate scholarly discussions – on the meaning of righteousness/justification in Paul. Thinking through your own understanding of the matter will require careful and extended study of the letters, as well as of the books written about them. And, as the comments above will have shown, even the introductory books on Paul give you different interpretations and perspectives on this central theme. Many recent interpreters would agree that Paul's 'justification' language is not so much concerned with how a guilty individual finds mercy, but about how the people of God are to be defined: who is a member, and on what basis? If this is right, then being 'justified' (or 'righteoused') is not so much about being declared 'not guilty', nor about being made morally perfect, but about being 'in' the people of God, whether we see that in terms of being transferred in (so Sanders) or anticipating the eschatological verdict (so Wright). But Westerholm makes a strong case for the more traditional focus: Paul is, contrary to much modern scholarship, interested precisely in the question as to how a guilty person finds mercy.[47] Fundamental debates continue. So much, then, for justification. The next phrases of Paul's declaration in Gal 2.16 concern the means by which this state of being 'justified', or 'righteoused', comes about.

2. 'Not by the works of the law'

Before mentioning the positive basis on which a person *can* be 'justified', or 'righteoused', Paul emphasizes the negative basis on which such justification is *not* possible. This order may well reflect the fact that the statement is made in a context where Paul is arguing precisely against those who do think that 'the works of the law' are necessary for everyone who would be a member of God's people. What Paul actually *means* by this phrase is a subject we shall defer until the following chapter, when we shall consider in some detail Paul's attitude to the Jewish law and to the people of Israel. For now we can pass on, noting only that it is *not* by 'works of the law' – whatever they may be – that a person is 'justified'.

3. By 'faith in' or 'the faith of' Jesus Christ?

Following the negative part of his declaration about justification, Paul proceeds straight to the positive – the basis on which people *are* justified, or righteoused. The NRSV translation, like most other English translations, renders this positive phrase, 'but through faith in Jesus Christ'. Yet the King James Version has 'But by the faith of Jesus Christ', in this case a quite literal rendering of the Greek. Why the differences and what are the issues underlying the choices in translation? The crucial words in Greek, found a number of times elsewhere in Paul, are *pistis Christou*, literally, '(the) faith of Christ'. (Along with Gal 2.16, the key texts are Rom 3.22, 26; Gal 2.20; 3.22; Phil 3.9.) The problem for translators and interpreters is to decide how to understand this phrase. In technical terms, the two alternatives are to take it as either a 'subjective genitive' or an 'objective genitive' (*Christou*, 'of Christ', is in the genitive case). The ambiguity in the Greek is not common in contemporary English, but can nonetheless be illustrated. Compare the following phrases:

(a)   He was inspired by the love of God.
(b)   She did it for the love of God.

Both are ambiguous: in each case, the phrase 'the love of God' might mean the love which God has for other people, for creation, or whatever (that is a 'subjective' genitive: God is the *subject*, the one who loves), or it might mean the love which the person has for God, their love of God (that is an 'objective' genitive: God is the *object* of their love). So phrase (a) might mean that he did whatever he did because he was inspired to do so by his sense of God's love for him and for others (subjective genitive), or that he was inspired by his own love for God, which led him to devotion, action, etc. (objective genitive). Phrase (b) might mean that she acted because of her sense of God's love for her and/or others, or because of her love for God.

The phrase *pistis Christou* is in most English translations taken as an objective genitive: Christ is the object of faith, faith placed in Christ, hence the translation 'faith in Christ'. However, in recent years a number of scholars have been arguing that it should be interpreted as a subjective genitive, that is, as the faith which Christ himself has. Particularly influential, again, is the work of Hays, in *The Faith of Jesus Christ*.[48] In considering this proposal we need to bear in mind that the noun *pistis* can mean 'faith' in the sense of belief, or (more often) trust (its usual meaning in Greek of the period), but it can also mean 'faithfulness', as in Rom 3.3: 'the faithfulness (*pistis*) of God' (KJV has 'the faith of God'). If these scholars are right, then Paul may be making a somewhat different argument than the usual translations imply. Namely, that the possibility of being 'righteoused' comes through the faithfulness of Jesus Christ, that is, through the faithful obedience of Jesus to the will of God (cf. Phil 2.8). If this is correct, it does not mean that Paul sees no need for Christians to have faith, for their faith is often mentioned alongside the crucial phrase 'the faith of Christ' (e.g. Rom 3.22; Gal 2.16). What it would mean, however, is that the emphasis shifts from saying that justification comes about through a person's faith in Jesus Christ to saying that the creation of a righteous people (if that is how we should interpret the idea of justification) was achieved through the faithfulness of Jesus Christ, who (unlike Adam) was obedient to the will and purpose of God.

It may be going too far to see this as a major change in our whole understanding of Paul's gospel, but it certainly shifts the focus, and leads to a very different reading of the key texts such as Gal 2.16; now the stress is not on the believer's response but on the action of Christ, or, more precisely, on what God has done in Christ. Unsurprisingly, however, these recent arguments in favour of the subjective genitive interpretation have not gone unchallenged. Barry Matlock and James Dunn, both defenders of the objective genitive reading, have rightly warned that, however attractive the theology that results from the subjective genitive reading, this cannot itself determine what Paul intended the phrase to mean. That must be decided on the basis of grammatical, linguistic, and exegetical arguments – and at present neither side of the debate can claim outright victory on those grounds.[49]

One final point of translation should be noted. Just as the links between the group of *dik-* words are obscured by translation (see above) so too are the links between the *pist-* words, which have to do with faith:

Noun: *pistis*	faith
Adjective: *pistos*	faithful
Verb: *pisteuein*	to believe (or 'to have faith')

It is probably better, therefore, to translate the verb *pisteuein* 'to have faith' (or 'to trust') rather than 'to believe', partly because the links with the other *pist-* words are thereby clearer, but also because the words for Paul have less to do with the notion of believing in the existence of, or accepting certain propositions about, and more to do with entrusting and committing oneself to the object of faith.

We can now see how different interpretations of a key phrase in Paul's formulation of the gospel might lead to rather different translations. Compare, for example, the following two renderings of the verse with which we began this whole section, Gal 2.16:

> Yet we know that a person is justified not by the works of the law but through faith in Jesus Christ. And we have come to believe in Christ Jesus, so that we might be justified by faith in Christ, and not by doing the works of the law, because no one will be justified by the works of the law.
>
> (NRSV)

> We know that a person is righteoused not by the works of the law, but through the faithfulness of Jesus Christ; and we have put our faith in Christ Jesus, so that we might be righteoused by the faithfulness of Christ and not by the works of the law, because no one will be righteoused by the works of the law.
>
> (DGH)[50]

Whatever translation we opt for, we still of course need to work out our view of what Paul *means* by being 'justified' or 'righteoused', by 'works of the law', and so on. Unpacking this important phrase in Paul's letters turns out to be rather complicated and may lead to a variety of interpretations. Being made aware of all these different interpretations may seem to some to be rather a negative exercise: something they once thought they understood clearly might now seem more complex and less clear! But all too often, our seemingly 'clear' interpretations result from reading Paul through the lens – or even squeezing Paul into the mould – of a particular theological perspective. Trying to look afresh at the letters is one way of attempting to do justice to what Paul actually wrote and what he may have meant by it in its context. And grappling with these central concepts in Paul's theology remains at the heart of contemporary scholarly debate.

Ethics

It is clear that among the basic elements of Paul's gospel proclamation is an exhortation to his converts to live holy lives, to be set apart and distinctive from what Paul regards as the evil age in which they lived (Rom 12.1–2; 1 Thess 4.1–8). A number of times in his letters Paul paints in stark colours the contrast between his converts' former and present lives, between evil things and good things (Rom 13.11–14; 1 Cor 6.9–11; Gal 5.19–23). Yet Paul does not simply urge people to be good; he reminds them that they are now changed people and should live accordingly. Their conduct, in other words, should flow from their identity. This understanding of Pauline ethics has often been epitomized in the phrase: 'Be what you are!' In order to understand this foundation of Paul's ethical instruction it is important to look at the relationship between what scholars term the indicative and the imperative in Paul.[51]

An indicative phrase is a statement of what is the case: 'She sits (or is sitting) on the chair', for example. An imperative is a command, instruction or exhortation: 'Sit on the chair!' Paul often seems to base his ethical exhortation upon indicative statements. Clear examples can be found in Romans 6.1–14 (where verses 2–10 are primarily indicative, though sometimes phrased as rhetorical questions, verses 11–14 imperative):

> Indicative statements: 'We have been buried with him by baptism into death ... We know that our old self was crucified with him so that the body of sin might be destroyed.'

> Imperative exhortations: 'So you also must consider yourselves dead to sin and alive to God in Christ Jesus. Therefore, do not let sin exercise dominion in your mortal bodies, to make you obey their passions. No longer present your members to sin as instruments of wickedness, but present yourselves to God ...'

Paul thus describes Christians as people who have died with Christ; they have died to sin and begun a new life in Christ. These are indicative statements about their new identity. Yet living in a way appropriate (in Paul's view) to being a new person in Christ clearly did not come automatically. Indeed, Paul was sometimes scandalized at the conduct of some of his converts, to the extent that their status as members of the community was put in question (1 Cor 5.1–13). He had to urge them to act rightly, to live in a holy manner; and so, along with the indicatives, we find imperatives (Rom 6.11–14; 1 Cor 10.14; 1 Thess 4.9–12). For Paul it is profoundly true to say that a believer *has* already died with Christ and is already a new person; yet in the in-between times, the (short) time between the resurrection of Christ and his final return, there is also a sense in which this dying and rising has not yet occurred ('already but not yet'; see above on eschatology). The final act in the drama, the defeat of death itself and the day of resurrection, lies in the future, and so the completion of the process of redemption, the redemption of the body (Rom 8.23), is still awaited. While dying with Christ can be spoken of as having already happened, the believer's resurrection seems to remain for Paul a future hope (see Rom 6.4–5; 8.22–25; contrast Col 2.12; 3.1). In the here and now, Christians must make a commitment; they must 'set their minds' one way and not the other, must live in the power of the Spirit and not allow sin to reign over them (Rom 8.5–13). They must anticipate what will soon be complete.

That outline gives some indication of the theological basis of Paul's ethics. But what influences the substance of his ethical instruction? Here there is even more room for debate and disagreement. Four key influences on Pauline ethics may be mentioned, though scholars disagree about the relative importance of each of them (and the order below is not meant to indicate their comparative significance).

Firstly, Paul's ethical instruction is shaped by the teaching and example of Jesus Christ. The number of clear allusions to Jesus' teaching in Paul's letters is in fact quite small (see above, pp. 28–30), and while Jesus' instruction seems to play a significant role in Paul's instruction in 1 Cor 7.10–11, it would be hard to claim that Jesus' teaching itself underlies much of Paul's ethics. Paul certainly does not quote Jesus in order to supply the answer to moral dilemmas or disputes in his churches. More important, perhaps, is Paul's emphasis on Jesus as an example, with the pattern of Christ's self-giving serving as a paradigm for Christian morality (see Rom 15.2–3; Phil 2.3–8; 1 Cor 11.1).[52] Indeed, Christ's love (Gal 2.20) serves as a model for the love Paul desires to see among members of the Christian communities; love for one another is a prominent theme in his instruction (1 Thess 4.9–10; Gal 5.13–14).

Secondly, there are the Jewish scriptures and the Jewish traditions of ethical instruction. Paul himself, writing to the Corinthians (most of whom were not Jewish: 1 Cor 12.2), describes the Jewish scriptures as 'written for our instruction' (1 Cor 10.11). Quotations from scripture are common in Paul's letters, and are used to justify and support points of ethical teaching (e.g. Rom 12.19–20; 14.10–12; 1 Cor 5.13; 6.16). His strong aversion to idolatry and sexual immorality certainly reflects his Jewish heritage (cf. Rom 1.18–31 and Wisd 13–15). And although Paul is adamant that justification does not come through the works of the law (see Chapter 6) he does insist that Christians fulfil the heart of what the law, recorded in scripture, requires:

Owe no one anything, except to love one another; for the one who loves another has fulfilled the law. The commandments, 'You shall not commit adultery; You shall not murder; You shall not steal; You shall not covet'; and any other commandment, are summed up in this word, 'Love your neighbour as yourself'. Love does no wrong to a neighbour; therefore, love is the fulfilling of the law.

(Rom 13.8–10; cf. Rom 8.3; Gal 5.14)

Thirdly, some scholars suggest that various Greek and Roman traditions of moral instruction have a significant influence on Paul's ethics. Paul's lists of 'vices and virtues' (e.g. Gal 5.19–23), his emphasis on the need for self-control and discipline (1 Cor 7.5; 9.25–27), for example, are paralleled in Greco-Roman writings. In one text, admittedly unique in Paul, he describes what is 'good' using terms well known from Greco-Roman moral discourse, most notably the central term of Greek ethics: *aretē*, virtue (Phil 4.8). Indeed, Paul's argument in Philippians, that Christians should 'run the race' with single-minded focus and determination so as to attain the 'goal' (Greek: *telos*), which is Christ, closely parallels the structure and imagery of much moral philosophical argument about attaining the 'goal' of a good and virtuous life.[53] For example, compare the following text from Philippians with one from Lucretius, a Roman philosopher of the first century BCE:

I want to know Christ and the power of his resurrection and the sharing of his sufferings by becoming like him in his death, if somehow I may attain the resurrection from the dead. Not that I have already obtained this or have already reached the goal; but I press on to make it my own, because Christ Jesus has made me his own. Beloved, I do not consider that I have made it my own; but this one thing I do: forgetting what lies behind and straining forward to what lies ahead, I press on toward the goal for the prize of the heavenly call of God in Christ Jesus.

(Phil 3.10–14)

And so he [Epicurus] purged people's hearts with his truthful words, and established the limit of desire and fear, and laid out the nature of the highest good to which we all strive, and indicated the way by whose narrow path we may press on towards it on a straight course.

(Lucretius, *On the Nature of Things* 6.24–28)[54]

On more specific and substantive topics, Will Deming has explored the parallels between Paul's teaching on marriage and celibacy in 1 Corinthians 7 and the discussions of this topic among Stoics and Cynics. Deming argues that Paul's opinions show clearly the influence of these philosophical traditions.[55] In other words, in relation to his ethics, Paul's thought is shaped not only by Jewish traditions but also by Greek and Roman philosophical and ethical traditions – which also influenced many other Jewish writers of the time, including Philo, Josephus and the author of *The Wisdom of Solomon*. Like many other Jews of his time, as we have already seen (pp. 6–7), Paul was 'Hellenized', with various influences combining to shape his thought. Indeed, as we noted above, it is not possible to draw clear or sharp lines separating Judaism on the one hand and Hellenism on the other. Importantly, these parallels also show that Paul's ethics did not stand in as stark a contrast with those of his wider society than his own rhetoric sometimes suggests.[56]

Fourthly, Paul's ethics are influenced to some degree by his sense of the nearness of the end, by his eschatology (see above).[57] One reason he gives for not marrying, for example, is that 'the appointed time has grown short' (1 Cor 7.29). The fact that the day of salvation is drawing nearer is also cited by Paul as a reason for upright moral behaviour:

you know what time it is, how it is now the moment for you to wake from sleep. For salvation is nearer to us now than when we became believers; the night is far gone, the day is near. Let us then lay aside the works of darkness and put on the armour of light; let us live honourably as in the day, not in revelling and drunkenness, not in debauchery and licentiousness, not in quarrelling and jealousy.

(Rom 13.11–13)

How these various influences should be evaluated in terms of their influence on Paul is a matter for debate; but it is clear that Paul urged and expected his converts to live holy lives. This holy living, for Paul, entailed turning from idolatry and avoiding sexual immorality – which specifically meant not participating in sacrifices to other gods (1 Cor 10.14–22), and avoiding divorce and sexual unions outside the marriage bond (1 Cor 6.12–7.16). It also required the demonstration of love and goodness towards fellow Christians, and indeed towards all people, and specifically imitating Christ's self-giving in placing the needs and interests of others before one's own. Paul was, however, sometimes disappointed by his converts' failure to realize what such a holy life entailed (e.g. 1 Cor 5.1–13) and one of the main purposes behind his letters was to reiterate and develop his ethical instruction, sometimes by encouraging converts to continue doing as they are doing, sometimes to clear up points of confusion or to add further instruction.

Conclusion: what is the key to Paul's theology?

Although there is a great deal more that might usefully be said, we have surveyed briefly the major themes in Paul's theology and seen something of the debates over their interpretation. The discussions above will have made it clear that virtually every theme is the subject of extended and intricate debate. What is Paul's view of Christ? What does he mean by 'justification'? Can we legitimately abstract an overall Pauline theology from Paul's varied and distinctive letters? Many other questions could easily be added.

And what about the question of the 'key' to Paul's theology? Is there a central key or core? As we have already seen, one major division among interpreters has been between those who see 'justification by faith' as the key to Paul's theology and those who believe that 'participation in Christ' comes much closer to expressing the distinctive idea around which Paul's thought revolves. Would it be more true to say that the heart of Paul's gospel is that through Christ's sacrificial death the guilty sinner can be freed from condemnation, or that because of Christ's representative death the one who has faith in Christ can also die with him, die to sin, and live anew 'in Christ'? Or is this a false either/or? Are there better ways of expressing what lies at the heart of Paul's gospel? Can we find ways of incorporating the various aspects of Paul's understanding of what God has done in Christ under a different overall umbrella, such as Beker's idea of the triumph of *God*? Or perhaps the search for a single 'key' is misguided and inappropriate, especially given the character of the Pauline letters; perhaps there are several key themes in Paul's theology?

It will certainly be clear – but hopefully not too much of a disappointment! – that this chapter has not fully *answered* the questions about the heart of Paul's theology. I have sought to outline various themes which are central in that theology, but have not sought to propose one particular view as to how they should be interpreted or combined. Rather than try to convince you of a certain view, I have tried to show some of the different ways in which Paul can be understood, and to explain where and why scholars propose different interpretations. The task of putting Paul's theology together again I leave to you and your studies of Paul. Hopefully this chapter has enabled you to understand some of the questions and some of the tools you will need to use in order to assess the various scholarly proposals critically and to work out your own answers to those questions.

Further reading

The short introductions to Paul, listed at the end of Chapter 1, offer an overview of the major themes in Paul's theology. These are well worth reading, not least because it will rapidly become clear how *different* are their interpretations of central ideas such as justification and righteousness. C.J. Roetzel's book *Paul: The Man and the Myth* (Columbia: University of South Carolina Press, 1998) contains a valuable chapter on Paul 'The Theologizer', which looks in turn at the theology in 1 Thessalonians, 1 Corinthians and Romans, rather than amalgamate the varied material of the letters into a single scheme.

Another book which approaches Paul's theology by first examining the individual letters in turn is Jürgen Becker's *Paul: Apostle to the Gentiles* (Louisville: Westminster John Knox, 1993). Gorman, *Apostle of the Crucified Lord* (see Chapter 1 for details), also offers a detailed treatment of each letter.

There are many studies of Paul's theology, and of various aspects of it, and only a few major works can be listed here (see also the notes to this chapter). J.D.G. Dunn's, *The Theology of Paul the Apostle* (Edinburgh: T&T Clark/Grand Rapids: Eerdmans, 1998), taking Romans as its main basis, discusses in depth the major areas of Paul's theology. Even larger are the recent volumes by Douglas Campbell and N.T. Wright: the former of these presents an assault on 'justification theory' – D.A. Campbell, *The Deliverance of God* (Grand Rapids: Eerdmans, 2009) – while Wright offers a massive and comprehensive treatment of Paul – N.T. Wright, *Paul and the Faithfulness of God* (2 vols, London/Minneapolis: SPCK/Fortress, 2013). A major treatment representing a perspective from German scholarship is U. Schnelle, *Apostle Paul: His Life and Theology* (Grand Rapids: Baker, 2005). Various presentations of the heart of Paul's theology are also found in M.D. Hooker, *From Adam to Christ: Essays on Paul* (Cambridge: CUP, 1990); J.C. Beker, *The Triumph of God: The Essence of Paul's Thought* (Minneapolis: Fortress, 1990); E.P. Sanders, *Paul and Palestinian Judaism* (London: SCM, 1977), pp. 429–556; S. Kim, *The Origin of Paul's Gospel* (Grand Rapids: Eerdmans, 1982); and D.A. Campbell, *The Quest for Paul's Gospel* (London and New York: T&T Clark, 2005), see esp. Ch. 2 (pp. 29–55).

The best place to begin a study of Paul's ethics is with the collection of essays in B.S. Rosner (ed.), *Understanding Paul's Ethics: Twentieth-Century Approaches* (Grand Rapids: Eerdmans, 1995). An important and classic study of Paul's ethics is V.P. Furnish, *Theology and Ethics in Paul* (Nashville: Abingdon, 1968), reissued with an introductory essay by Richard Hays in 2009 (Louisville: Westminster John Knox). A rather different study, bringing Paul's ethics into dialogue with contemporary approaches to ethics, is D.G. Horrell, *Solidarity and Difference: A Contemporary Reading of Paul's Ethics* (London and New York: T&T

Clark, 2005). Also focused on Paul's ethics are J.P. Sampley, *Walking Between the Times: Paul's Moral Reasoning* (Minneapolis: Fortress, 1991) and J.W. Thompson, *Moral Formation According to Paul* (Grand Rapids: Baker, 2011). Valuable briefer treatments of Paul's ethics can also be found in a number of works on New Testament ethics; among the best are W. Schrage, *The Ethics of the New Testament* (Edinburgh: T&T Clark, 1988) and R.B. Hays, *The Moral Vision of the New Testament* (New York: HarperCollins, 1996; Edinburgh: T&T Clark, 1997). An argument for Paul's ethics as following the pattern of inclusiveness practised by Jesus is presented by R.A. Burridge, *Imitating Jesus: An Inclusive Approach to New Testament Ethics* (Grand Rapids: Eerdmans, 2007), pp. 81–154. On some of the concrete moral issues addressed by Paul, see V.P. Furnish, *The Moral Teaching of Paul* (3rd edn; Nashville: Abingdon, 2009).

Questions for further study

- How does Paul regard and depict the person of Jesus Christ? What are Paul's main sources and influences here, and to what extent does his Christology differ from that of later Christian orthodoxy?
- What would you see as the heart of Paul's theology? Is it right to see 'justification by faith' and 'participation in Christ' as the two main, and opposed, possibilities?
- What would you see as the main influences on Paul's ethics? In what respects, if any, are Paul's ethics distinctive compared with those of his contemporaries, Jewish and non-Jewish?

Notes

1 See R.B. Hays, *The Faith of Jesus Christ* (Chicago: Scholars Press, 1983; 2nd edn, Grand Rapids: Eerdmans, 2002); B. Witherington III, *Paul's Narrative Thought-World* (Louisville: Westminster/John Knox, 1994); N.T. Wright,

The New Testament and the People of God (London: SPCK, 1992), esp. pp. 403–9. For an overview, see B.W. Longenecker, 'Narrative Interest in the Study of Paul: Retrospective and Prospective', in B.W. Longenecker (ed.), *Narrative Dynamics in Paul* (Louisville: Westminster John Knox, 2002), pp. 3–16.

2   N.T. Wright, *Paul and the Faithfulness of God* (Christian Origins and the Question of God; London/Minneapolis: SPCK/Fortress, 2013), p. 461. On the narrative structure of Paul's theology, see pp. 456–537.

3   B.W. Longenecker (ed.), *Narrative Dynamics in Paul* (Louisville: Westminster John Knox, 2002).

4   R.B. Hays, 'Is Paul's Gospel Narratable?', *Journal for the Study of the New Testament* 27 (2004), pp. 217–39.

5   For a valuable introduction, see S. Moyise, *The Old Testament in the New: An Introduction* (London and New York: Continuum, 2001), pp. 75–97; and, in somewhat more detail, S. Moyise, *Paul and Scripture* (London: SPCK, 2010).

6   R.B. Hays, *Echoes of Scripture in the Letters of Paul* (London and New Haven: Yale University Press, 1989).

7   F. Watson, *Paul and the Hermeneutics of Faith* (London and New York: T&T Clark, 2004).

8   C.M. Tuckett, 'Paul, Scripture and Ethics: Some Reflections' *New Testament Studies* 46 (2000), pp. 403–24; C.D. Stanley, *Arguing With Scripture: The Rhetoric of Quotations in the Letters of Paul* (London and New York: T&T Clark, 2004).

9   These issues and others were debated and addressed in a six-year programme in the 'Paul and Scripture' Seminar of the SBL. The results are published in S.E. Porter and C.D. Stanley (eds), *As It Is Written: Studying Paul's Use of Scripture* (Atlanta: Society of Biblical Literature, 2008), and C.D. Stanley (ed.) *Paul and Scripture: Extending the Conversation* (Atlanta: Society of Biblical Literature, 2012).

10 For a recent study of this use of Jewish 'messiah' language in Paul, see M.V. Novenson, *Christ among the Messiahs: Christ Language in Paul and Messiah Language in Ancient Judaism* (Oxford & New York: OUP, 2012).

11 E.P. Sanders, *Paul and Palestinian Judaism* (London: SCM, 1977), pp. 467–68; italics original. Sanders cites passages such as Rom 6.3–11; 7.4; Gal 2.19–20; 5.24; Phil 3.10–11 in support, claiming that: '*It is these*

passages which reveal the true significance of Christ's death in Paul's thought' (italics original).

12 A.Schweitzer, *The Mysticism of Paul the Apostle* (2nd edn, London: A&C Black, 1953), p. 3.

13 On this point, see M. Gorman, *Inhabiting the Cruciform God: Kenosis, Justification, and Theosis in Paul's Narrative Soteriology* (Grand Rapids: Eerdmans, 2009), pp. 40–104.

14 J.D.G. Dunn, *Christology in the Making* (London: SCM, 1980, 2nd edn 1989).

15 Dunn, *Christology in the Making*, pp. 114–21; also J.D.G. Dunn, *The Theology of Paul the Apostle* (Edinburgh: T&T Clark, 1998), pp. 281–88.

16 E.g. P.M. Casey, *From Jewish Prophet to Gentile God* (Cambridge: James Clarke, 1991), pp. 112–13; G.D. Fee, *Paul's Letter to the Philippians* (Grand Rapids: Eerdmans, 1995), p. 203, n. 41.

17 Colossians may or may not be by Paul (see pp. 189–91). Nonetheless it is interesting that the text refers to Christ as the *image* of God, and to the fullness of deity dwelling in Christ, not to Christ as 'God with us' (Matt 1.23), nor as 'the Word (which was God) become flesh' (John 1.1–2, 14). We should also note that the Greek of Col 1.19 actually runs: 'in him all the fullness was pleased to dwell' – the NRSV adds 'of God'. Col 2.9 has the phrase 'the fullness of deity'.

18 The earliest New Testament Greek manuscripts contain no punctuation, so the intended punctuation and sentence structure is open to debate.

19 N.T. Wright, *The Climax of the Covenant* (Edinburgh: T&T Clark, 1991), pp. 120–36; *What Saint Paul Really Said*, pp. 65–75; *Paul and the Faithfulness of God*, pp. 619–737.

20 R. Bauckham, *Jesus and the God of Israel* (Milton Keynes: Paternoster, 2008), pp. 182–232.

21 An early and influential article is R. Bauckham, 'The Worship of Jesus in Apocalyptic Christianity', *New Testament Studies* 27 (1981), pp. 322–41. See further L.W. Hurtado, *One God, One Lord: Early Christian Devotion and Ancient Jewish Monotheism* (London: SCM, 1988; 2nd edn, Edinburgh: T&T Clark, 1998); L.W. Hurtado, *Lord Jesus Christ: Devotion to Jesus in Earliest Christianity* (Grand Rapids: Eerdmans, 2003), with pp. 79–153 on the early Pauline material; Bauckham, *Jesus and the God of Israel*.

22 See J.C. Beker, *Paul the Apostle* (Edinburgh: T&T Clark, 1980), pp. 362–67; *The Triumph of God* (Minneapolis: Fortress, 1990), pp. 21–24, 115.

23 The Hebrew word *ruach* means spirit, breath or wind, hence the NRSV's rendering of Gen 1.2 'a wind from God'.

24 For a comprehensive study, see G.D. Fee, *God's Empowering Presence: The Holy Spirit in the Letters of Paul* (Peabody: Hendrickson, 1994), and the briefer treatment in G.D. Fee, *Paul, the Spirit, and the People of God* (Peabody: Hendrickson, 1996).

25 Beker, *Paul the Apostle*, p. 362.

26 For a discussion of these contrasting eschatological perspectives, see also J.D.G. Dunn, *The Theology of Paul the Apostle* (Edinburgh: T&T Clark, 1998), pp. 461–66.

27 C.H. Dodd, *New Testament Studies* (Manchester: Manchester University Press, 1953), pp. 83–128. Cf. also A.E. Harvey, *Renewal Through Suffering: A Study of 2 Corinthians* (Edinburgh: T&T Clark, 1996), who argues that Paul's near-death experience recounted in 2 Cor 1.8–10 caused him to develop a new perspective on suffering and its significance.

28 On this topic, see further D.G. Horrell, C. Hunt and C.C.B. Southgate, *Greening Paul: Rereading the Apostle in an Age of Ecological Crisis* (Waco: Baylor University Press, 2010).

29 E.P. Sanders, *Paul* (Oxford: OUP, 1991), pp. 126–27. For an extensive study of these contrasting perspectives see S. Hillert, *Limited and Universal Salvation: A Text-Oriented and Hermeneutical Study of Two Perspectives in Paul* (Stockholm: Almqvist and Wiksell, 1999).

30 W. Wrede, *Paul* (London: Philip Green, 1907); Schweitzer, *Mysticism*; both quoted by P.F. Esler, *Galatians* (London and New York: Routledge, 1998), p. 153.

31 See Esler, *Galatians*, pp. 154–59.

32 Stendahl, *Paul Among Jews and Gentiles*, p. 26.

33 See Schweitzer, *Mysticism*, p. 3, etc.; Sanders, *Paul and Palestinian Judaism*, pp. 447–74; also Sanders, *Paul*, pp. 74–75.

34 E.g. M. Seifrid, *Justification by Faith: The Origin and Development of a Central Pauline Theme* (Leiden: Brill, 1992); S. Westerholm, *Israel's Law and the Church's Faith* (Grand Rapids: Eerdmans, 1988), pp. 141–73, 221; S. Westerholm, *Perspectives Old and New on Paul* (Grand Rapids: Eerdmans, 2004), pp. 352–407. For a concise and recent articulation of this view, in critical dialogue with N.T. Wright and Douglas Campbell, among others, see S. Westerholm, *Justification Reconsidered: Rethinking a Pauline Theme* (Grand Rapids: Eerdmans, 2013).

35 See D.A. Campbell, *The Quest for Paul's Gospel* (London and New York: T&T Clark, 2005) and esp. *The Deliverance of God: An Apocalyptic Rereading of Justification in Paul* (Grand Rapids: Eerdmans, 2009). For a critically probing engagement with this massive book, see R.B. Matlock, 'Zeal for God but Not According to Knowledge: Douglas Campbell's War on Justification Theory', *Journal for the Study of the New Testament* 34 (2011), pp. 115–49.

36 Gorman, *Inhabiting*, p. 74; see further pp. 40–104.

37 See Wright, *Paul and the Faithfulness of God*, pp. 774–1042; or briefly, e.g., in Wright, *What Saint Paul Really Said*, pp. 113–33.

38 Westerholm, *Justification Reconsidered*.

39 For a similar but more detailed presentation, see Sanders, *Paul*, pp. 45–49.

40 See E.P. Sanders, *Paul, the Law and the Jewish People* (London: SCM, 1983), pp. 6–10, 13–14 n. 18; Sanders, *Paul*, p. 46.

41 See further J. Ziesler, *The Meaning of Righteousness in Paul* (Cambridge: CUP, 1972). See also the table of possible understandings of 'righteousness' in Wright, *What Saint Paul Really Said*, p. 101.

42 See e.g. Barrett, *Paul*, p. 99; Ziesler, *Pauline Christianity*, p. 88.

43 Sanders, *Paul*, pp. 47–48.

44 Wright, *Paul and the Faithfulness of God*, pp. 795–801. See also a concise overview in Wright, *What Saint Paul Really Said*, pp. 117–18.

45 Wright, *Paul and the Faithfulness of God*, p. 944.

46 See the extended treatment in Wright, *Paul and the Faithfulness of God*, pp. 774–1042. For a concise overview, see N.T. Wright, *Paul: Fresh Perspectives* (London: SPCK, 2005), pp. 108–29.

47 Westerholm, *Justification Reconsidered*, pp. 1–22.

48 See R.B. Hays, *The Faith of Jesus Christ: An Investigation of the Narrative Substructure of Galatians 3:1–4:11* (Chico: Scholars, 1983), pp. 139–91; M.D. Hooker, *From Adam to Christ: Essays on Paul* (Cambridge: CUP, 1990), pp. 165–86. For both sides of the debate, see the essays in D.M. Hay and E.E. Johnson (eds), *Pauline Theology, Vol.4* (Atlanta: Scholars, 1997), pp. 35–92, two of which (by Hays and Dunn) are also reprinted in the 2002 edition of Hays, *Faith of Jesus Christ*, pp. 249–97.

49 R.B. Matlock, 'Detheologizing the *PISTIS CHRISTOU* Debate: Cautionary Remarks from a Lexical Semantic Perspective', *Novum Testamentum* 42 (2000), pp. 1–23; J.D.G. Dunn, 'Once More, *PISTIS CHRISTOU*', in E.E. Johnson and D.M. Hay (eds), *Pauline Theology, Vol. 4* (Atlanta: Scholars

Press, 1997), pp. 61–81 (now reprinted in the second edition of Hays, *Faith of Jesus Christ*, pp. 249–71). Cf. also J.D.G. Dunn, *The Theology of Paul the Apostle* (Edinburgh: T&T Clark, 1998), pp. 379–85.

50 This translation should not be taken to represent my own interpretation of Gal 2.16, but is intended simply to illustrate the different possibilities.

51 See further V.P. Furnish, *Theology and Ethics in Paul* (Nashville: Abingdon, 1968), reissued with an introduction by Richard Hays (Louisville: Westminster John Knox, 2009).

52 See further D.G. Horrell, *Solidarity and Difference: A Contemporary Reading of Paul's Ethics* (London & New York: T&T Clark, 2005), pp. 204–45.

53 See B. Arnold, *Christ as the Telos of Life: Moral Philosophy, Athletic Imagery, and the Aim of Philippians* (Tübingen: Mohr Siebeck, 2014).

54 Quoted from A.A. Long and D.N. Sedley, *The Hellenistic Philosophers: Vol. 1: Translations of the Principal Sources with Philosophical Commentary* (Cambridge: CUP, 1987), p. 121.

55 W. Deming, *Paul on Marriage and Celibacy: the Hellenistic Background of 1 Corinthians 7* (Cambridge: CUP, 1995). See also A.J. Malherbe, *Paul and the Popular Philosophers* (Minneapolis: Fortress, 1989); F.G. Downing, *Cynics, Paul and the Pauline Churches* (London and New York: Routledge, 1998); T. Engberg-Pedersen, *Paul and the Stoics* (Edinburgh: T&T Clark, 2000).

56 On this point, see further Horrell, *Solidarity and Difference*, pp. 133–65, 246–72.

57 This theme is emphasized by J.T. Sanders, *Ethics in the New Testament* (London: SCM, 1975).

Paul, Israel and the Jewish Law

Introduction

Paul's theology, his gospel, is profoundly and thoroughly Jewish: it tells the story of how the God of Abraham, Isaac and Jacob, the God who spoke through Moses and the prophets, has now acted to fulfil the promises made long before and to enable God's people to inherit their long-awaited blessings through the coming of the Messiah. Yet according to Paul's gospel, the people who inherit these blessings, the people who are the true 'children of Abraham', are not all who are Jewish, but all who have faith in Christ, whether they be Jew or Gentile. Indeed, 'in Christ', according to Paul, 'there is no longer Jew or Greek' (Gal 3.28; cf. 1 Cor 12.13; Col 3.11). So Paul's theology is essentially Jewish, yet it claims Israel's identity, blessings and salvation for a community which is not comprised solely of Jews, but of Jewish and Gentile believers in Christ. There is then in Paul's theology a fundamental tension between continuity and discontinuity: Paul's message did not represent a rejection of his Jewish 'past', but neither was it simply a straightforward continuation of it. While Paul saw his gospel as the announcement of what the God of Israel had now done in order to fulfil the promise to bless all nations through Abraham (Gen 12.3), many of his Jewish contemporaries regarded it as dangerous, false and heretical – hence Paul's rejection by his own people and his repeated punishment in their synagogues (2 Cor 11.24; 1 Thess 2.14–16).

One of the most difficult and important areas in the study of Paul lies in trying to understand the ways in which, and the extent to which, Paul's perspectives on his ancestral faith were reconfigured in the light of his vision of Christ. Understanding these areas of Paul's thought is important for various reasons: from a historical perspective it is vital to answering the question as to how and why Christianity eventually (some time after Paul's death) became a separate religion from Judaism and did not remain as a Jewish messianic sect. For theological, social and cultural reasons these areas of Paul's thought are also of enormous significance: Did Paul think that God had rejected his people Israel? Was God unfaithful to the promises made to Israel? Did Paul consider that the Christian Church had replaced Israel as the people of God – was Judaism now superseded? All these questions are clearly of great relevance for those who attempt to wrestle with wider, contemporary questions: To what extent was the Christian gospel, or Paul's gospel in particular, responsible for the rise of anti-Semitism? Should Christians believe that they alone will be redeemed, or that members of other religions will also be saved? Should Christians actively seek the conversion of members of other religions, specifically the conversion of Jews? Can Christianity allow other religious and cultural groups – specifically Judaism – to retain their identity and value? Understanding Paul's views on such matters is of course only a small part of beginning to wrestle with these contemporary questions; yet it is an important part, particularly given Paul's enormous influence on the Christian Church, and on its most prominent thinkers throughout the centuries. Two particular aspects of Paul's thought have received considerable attention from scholars: his attitude to the Jewish law, and his views on the continuing status of Israel.

Paul and the Jewish law

It is clear from the Hebrew Bible that central to Israel's identity is her calling to be obedient to the commandments of God, to the way of life set down for her by God, to the *Torah* (the Hebrew word translated 'law') (see, e.g., Exod 19.7ff; Deut 6.1–9). The basic problem in interpreting Paul's Christian view of the Jewish law is that he seems to say both positive and negative things about it. For example, apparently negative statements include the following: 'For no human being will be justified in his sight by deeds prescribed by the law, for through the law comes the knowledge of sin' (Rom 3.20). 'The sting of death is sin, and the power of sin is the law' (1 Cor 15.56). 'The letter kills, but the Spirit gives life' (2 Cor 3.6). 'Christ redeemed us from the curse of the law . . .' (Gal 3.13).

But on the other hand, consider these positive statements: 'So the law is holy, and the commandment is holy and just and good' (Rom 7.12). 'Owe no one anything, except to love one another; for the one who loves another has fulfilled the law' (Rom 13.8); '. . . through love become slaves to one another. For the whole law is summed up in a single commandment, "You shall love your neighbour as yourself"' (Gal 5.13–14).

How then are we to make sense of these contrasting, even contradictory statements? Some scholars, notably Heikki Räisänen, have argued that Paul's various statements about the law cannot be harmonized into a coherent or systematic scheme: Paul is simply inconsistent.[1] Others suggest that Paul's thought developed between his different letters, notably between Galatians and Romans;[2] but since both positive and negative statements occur within the same letters (e.g., Galatians; see above) such an answer seems less than complete. As for Paul's consistency, few would want to argue that Paul was rigorously consistent or systematic in all that he wrote, but many scholars also believe that it is at least worth the attempt to understand what underlying convictions motivate Paul's varied statements about the Jewish law. The basic problem or dilemma surely results from the theological convictions which Paul seeks to hold together. He is convinced on the one hand that God gave the law, so unless God made a mistake, or was unable to bring the plans to fruition, or has simply had a change of mind, then the law must be a part of the divine purpose. Yet, on the other hand, Paul is convinced that God has now acted in Christ for the salvation of all who believe, and that salvation comes through Christ and not through the law.

1. A traditional 'Lutheran' perspective

A traditional interpretation of Paul's attitude to the law would run something like this: as a Jew, Paul had sought to earn his salvation through obedience to the law, even though he found this an impossible struggle (cf. Rom 7.7–25). His conversion brought about his liberation from this enslavement to a legalistic religion. From that point on, he realized that salvation came through grace alone, the grace of God manifested in the self-giving of Christ, through whom righteousness and eternal life were freely given. Paul thus criticizes the law – and indeed the Jewish religion as a whole – because obeying laws, doing good deeds, can never earn a person's salvation. The Jews were fundamentally mistaken on this point, and Paul's conversion marked the change from living under law to living under grace. God's main purpose in giving the law had been to make human beings conscious of their sin, and indeed to make them sin all the more, and so, ultimately, to make them aware of their need for salvation – a salvation which comes by grace alone, through faith in Christ.

Such a perspective on Paul and the law is generally associated with the name of Martin Luther (1483–1546), whose interpretation of Paul in the context of his own personal and religious struggles remains enormously influential, especially, of course, in Protestant Churches which stand in the Lutheran tradition. The summary above may be somewhat caricatured, yet similar statements regarding Paul and Judaism may be found in the writings of some of the most influential modern Lutheran interpreters of Paul: Rudolf Bultmann and Ernst Käsemann.

In his interpretation of Paul's view of the law, for example, Bultmann writes as follows:

> The way of works of the Law and the way of grace and faith are mutually exclusive opposites ... But why is this the case? Because man's effort to achieve his salvation by keeping the Law only leads him into sin, *indeed this effort itself in the end is already sin* ... Thus, the Law brings to light that man is sinful, whether it be that his

sinful desire leads him to transgression of the Law or that *that desire disguises itself in zeal for keeping the Law.*[3]

Käsemann presents a similarly Lutheran interpretation, in which the criticism of Judaism is more explicit:

> In fact, religion always provides man with his most thoroughgoing possibility of confusing an illusion with God. Paul sees this possibility realized in the devout Jew: inasmuch as the announcement of God's will in the law is here misunderstood as a summons to human achievement and therefore as a means to a righteousness of one's own. But that is for him the root sin, because now an image is set in the place of God ... in and with Israel he [Paul] strikes at the hidden Jew in all of us, at the man who validates rights and demands over against God on the basis of God's past dealings with him and to this extent is serving not God but an illusion.[4]

While we should be careful not to dismiss the exegetical insights of Luther and his followers too quickly, there are major problems with such an interpretation of Paul and particularly with the portrait of Judaism which emerges as the counterfoil to Paul's gospel. As Daniel Boyarin emphasizes, there is something profoundly disturbing about the negative portrayal of Judaism in the works of these German scholars writing after the horrors of the Holocaust had become apparent.[5] These problems in the presentation of Judaism did not go unnoticed by scholars, some of them Jewish, but they were not given their due attention until the late 1970s, and the publication of a major book on Paul, a book which many now see as inaugurating a new phase in the study of Paul: E.P. Sanders' *Paul and Palestinian Judaism* (London: SCM, 1977).

2. E.P. Sanders and the 'New Perspective' on Paul

In *Paul and Palestinian Judaism* Sanders investigates whether or not the Judaism of Paul's day can legitimately be characterized as a religion of 'legalistic-works-righteousness' – Sanders' term to summarize the portrait which emerged in much New Testament scholarship. Sanders argues that the available evidence demonstrates that such a label is little more than a pernicious Christian caricature. Judaism's pattern of religion is more adequately encapsulated, Sanders proposes, in the term 'covenantal nomism'. At the heart of Judaism's self-understanding is the idea of covenant, a binding relationship between God and God's people, initiated by God in an act of undeserved grace (hence 'covenantal'). The appropriate *response* for those who are members of this covenant people is to live in obedience to God's law (*nomos* is the Greek word for law, used by Paul; hence the term 'nomism'). In other words, obedience to the law was not regarded as a means of earning one's salvation, or of becoming a member of God's people, but as a response to the gracious act of God in making a covenant with the people of Israel. According to Sanders, there is virtually no evidence that Jews of Paul's time lost sight of the centrality of the covenant, nor that their religion was essentially legalistic. Indeed, Sanders suggests that the relation between grace and works is held in a very similar balance by both Paul and the Judaism contemporary with him: membership of the people of God is dependent on God's grace, but acting obediently is a condition for remaining 'in' God's people (cf. 1 Cor 6.9–11; Gal 5.19–21).

Following the publication of Sanders' work there has been quite widespread agreement that much previous New Testament interpretation did indeed misrepresent and caricature Judaism, and a willingness to admit that such misrepresentation perhaps bears some responsibility for the anti-Semitism which reached its zenith in the Holocaust. There is now a much greater concern to present the Judaism of Paul's time fairly, and to avoid the naive assumption that Paul's angry polemic is an unbiased source from which to reconstruct Jewish beliefs and practices.

However, lively discussion continues about many of the issues raised by Sanders' work, in terms of both its depiction of Judaism and especially its consequences for the reinterpretation of Paul. As we shall see below, debate between so-called 'new' and 'old' perspectives on Paul – and about possible ways beyond this opposition – remains a major issue in contemporary Pauline studies. For those who accept Sanders' insistence that first-century Jews did not place salvific weight on doing good deeds in obedience to the law – that is, did not ever think they would be saved by 'works' – a new interpretation of Paul is needed, one which does not see this as the target of his attack. If he was not attacking legalism and self-righteousness, what was he criticizing?

Sanders' own answer essentially turns on its head the direction in which Paul's thought is conventionally understood. Instead of seeing Paul as someone conscious of a problem (the impossibility of fulfilling the law well enough to be saved) who then finds the answer in Christ, Sanders proposes that Paul reasoned 'from solution to plight'. In other words, through his conversion experience Paul became convinced that God had acted in Christ to save the world. Reasoning 'backwards' from this new conviction, Paul concluded that all people must have needed saving (or otherwise Christ came for no good reason) and that the law was not the means by which they could be saved. (It's a bit like the popular Christian cliché, 'Jesus is the answer, now what's the question?') In an oft-quoted summary, Sanders expresses in a nutshell what he sees as Paul's 'criticism' of Judaism: *'this is what Paul finds wrong in Judaism: it is not Christianity'.*[6] Once convinced that Christ is the answer, Paul then concludes (and attempts to demonstrate) that Judaism, and specifically the Jewish law, is not the way. The apparent tension between Paul's positive and negative statements about the law can be resolved, Sanders suggests, by observing that Paul gives different answers to different questions.[7] To the question, 'How does someone join the people of God?', Paul's answer is emphatically, 'Not by works of law but by faith in Christ' (Rom 3.28; Gal 2.16). But on the question of what behaviour is appropriate for those who are members of God's people, and wish to remain so, the answer is that the law's demands must be fulfilled, not in all its particular requirements (specifically circumcision, food laws and sabbath observance), but in its basic demand of love for one's neighbour (Rom 8.4; 13.8–10; Gal 5.14).[8]

James Dunn, while accepting Sanders' portrait of Judaism at the time of Paul and warmly welcoming the 'new perspective' that this makes possible, argues that Sanders' reconstruction of Paul is less than satisfactory.[9] In a lecture first published in 1983 Dunn set out both his agreement with Sanders' work on Judaism and his new proposals for reinterpreting Paul, and, in using the phrase 'new perspective', established the catch-phrase for the various new, 'post-Sanders' readings of Paul, of which Dunn's is among the most prominent and developed. For Dunn, Sanders' Paul makes an arbitrary and inexplicable jump from one religious system to another, without there being any substantive reason for his criticism of his former position or any real sense of continuity with his Jewish faith. In his own influential proposal to reinterpret Paul in the light of Sanders' work, Dunn highlights the fact that Paul often focuses his critique not on 'the law' per se, but on 'the works of the law' (see Rom 3.28; Gal 2.16; 3.2, 5, 10 etc.). What Paul objects to, Dunn proposes, is the way in which the Judaism of Paul's time used the law as a boundary marker, defining a particular ethnic and cultural group as inside the covenant and others as 'out'. Circumcision, food laws and sabbath observance were the most prominent examples of the 'works of the law' which served as the badges of covenant membership and thus functioned to demarcate Jews from Gentiles. Paul is not therefore criticizing legalism, nor the doing of good deeds, when he criticizes those who depend on the works of the law. Rather he is criticizing the use of the law to mark out certain people as belonging, as coming exclusively within the sphere of God's grace. To this nationalistic and ethnocentric exclusivism Paul opposes his gospel message that salvation is available to all who have faith in Christ, both Jew and Gentile, without the need for Gentile converts to adopt the marks of Jewish belonging (circumcision etc.). The problem Paul confronted, in a nutshell, was not legalism but ethnocentrism or nationalism. This, in essence, is the 'New Perspective' on Paul that Dunn proposes, and has worked out in great detail in commentaries on Romans and Galatians, as well as in his major summary work on Paul's theology.[10]

Dunn in turn has also been criticized. Does his interpretation of the 'works of the law' stand up to scrutiny? Does his reconstruction of Paul still depend on a Christian bias that somehow presents Christianity as open and universalistic in contrast to a Judaism which is narrow, nationalistic and ethnocentric? Two kinds of critical reaction to the New Perspective may be distinguished in recent scholarship: one is what has been termed the 'radical new perspective' that argues for a more thoroughly 'Jewish' Paul (see further below); the other is the reassertion of a more traditional, 'Lutheran' understanding of Paul. From this latter perspective, counter-arguments have been mounted against Sanders, Dunn and others. Indeed, the New Perspective has, in some (Christian) circles at least, proved highly controversial and is perceived as challenging fundamentally the Reformation-based, Protestant understanding of Paul's gospel as a message about justification by faith and not by works. A flavour of the extent to which fundamental issues are felt to be at stake may be gained from the comments of Seyoon Kim, in a book which is both a vigorous defence of his earlier work and a sharp critique of the New Perspective, particularly of Dunn:

> Since the Reformation ... no school of thought ... has exerted a greater influence upon Pauline scholarship than the school of the New Perspective ... [This school] is in many respects overturning the Reformation interpretation of Paul's gospel. The potential significance of the school for the whole Christian faith can hardly be exaggerated.[11]

3. A 'Lutheran' interpretation reasserted: Stephen Westerholm

Among those who have argued for a position which retains more in common with the traditional Lutheran perspective is Stephen Westerholm, in a book published in 1988 and republished in 2004 in an extensively revised and expanded form, as well as in a recent (2013) brief study of the theme of justification.[12] Westerholm accepts an important point arising from the work of Sanders and others: that Paul's writings must not be taken as an accurate source for reconstructing

Jewish self-understanding; Jewish attitudes to the law cannot simply be read off from Paul's letters. Paul is writing *Christian* theology, arguing out a position on the Jewish law from the perspective of his conviction about God's action in the death and resurrection of Christ. Moreover, Westerholm accepts and affirms as 'the most important and salutary emphasis of the new perspective on Paul ... that Judaism was not "legalistic"'.[13]

Westerholm argues that by the 'law' Paul generally means the commandments given to Moses at Sinai – the basic legal code by which Jews were obligated to live. This law, Westerholm suggests, is indeed presented in the Hebrew Bible as a means to life for those who follow it; hence it is not inaccurate to conclude that obedience to the law was seen as the means to obtain salvation. According to Paul, human beings have simply proved incapable of obeying the law, and thus have failed to obtain the life that it promised. Salvation for sinful human beings cannot be attained by doing good deeds, by 'works', and the law ultimately only leads people to this realization. Thus, according to Westerholm, Paul is more pessimistic than Judaism about the possibility that people could embody the kind of obedience necessary to maintain God's favour towards them. Salvation can thus come only by an act of God's undeserved grace, precisely what Paul sees as God's gift in Christ. God's purpose in giving the law, then, was to make sin visible, accountable, and indeed to increase it, such that the need for salvation in Christ might become apparent. Paul's theology is therefore, as Luther saw, fundamentally based upon a contrast between justification by grace (through faith alone) and the impossible attempt at justification by works.

Westerholm thus defends and rearticulates a fundamentally Lutheran view of Paul and the law. However, his clear insistence that this is an articulation of Paul's *Christian* theology is important in order to avoid the false and pernicious conclusions which might otherwise be implied about Judaism at the time of Paul. The logic of Paul's Christian convictions may have driven him to the argument that Judaism was based on an attempt to achieve righteousness by works and to decry this attempt as impossible; but that does *not* mean that Paul's Jewish contemporaries would have understood their covenantal responsibilities in anything like the same way.[14]

Westerholm's attempt to reassert the validity of a broadly Lutheran understanding of Paul has of course also been subject to criticism. Dunn, for example, criticizes Westerholm's argument that Paul's critique of 'works' applies to works in general and not (as Dunn maintains) specifically to the observances of the Mosaic law which set Jews apart from Gentiles. According to Dunn, Westerholm fails to appreciate the social function of the law as a boundary marker around the people of Israel, and thus deals with Paul's theology in abstraction from the specific social context - the incorporation of Gentiles as Gentiles into the covenant people of God – within which Paul's arguments were expressed.[15] Nevertheless, Westerholm's arguments should be considered carefully, and show that a 'Lutheran' interpretation of Paul cannot simply be dismissed in the current phase of Pauline interpretation.

Indeed, the so-called 'Old Perspective' has been rearticulated and reasserted with considerable energy – though not in ways that ignore or refute all the insights of the New Perspective. Along with the books by Westerholm and Kim, another weighty example is the two-volume project edited by D.A. Carson, Peter O'Brien and Mark Seifrid, which has as its main target Sanders' characterization of Judaism's religion as one of covenantal nomism and the consequent interpretation of Paul against the background of this controlling concept.[16]

Vigorous debate continues, then, between the so-called 'Old' and 'New' Perspectives on Paul, and fundamental historical and theological issues are felt to be at stake. However, it is worth noting that there is a considerable diversity of interpretations of Paul on both sides of the debate; there is no single 'New' or 'Old' Perspective. Also worth considering is the extent to which, despite their vigorous opposition, prominent versions of both 'Old' and 'New' Perspectives on Paul share a structurally similar analysis of Paul's theology in relation to Judaism, in arguing, though in different ways, that there really was substance to

Paul's criticism of Judaism.[17] In this they differ from Sanders, who, we recall, maintained that Paul only saw a 'problem' with Judaism once he became convinced that Christianity was now the way to salvation. In other words, there was no real 'substance' to his criticism. By contrast, for some defenders of the Old Perspective, Judaism really did place weight on doing good deeds as contributing to salvation, while for Dunn Judaism really did use the law to demarcate a particular ethnic, national group as the people of God, and thus misunderstood the purpose of the law. As Barry Matlock has astutely observed: 'Substitute for "legalism" in the traditional reading "nationalism" in Dunn's, as the perverted attitude toward the law and its observance that is the real target of Paul's attack, and the old perspective fits Dunn right down to the ground'.[18] One key question at issue in historical analysis is whether it is convincing to argue that the Judaism of Paul's time placed salvific weight on doing good deeds in obedience to the law ('legalism'; the 'Old Perspective') or placed weight on the identity-defining 'works of the law' as determining the boundary around who was 'in' and who was 'out' ('ethnocentrism'; the 'New Perspective'). A question that remains for theological reflection is whether, and how, the Pauline gospel can (or should) be narrated without implying a relation of superiority between Christianity and Judaism.

4. A radical 'Jewish' perspective: two covenants?

This very issue – the relation between Christianity and Judaism – is in a sense central to another perspective on the questions about Paul's attitude to the Jewish law, namely one which argues that Paul's gospel, his letters, and specifically his comments about the law, were essentially directed towards Gentiles. This is what some have seen as offering a more 'radical' kind of new perspective, one in which Paul remains much more thoroughly Jewish even as an apostle of Christ. Another way of labelling this approach is to call it a 'two covenant' perspective, since it is Gentiles who are saved through Christ, while Jews are saved as Jews. Lloyd Gaston's book, *Paul and the Torah* – a collection of essays which opens with a programmatic chapter bearing that same title – presents an influential early articulation of this position, which others have since developed in various ways.[19] Gaston stresses that 'Paul is ... concerned to argue for the full right of Gentiles to be equal members of the people of God' but also that Paul assumes 'the right of Israel to remain Israel'. In short: 'All of the positive things Paul has to say about the righteousness of God effecting salvation for Gentiles in Christ need not at all imply anything negative about Israel and the Torah'.[20] Gaston's key claims about Paul's focus on Gentiles are firmly supported, and further developed, by John Gager, who also insists that Paul affirmed the continuing validity of the Jewish law for Jews and the certainty of Israel's salvation, and that his message about salvation in Christ was a message for Gentiles.[21]

More recently still, similar claims about Paul are central to Pamela Eisenbaum's book, *Paul Was Not a Christian*. According to Eisenbaum, Paul 'lived and died a Jew' but came to the conviction that Jesus, by his faithful obedience to God, had accomplished what was necessary for Gentiles to be incorporated into the family of God, and saw it as his divinely given mission to take this message to the Gentiles.[22] As Eisenbaum puts it elsewhere: 'whatever Paul says applies specifically to Gentiles ... Christ has provided an alternative to Torah observance for Gentiles ... Paul certainly never condemns Jews' observation of Torah, never advocates their abstaining from circumcision'.[23] In this view, Paul's insistence that no one is 'justified' by works of the law is intended to make clear that Gentile converts could find salvation (in Christ) without being required or expected to adopt the entire Jewish law, with its regulations concerning circumcision, sabbath observance, and clean and unclean foods. But equally, so the argument goes, Paul does not intend that Jewish believers in Christ should cease their practice of law observance. In short, it is Gentiles who can now be saved 'apart from the Law' (cf. Rom 3.21, 28) through Christ, while Jews retain their status as God's people on the basis of God's earlier covenant promises (see further below). Eisenbaum expresses the point sharply: 'Jesus saves, but he saves only Gentiles ... what was accomplished by Jesus' death was the reconciliation of *Gentiles* to God, and . . . that is all Paul ever claimed Jesus accomplished'.[24]

Some scholars, such as Magnus Zetterholm, regard this view – articulated in different ways by various proponents of it – as a major alternative position alongside those of the 'Old' and 'New' perspectives.[25] According to Zetterholm, both Old and New Perspectives treat Paul as someone who has in some way moved beyond Judaism, while this alternative, 'radical new perspective' treats Paul as remaining thoroughly within Judaism.[26] In some ways this is also a perspective that sits more easily with some modern sensitivities about the equal and abiding validity of Judaism and Christianity. For Gaston, it is important to note that the 'context' for doing Christian theology is decisively shaped both by the Holocaust and the refounding of the state of Israel; yet he also insists that his aims are rigorously historical, attempting to understand Paul better in his own context.[27] Gager likewise sees 'the Nazi Holocaust, together with the founding of the state of Israel' as the modern conditions that have enabled a new – and, in Gager's view, more historically accurate – reading of Paul to arise.[28] A concern about the anti-Judaism to which Paul's writings have often given foundation is an explicit motivation for such readings. Eisenbaum, for example, suggests that 'a reading of Paul capable of demonstrating that he did not condemn Judaism, and that he did not reject Jews and replace them with Gentiles, would be welcome to many Christians and perhaps others'. Paul could instead offer 'a vision of inclusion that recognizes the validity of difference' and 'a model for thinking about religious pluralism'.[29] It is important, nonetheless, to sustain a careful distinction between the most historically and exegetically plausible interpretation of Paul's letters and the most theologically and ecumenically attractive interpretation. It is a striking illustration of the diversity in contemporary Pauline studies that some can declare this perspective the most promising direction, accepted by 'an increasing number of scholars', while others can refer to it as a 'now surely discredited position'![30]

Indeed, the so-called 'radical new (Jewish) perspective' on Paul outlined briefly above has been subjected to serious criticism, not least on the basis that Paul's argument in Romans, his most extensive and mature treatment of such issues, seems – though some would certainly argue otherwise – to make clear that both Jews and Gentiles are equally in need of salvation and that this salvation comes to both without reference to works of law and only through Christ, in whom, Paul believes, God has fulfilled his promises to Israel.[31] Likewise, referring to Gal 3.10–12, Andrew Das insists that Paul is 'grounding his conclusions for *all people* in biblical passages that employ *universal* language. At a minimum the Jewish scriptural passages he provides in support require the *inclusion* of the Jews'.[32] Paul's comments on his former life and Jewish identity in Gal 2.16–21 and Phil 3.3–9 may also suggest a more radical shift in his sense of identity than the 'Jewish perspective' on Paul allows.

This difficulty for the more 'Jewish' interpretation of Paul may be somewhat alleviated by distinguishing between salvation and behaviour, or, in more technical terms, between soteriology and ethics: Markus Bockmuehl, for example, argues that Paul's view is that both Jews and Gentiles are equally 'saved' by Christ and not on the basis of works of law, but that in terms of behaviour, Paul expects Jews to continue to observe the law, and Gentiles to observe only those aspects of the law relevant to Gentiles (such as abstaining from idolatry and sexual immorality): '[t]he apostle in 1 Corinthians 7:17ff makes clear that his "rule for all the churches" is for Jews to keep the Torah … and for Gentiles to keep what pertains to them'.[33] A similar position is argued by Peter Tomson, namely, that what Paul is developing in his letters is *halakah* – ethical instruction based on the law – specifically for Gentiles.[34] Again, though, there are questions about how far Paul's own practice, and that which he expects of other Jewish Christians, implies a move away from obedience to the law, particularly when the unity of the Christian community is at stake (cf. Gal 2.11–19; Rom 14.14; 1 Cor 9.20–21).[35]

Issues concerning Paul and the law, then, and specifically questions about how to understand Paul's insistence that no one will be justified (or righteoused)[36] by the works of the law, remain central to contemporary discussion of Paul.

5. Why did God give the law?

If the law is not the means to salvation, if it is unable to bring the life that it promised, then why did God give the law in the first place? This is not an insignificant question for Paul, who would never have countenanced the route taken by the second-century heretic Marcion, separating sharply the God of the Old Testament from the God of the New, and rejecting the former in favour of the latter. Paul never denies that the law was given by God and was part of God's purpose, although he comes closest to demoting the law's divine status in Gal 3.19, where he presents it as given through angels (not directly from God) and thus as having a lower and temporary status compared to the promise to Abraham, which has now been fulfilled in Christ (see Gal 3.16–4.7). It will be no surprise to learn that interpretations of Paul's attempts to answer the question about the law's purpose are also varied and conflicting – and the full range of scholarly proposals cannot be reviewed here.

In Gal 3.23–25, Paul makes clear that the law was given for a time: it played its role as a guardian (Greek: *paidagōgos*) up until the time when Christ came, when God's children now come into their true inheritance and so no longer (need to) live under the law. He suggests that the law was given 'because of transgressions' (Gal 3.19). Interpreting this phrase, and other texts where similar ideas seem to emerge, is difficult. Does Paul mean that the law was intended to restrict or limit sin, to provide a means of recording and reckoning sins, or even to *increase* sin? This last suggestion would of course raise theological problems – does God then promote sin? – but they are problems which Paul acknowledges and wrestles with in Rom 7.7–25, where he is explicitly concerned to defend the law against the charge that it is itself 'sin' (7.7). The fault lies not with the law but with 'sin' – a more or less personified power here – which, however, was given 'opportunity' by the commandments of the law (7.7–12). Paul goes further in his efforts to clear the law (and thus God) of direct blame for the enslavement of human beings under sin, by presenting the picture of a divided human self: an inner self that delights in the law of God and wants to do good; a fleshly self that is captive to the law of sin. In the following chapter of Romans, Paul goes on to show how, in Christ, God has provided a solution to this wretched situation, a solution which the law, weakened by the flesh, could not achieve (Rom 8.1–4).

Paul then has taken up thoroughly Jewish themes, themes known from his scriptures, and developed them in the light of his new conviction that God's saving grace is now manifest in Christ. From this Christian perspective, he reasons that the law itself cannot save, and thus has to rethink the purpose for which God gave it. Paul here finds himself facing a well-known theological dilemma, one hardly unique to Paul's thought alone: namely, that if God is the all-powerful sovereign creator, and foresaw all that would happen, then how can God not bear responsibility for sin? Paul rejects the idea that God (or God's law) is directly the agent of sin; he remains insistent that God's purposes are being worked out, and that the law has played its part in the cosmic drama of salvation that now finds its culmination in Christ. Another nagging question however remains: what then has become of Israel, the chosen people of God?

What has become of Israel?

Since Paul is adamant that salvation is found in Christ alone, and does not come by obedience to the law, that seems to leave 'unbelieving' Jews, as well as Gentiles, under sin and in need of salvation (cf. Rom 1.18–3.20). But if Paul's gospel implies that unbelieving Jews are now outside the community of the 'children of Abraham', excluded from the promised blessings, what has become of God's promises to the covenant people? The question is by no means marginal or trivial for Paul. On the contrary, it is a source both of personal anguish (Rom 9.1–5) and of intense theological deliberation (Rom 9–11). For if Israel has indeed been abandoned, does that not mean that God has been unfaithful to God's word, has reneged on a promise (cf. Rom 3.3–4; 9.6; 9.14; 11.1)?

It is clear, first of all, that Paul claims for the Christian believers, both Jewish and Gentile, the status which Israel claims as her own. There is only one place where Paul refers to the Church as 'the Israel of God' (Gal 6.16) – and the interpretation of that text is disputed – but he does clearly imply that this new community of believers in Christ has a distinct identity (1 Cor 10.32), distinct from that of 'Israel according to the flesh' (*kata sarka*; 1 Cor 10.18; cf. Rom 9.4–8), and that it inherits the blessing and status promised to Israel. In particular, Paul spends some time in Galatians arguing that the true descendants of Abraham, the father of the Jewish people, are those who have faith, specifically faith in Christ (Gal 3.6–4.31). The promise of blessing was made to Abraham and his seed (Gen 13.15; 17.8 etc.), 'seed' being clearly a collective noun referring to Abraham's descendants. Paul however rather cleverly – if somewhat unconvincingly – points to the fact that the noun is singular (as collective nouns generally are!) and claims that *the* seed of Abraham is Christ (Gal 3.16). Consequently, all who are 'in Christ' are the descendants of Abraham, and thus are inheritors of the promised blessing. By contrast, those who belong to 'the present Jerusalem', the Israelites, Paul claims, reversing the traditional Jewish interpretation of the story of Sarah and Hagar (Gal 4.21–31), are in slavery. The children of the promise, those who are 'in Christ', are free.

Abraham is also central to Paul's argument in Romans 4, where he seeks to demonstrate, probably in opposition to the Jewish interpretation which would have upheld the scriptural injunction that all of Abraham's descendants must be circumcised (Gen 17.10–14), that Abraham was justified by faith, and thus is the ancestor of all who have faith, whether they be circumcised or not (Rom 4.11–12). In other words, Abraham's descendants, according to Paul, are not those who are circumcised (i.e., Jews) but all who have faith (in Christ – i.e., Christians).[37]

Here then is the central point from which the question of Israel's continuing identity emerges: Paul has claimed for his Christian converts the status of children of Abraham, and simultaneously denied that exclusive status to those who conventionally claim it, the Jewish people. Jews who do not believe in Christ, it seems, are enslaved under sin, and face the prospect of God's wrath (Rom 2.17–3.20). Indeed, in 1 Thess 2.14–16, Paul speaks of the wrath of God coming upon the Jews at last – a puzzling and unique passage in Paul, which some have argued was added later to the letter and is not in fact from Paul himself.

All of this creates a profound dilemma for Paul: how can God offer salvation in Christ to Jew and Gentile without distinction, yet also remain faithful to the promises made to Israel? Romans is the letter in which this theological dilemma is most apparent, where Paul is most insistent that the gospel is an offer of salvation equally available to Jew and Gentile without distinction (Rom 10.12; cf. Rom 1.16; 3.22 etc.), but is also concerned to insist that God has not been unfaithful to Israel. The pressing question, 'What has become of Israel?' is one that Paul turns to specifically in chapters 9–11, where he wrestles at length with this issue. While scholars of a former generation (notably C.H. Dodd) regarded this section of Romans as something of a digression, less than central to the overall argument, recent commentators have generally come to the view that it is in fact integral and important to the whole letter.[38]

Paul begins this complex and difficult passage by expressing his genuine anguish over the fate of Israel, over his kinspeople whom he recognizes are the rightful heirs of God's adoption, promises, and so on (Rom 9.1–5). In his basic concern to defend God's faithfulness, using scriptural citations frequently throughout, Paul presents various arguments as to why the situation is as it is. First of all he suggests that only some Israelites are 'true' Israelites and that this is due to the election of God (9.7–13). The question then arises as to whether God is being unjust in choosing some and rejecting others (9.14–29). Paul's response, that God can do whatever God chooses and that people, like pots made by a potter, have no right to question the decision of their creator, was famously regarded by Dodd as 'the weakest point in the whole epistle': 'man is not a pot; he *will* ask, "Why did you make me like this?" [Rom 9.20] and he will not be bludgeoned into silence'.[39]

Paul proceeds to reiterate his conviction that both Gentiles and Jews can be saved in Christ but that Israel as a whole has missed the way due to her attempt to establish her righteousness based on works and not on faith (Rom 9.30–10.21). However, he then returns to his insistent refrain: 'has God rejected his people? By no means!' (11.1). This time the explanation proposed is based on the Jewish idea of the faithful remnant. As at other times in her history, so now, only an elect remnant of Israel (including Paul, a Jew) has obtained what Israel as a whole sought (11.1–10).

The long and complex argument comes to its climax in 11.11–36, where Paul asks whether Israel's 'stumbling' means her permanent falling away. Again his emphatic answer is 'No!', and he claims to see in the purposes of God a profound plan, a mystery, which will lead to salvation for Gentiles and for Israel. Israel's rejection of the gospel, Paul suggests, led to its proclamation among the Gentiles (11.11–12), but the Gentiles' salvation will in turn make Israel jealous such that some of the Israelites too will be saved (11.14). Paul warns his Gentile readers not to become arrogant about their salvation and Israel's (temporary) rejection: he uses the illustration of natural branches broken off from a tree, and unnatural branches grafted in (11.17–24). Even though Paul claims that the gospel is offered to all without distinction, there remains for him something essentially 'natural' about Israel's belonging – after all, the roots of the tree are hers – compared with the grafting in of the Gentiles (11.17, 24). And finally, Paul declares a mystery, a mystery which should serve to warn Gentile Christians against becoming boastful and arrogant: the hardening of Israel has been allowed for a time, in order for 'the full number of the Gentiles' to come in. But then 'all Israel will be saved' (11.26). Indeed, the climactic conclusion of all Paul's wrestling to explain the purposes of God is reached in the affirmation that God's purpose in all this is to have mercy upon all (11.32), both Jew and Gentile (though Paul does not say whether he means 'all' in the sense of every single person, or 'all' in some collective representative sense – cf. 11.25: 'the full number of the Gentiles'). God's amazing plan of salvation leaves Paul lost for words and he ends with an outburst of praise to God, whose judgements are unsearchable and whose ways are inscrutable (11.33–36).

As regards the specific question of the salvation of Israel, Paul's statement in 11.26 – the 'mystery' that 'all Israel will be saved' – is open to various interpretations and has been much discussed. What does he mean by *all Israel*? Does he mean every individual Israelite who has ever lived, or only the 'true' Israelites he referred to earlier? Does he mean the Jews themselves, or the 'new' Israel defined as those who have faith in Christ? Equally important, and of obvious relevance to the contemporary Jewish-Christian dialogue, is the question as to whether Paul implies that Israel will be saved when she finally comes to have faith in Christ (cf. Rom 11.23), or simply as Israel, since God's gifts and call are 'irrevocable' (Rom 11.29). Some have argued that there is a 'special way' (the German term *Sonderweg* is sometimes used in the discussion) for Jews to be saved – simply as Jews, on the basis of God's covenant with them, apart from faith in Christ. From this perspective, Paul's gospel message is directed specifically to Gentiles, who can now be saved without adopting the Jewish law and becoming Jewish; but it does not imply that Jews themselves need to be saved or need abandon their commitment to a way of life based around the law (see also pp. 136–39 above, on this Jewish perspective on Paul and the law).[40] Others maintain that Paul's argument implies, whatever our contemporary preferences might be, that his view was that the Jewish people would be saved (only) through Christ.[41]

Once again we see Paul wrestling with theological dilemmas: attempting to hold together his belief concerning the need for people to turn to Christ with his belief in God's promises to Israel and his conviction that God's sovereign plan of salvation will ultimately be unstoppable; attempting to do justice to both human responsibility and the sovereignty of God. Moreover, Paul insists on holding onto two basic convictions, though they stand in some considerable tension: (a) that salvation is available to Jew and Gentile, without distinction, only in Christ; and (b) that God's promises to Israel – the people of Israel, the Jews – are irrevocable. As the Church over time became more distanced from its Jewish roots, it is understandable, though unfortunate, that the second of these convictions faded from view, and only the first was strongly asserted. Doing justice to Paul requires that we appreciate how deeply he holds both of these convictions, despite the apparent difficulties involved in trying to reconcile them.

Conclusion

In this chapter we have surveyed briefly some of the most difficult and important themes in Paul's thought, themes which concern the extent to which there is both continuity and discontinuity between Paul's Jewish and Christian theology. Paul seems clear that the Jewish law remains a source of authority and ethical instruction, yet equally insists that no one will be justified/righteoused by works of the law. Similarly, he insists that God's promises to Israel are irrevocable, yet sees these promises fulfilled in Christ, and available (only) to those who have faith in Christ. For both historical and theological reasons these themes are of enormous significance, and have been among the most studied aspects of Paul's theology. In the post World War II period, the increasing realization that Christian perspectives on Judaism bear some responsibility for the rise of violent anti-Semitism has given heightened urgency to the task of understanding sympathetically not only Paul, but also the varieties of Judaism contemporary with him. Moreover, as we have seen, deciding how to interpret Paul's own statements is difficult enough – and scholars continue to propose various possibilities – but deciding what place (if any) Paul's ideas should have in the contemporary search for understanding among Jews and Christians is another, even harder, task.

Further reading

The two important books mentioned above by E.P. Sanders are *Paul and Palestinian Judaism* (London: SCM, 1977) and *Paul, the Law and the Jewish People* (London: SCM, 1983); the second of these deals particularly with the two themes addressed in this chapter. Another influential book, which did much to challenge traditional presentations of Paul, is K. Stendahl's, *Paul Among Jews and Gentiles* (Philadelphia: Fortress, 1976). James Dunn's reaction to Sanders' earlier book, and his own ideas on the 'New Perspective' which it opens up, are best summarized in his essay 'The New Perspective on Paul', first published in the *Bulletin of the John Rylands Library* 65 (1983), pp. 95–122, and reprinted in Dunn's *Jesus, Paul and the Law* (London: SPCK, 1990), which contains additional notes responding to subsequent debate, as well as other relevant essays. Many of Dunn's essays related to the New Perspective are also collected in his *The New Perspective on Paul: Collected Essays* (Tübingen: Mohr Siebeck, 2005; revised edn, Grand Rapids: Eerdmans, 2008). Another major figure in what may loosely be termed the New Perspective on Paul is N.T. Wright, whose view of Paul is briefly set out in *What Saint Paul Really Said* (Oxford: Lion, 1997), and in *Paul: Fresh Perspectives* (London: SPCK, 2005), and extensively articulated in *Paul and the Faithfulness of God* (London/ Minneapolis: SPCK/Fortress, 2013). The flow of monographs on Paul and the law shows no signs of abating: among those which include surveys of previous scholarship are C.G. Kruse, *Paul, the Law and Justification* (Leicester: Apollos, 1996) and V. Kopalski, *What Are They Saying About Paul and the Law?* (New York: Paulist, 2001). A useful concise survey is also provided by C.J. Roetzel, 'Paul and the Law: Whence and Whither?', *Currents in Research: Biblical Studies* 3 (1995), pp. 249–75.

Stephen Westerholm's *Perspectives Old and New on Paul* (Grand Rapids: Eerdmans, 2004), which supersedes his earlier *Israel's Law and the Church's Faith* (Grand Rapids: Eerdmans, 1988) contains a thorough and careful survey of previous works as well as Westerholm's own defence of a broadly 'Lutheran' perspective. Magnus Zetterholm's *Perspectives on Paul: A Student's Guide to Recent Scholarship* (Minneapolis: Fortress, 2009) also offers a thorough survey of scholarship on Paul's relationship to Judaism, but places particular emphasis (and value) on those scholars who locate Paul firmly *within* Judaism. These two valuable surveys, with their rather different priorities and preferences, may be used in conjunction, not least given the contrasts between them. For the perspective that locates Paul firmly within Judaism, see in particular J.G. Gager, *Reinventing Paul* (Oxford & New York: OUP, 2000) and P. Eisenbaum, *Paul Was Not a Christian: The*

Original Message of a Misunderstood Apostle (San Francisco: HarperCollins, 2009).

On Paul's view of Israel, and on Romans 9–11 specifically, in addition to the commentaries on Romans, see A. Das, *Paul and the Jews* (Peabody: Hendrickson, 2003); Stendahl, *Paul Among Jews and Gentiles*, pp. 1–7; N.T. Wright, *The Climax of the Covenant: Christ and the Law in Pauline Theology* (Edinburgh: T&T Clark, 1991), pp. 231–57 (see also Wright's *Paul and the Faithfulness of God*, pp. 1156–258); R. Hvalvik, 'A "Sonderweg" for Israel. A Critical Examination of a Current Interpretation of Romans 11.25–27', *Journal for the Study of the New Testament* 38 (1990), pp. 87–107, and D. Harink *Paul Among the Postliberals* (Grand Rapids: Brazos, 2003), pp. 151–207, which particularly criticizes Wright's reading of Romans 9–11 and the resulting view of Paul and Israel. A stimulating book investigating how Paul's Jewish convictions were reconfigured following his conversion to Christ is T.L. Donaldson's *Paul and the Gentiles* (Minneapolis: Fortress, 1997).

One of the most challenging and interesting books on Paul and the implications of his thought for Jewish faith and identity is D. Boyarin, *A Radical Jew: Paul and the Politics of Identity* (Berkeley and Los Angeles: University of California Press, 1994). On the origins of anti-Semitism, including a reconsideration of Paul's impact on this, see J.G. Gager, *The Origins of Anti-Semitism* (Oxford & New York: OUP, 1983). On the range of modern Jewish engagement with Paul, both critical and appreciative, see D.R. Langton, *The Apostle Paul in the Jewish Imagination* (Cambridge: CUP, 2010).

Questions for further study

- Do you think Paul has a coherent view of the Jewish law? If so, what exactly is that view?
- What would you see as the key points that distinguish 'New' and 'Old' Perspectives on Paul? Do you agree with Kim that the New

Perspective presents a fundamental challenge to the Protestant Reformation's interpretation of Paul's gospel?

- How successfully does Paul hold together his convictions that on the one hand both Jew and Gentile will be saved in Christ and on the other hand God's promises to Israel are irrevocable? Is Paul susceptible to the charge of Christian supersessionism?

Notes

1 See H. Räisänen, *Paul and the Law* (Tübingen: Mohr Siebeck, 1983).

2 E.g. H. Hübner, *Law in Paul's Thought* (Edinburgh: T&T Clark, 1984).

3 R. Bultmann, *Theology of the New Testament. Vol. 1* (London: SCM, 1952), pp. 264–65; see further pp. 259–69. I have altered the emphases from the original.

4 E. Käsemann, 'Paul and Israel', in *New Testament Questions of Today* (London: SCM, 1969), pp. 184, 186.

5 D. Boyarin, *A Radical Jew: Paul and the Politics of Identity* (Berkeley and Los Angeles: University of California Press, 1994), pp. 212–14.

6 E.P. Sanders, *Paul and Palestinian Judaism*, p. 552, italics original.

7 E.P. Sanders, *Paul, the Law and the Jewish People* (London: SCM, 1983), pp. 3–167.

8 Sanders, *Paul, the Law and the Jewish People*, pp. 93–135.

9 See J.D.G. Dunn, *Jesus, Paul and the Law* (London: SPCK, 1990), esp. pp. 183–241.

10 Dunn, *Theology of Paul*.

11 Kim, *Paul and the New Perspective*, p. xiv. It should be noted, however, that the New Perspective has dominated Anglo-American discussion of Paul more than German discussion.

12 Westerholm, *Israel's Law and the Church's Faith; Perspectives Old and New; Justification Reconsidered*.

13 Westerholm, *Perspectives Old and New*, p. 443.

14 See Westerholm, *Israel's Law and the Church's Faith*, p. 173; also *Justification Reconsidered*, pp. 23–34.

15 Dunn, *Jesus, Paul and the Law*, pp. 237–41.

16 D.A. Carson, P.T. O'Brien and M. Seifrid (eds), *Justification and Variegated Nomism, Vol. 1: The Complexities of Second Temple Judaism* (Tübingen: Mohr Siebeck; Grand Rapids: Baker Academic, 2001); *Vol. 2: The Paradoxes of Paul* (Tübingen: Mohr Siebeck; Grand Rapids: Baker Academic, 2004). For another significant work arguing that Judaism at the time of Paul did place weight on obedience to *Torah* in relation to vindication at the Eschaton, see S.J. Gathercole, *Where then is Boasting? Early Jewish Soteriology and Paul's Response in Romans 1–5* (Grand Rapids: Eerdmans, 2002).

17 For a fuller analysis of the range of views on Paul's 'criticism' of Judaism, see S. Westerholm, 'The New Perspective at Twenty-Five', in Carson *et al.*, *Justification and Variegated Nomism, Vol. 2*, pp. 1–38.

18 R.B. Matlock, 'Sins of the Flesh and Suspicious Minds: Dunn's New Theology of Paul', *Journal for the Study of the New Testament* 72 (1998), p. 86.

19 L. Gaston, *Paul and the Torah* (Vancouver: University of British Columbia Press, 1987).

20 Gaston, *Paul and the Torah*, p. 34.

21 J.G. Gager, *Reinventing Paul* (Oxford & New York: OUP, 2000).

22 P. Eisenbaum, *Paul Was Not a Christian: The Original Message of a Misunderstood Apostle* (New York: HarperCollins, 2009), p. 5; cf. pp. 207, 240, 247 etc.

23 P. Eisenbaum, 'Jewish Perspectives: A *Jewish* Apostle to the Gentiles', in J.A. Marchal (ed.), *Studying Paul's Letters* (Minneapolis: Fortress, 2012), pp. 139–40; cf. Eisenbaum, *Paul Was Not a Christian*, pp. 216–19, 224.

24 Eisenbaum, 'Jewish Perspectives', p. 142; cf. Eisenbaum, *Paul Was Not a Christian*, p. 242.

25 See M. Zetterholm, *Approaches to Paul* (Minneapolis: Fortress, 2009), pp. 127–63, for an overview of works in this area.

26 Zetterholm, *Approaches to Paul*, pp. 125–26, 161–63.

27 Gaston, *Paul and the Torah*, pp. 2–3, 15.

28 Gager, *Reinventing Paul*, pp. 150–51.

29 Eisenbaum, 'Jewish Perspectives', pp. 135, 150.

30 Zetterholm, *Approaches to Paul*, p. 239, regards the 'radical new perspective' as getting closest to 'the truth about Paul'. Eisenbaum, 'Jewish Perspectives', p. 142, regards this Jewish perspective on Paul as one held by 'a growing number of scholars'. By contrast, Wright, *Paul and the Faithfulness of God*,

refers to 'the now surely discredited position of saying that Paul's gospel was *only* for Gentiles, not at all for Jews' (p. 401 n. 175).

31 See, e.g., R.B. Hays, ' "The Gospel is the Power of God for Salvation to Gentiles Only?" A Critique of Stanley Stowers' *A Rereading of Romans*', *Critical Review of Books in Religion* 9 (1996), pp. 27–44. The book to which Hays is responding here is S.K. Stowers, *A Rereading of Romans: Justice, Jews and Gentiles* (New Haven & London: Yale University Press, 1994). For further critique of such perspectives see also Wright, *Paul and the Faithfulness of God*, pp. 804–51, 1426–49 etc.

32 A.A. Das, *Paul and the Jews* (Peabody: Hendrickson, 2003), p. 99; see pp. 96–106 for a critique of the 'two covenant' approach.

33 M. Bockmuehl, *Jewish Law in Gentile Churches* (Edinburgh: T&T Clark, 2000), pp. 170–71.

34 P.J. Tomson, *Paul and the Jewish Law* (Assen & Maastricht/Minneapolis: Van Gorcum/Fortress, 1990).

35 See further Horrell, *Solidarity and Difference*, pp. 15–19; B. Holmberg, 'Jewish *Versus* Christian Identity in the Early Church', *Revue Biblique* 105 (1998), pp. 397–425.

36 See pp. 102–106.

37 We should recall that Paul never uses the term 'Christian', which appears only in what are probably among the later New Testament writings, and then only infrequently (Acts 11.26; 26.28; 1 Pet 4.16). See the discussion in Sanders, *Paul, the Law and the Jewish People*, pp. 171–99, esp. p. 175.

38 See K.P. Donfried, *The Romans Debate: Revised and Expanded Edition* (Edinburgh: T&T Clark, 1991) p. lxx.

39 C.H. Dodd, *The Epistle to the Romans* (London: Fontana, 1959), p. 171.

40 See also the discussion in Zetterholm, *Approaches to Paul*, pp. 127–63.

41 See discussion in Sanders, *Paul, the Law and the Jewish People*, pp. 192–98; R. Hvalvik, 'A "Sonderweg" for Israel. A Critical Examination of a Current Interpretation of Romans 11.25–27', *Journal for the Study of the New Testament* 38 (1990), pp. 87–107; N.T. Wright, *The Climax of the Covenant: Christ and the Law in Pauline Theology* (Edinburgh: T&T Clark, 1991), pp. 231–57, who sees 'all Israel' as a 'polemical redefinition', referring to the Church (p. 250).

7

Perspectives on the Pauline Assemblies

Introduction

Since the early 1970s a wide range of new methods and approaches has come into biblical studies, which is now (like many other humanities disciplines) a very diverse and often contested field: what some scholars regard as important and cutting-edge, others regard as faddish. Alongside the traditional focus on historical-critical study of mostly theological themes has come an enormous range of perspectives, from social-scientific and rhetorical to postcolonial and queer. Pauline studies has not always been in the vanguard of such experimental methods, but plenty of these new perspectives have been used to shed new light on Paul's letters and the churches to which they were sent. Some, such as the rhetorical criticism we encountered briefly in Chapter 4, have already been discussed. In this chapter I want to focus in particular on those approaches which have opened up new angles on the communities which Paul addressed. The focus thus shifts somewhat away from the single figure of Paul and his ideas, and onto others who were involved in the Christian movement, and the concrete circumstances of their gatherings. Indeed, one of the explicit motivations for the pioneers of social-scientific criticism of the New Testament was to redress what was seen as an over-emphasis on theological ideas and their interpretation, to the exclusion of the social context within which these ideas were formulated. Taking up both the concerns and the methods of the social sciences led to a rather different set of perspectives, and to a focus less exclusively on Paul and his 'grand' ideas and more on the people who comprised the membership of the Pauline communities. Thus questions have been asked about the cultural and social world which the early Christians inhabited (see also pp. 4–6 above), about the relationship between the early Christian groups and the wider society within which they were located, about the kinds of people who joined the Christian movement, about the rituals and structures of the earliest congregations, about how power and authority were exercised and legitimated within them, and so on. With such a wide range of questions and issues, and such a diversity of work done, what follows can only be a restricted review of a few of the areas covered in recent studies.

The socio-economic level of the early Christians

One question of obvious sociological interest concerns the kind of people who joined the Pauline churches, specifically their social level, class or status. Broadly speaking, until the 1970s, the consensus was – or was said to be[1] – that the Pauline Christians came from among the poor and lowly of Greco-Roman society. However, following an initial challenge by Edwin Judge, in a book published in 1960,[2] this consensus was widely rejected and largely replaced by what came to be known as the 'New Consensus'. This New Consensus owes a great deal to a study by Gerd Theissen, first published in 1974, in which Theissen examines the evidence concerning the social status of the Pauline Christians in the church at Corinth.[3] Looking both at statements concerning groups within the congregation and at data relating to named individuals among the Corinthian Christians, Theissen concludes that the Corinthian congregation was marked by what he calls 'internal stratification': 'The majority of members, who come from the lower classes, stand in contrast to a few influential members who come from the upper classes'.[4] The individuals named in the Corinthian correspondence, Theissen suggests, probably came from the upper class – a conclusion Theissen draws from evidence pointing to their owning of houses, the offices they held and their ability to travel and to provide support for others.

Theissen's work was taken up and further developed by Wayne Meeks, in his wide-ranging and influential book *The First Urban Christians*.[5] Looking at the evidence for the Pauline movement as a whole, Meeks confirms Theissen's picture of the Pauline congregations as containing a wide mix of social levels, with only the very top and bottom levels missing. While subsequent work has modified Theissen's and Meeks' work in various respects, the general picture of social diversity within the Pauline congregations has been very widely accepted.

However, a book published in 1998 by Justin Meggitt presents a sharp challenge to this so-called New Consensus.[6] Meggitt argues that the available evidence is not sufficient to substantiate Theissen's and Meeks' arguments; he claims that the Pauline Christians, Paul included, did in fact come from among the poor, the non-elite, of Roman society – the 99 per cent of the population who, Meggitt maintains, lived close to subsistence level. The question of the social and economic level of the Pauline Christians was thus once again opened up to debate.[7] A 2004 article by Steven Friesen, for example, develops a position somewhat akin to Meggitt's, but attempts to nuance and refine the approach by building a 'poverty scale' for various economic groups in the Roman Empire and allocating the Christians mentioned in Paul's letters to different groups.[8] They are all 'poor' – here Friesen basically agrees with Meggitt – but while some lived around or below subsistence level, a few had at least some surplus resources.

An informed judgement on this question requires of course a clear understanding, as far as such is possible, of the social and economic structure of the Roman Empire itself. It also depends on the interpretation of evidence from the Pauline epistles, and on the possible correlations between this evidence and that available from inscriptions and other literary and archaeological data. For example, there is the question as to whether the Erastus Paul mentions in Romans 16.23 can be identified with the Erastus named on an inscription found in excavations at Corinth – in which case Paul's Erastus would be wealthy and of high social standing. There is also the question as to what is implied by Paul's words near the opening of 1 Corinthians: 'Consider your own call, brothers and sisters: not many of you were wise by human standards, not many were powerful, not many were of noble birth' (1 Cor 1.26).

Does the indication that there were a few ('not many') wise, powerful and well-born members of the Corinthian community imply that this minority were of high social status, as Theissen and Meeks conclude? Or is Meggitt right to argue that the verse really gives very little concrete information about their precise socio-economic standing? Indeed, does the limited data in the Pauline epistles enable us to say much at all about the precise economic level of the early Christians? Similar debate surrounds the interpretation of the conflict over the Lord's Supper, which Theissen argues represents a conflict between rich and poor members of the congregation.[9] Again Meggitt offers a different interpretation: that 'those who have nothing' at the Lord's Supper (1 Cor 11.22) are not the poor, but simply those who do not receive the bread and wine of the Eucharist.[10] The whole discussion is significant not only in terms of the perspective it suggests on the composition and character of the earliest Christian groups but also with regard to the implications for understanding early Christian ethics and practice: Were the groups socially diverse, with relatively wealthy patrons opening their homes and providing meals for the poorer members? Or were they essentially groups of the poor, who offered one another forms of mutual support? It seems in my view unlikely that there were members of the wealthy elite among the earliest Christian congregations; but there was most likely some degree of socio-economic diversity encompassed within these communities. Moreover, as Peter Oakes has shown, through the use of historically-informed imagination, our sense of where the early Christians were located in terms of socio-economic status, occupation and accommodation can help us to see what Paul's letters may have meant to such people, when they were heard 'on the ground'.[11]

The character and location of the Pauline assemblies

Social-scientific interpretation has attempted to bring to the centre of attention realities all too often forgotten in the quest to understand Paul's theology: that Paul's letters are addressed to groups of ordinary people who met together, mostly in their homes and workplaces, and shared a common identity as brothers and sisters 'in Christ'. How then were membership, identity and community boundaries indicated? What kind of groups were the Pauline congregations? (As an aside, we should also beware the label 'Pauline' congregations – or churches, or assemblies – since this, while useful as a shorthand, can too easily give the impression that there were distinctly 'Pauline' groups which related only or primarily to Paul, when the New Testament evidence suggests otherwise.)[12] Investigating such questions from a social-scientific perspective involves, for example, studying the 'sacraments' of baptism and Lord's Supper as 'rituals', socially-significant acts which serve to initiate and confirm people in their membership of a group. Meeks, for example, has outlined the ways in which baptism works as a 'ritual of initiation', symbolizing and enacting the believer's separation from the former world of their existence and their integration into a new one. Similarly, Meeks shows how the Lord's Supper serves not only as a dramatized reminder of the story which is central to the faith of the Christian community but also as a 'ritual of solidarity', binding the members of the community together as one body in Christ (1 Cor 10.16–17).[13] But what kind of community was formed by these converts to Christ?

Some valuable information may be gained by comparing the Pauline assemblies with the various other kinds of groups and associations contemporary with them: Meeks examines the household, the voluntary association or club, the synagogue and the philosophical or rhetorical 'school', arguing that each of these four models bears some analogy with a Pauline *ekklēsia* (assembly) but that none fits it exactly.[14] Subsequent work has explored these ancient analogies further, especially focused on ancient associations, which were of diverse kinds.[15] Some associations, for example, were based around particular trades or occupations, such as bakers, coppersmiths or merchants. Others were more ethnic or religious in their composition and character. Philip Harland has argued that Jewish and Christian groups would have looked essentially like associations, and that we should study them among the various associations of antiquity.[16]

The importance of the household as a context for early Christian groups and meetings is also clear: a number of what are most likely household groups are referred to in Paul's letters (e.g., Rom 16.10–15; 1 Cor 16.15) and he also speaks of 'the church/assembly that meets in so-and-so's house' (Rom 16.5; 1 Cor 16.19; Col 4.15; Phlmn 2).[17] Among the leading figures in the early Christian communities the heads of households probably played a significant part. Scholars have long presumed that houses almost exclusively formed the earliest Christian meeting places, and have tended to focus in particular on Roman villas or *domus*-style houses as the likely setting for such meetings. However, more recent work has challenged this focus in various ways. One challenge has been to broaden the kinds of domestic space that are considered, and in particular to consider the kinds of accommodation that would more likely have been occupied by people who were not from the rich or elite groups in society (see above, on their likely socio-economic level).[18] A second challenge, by Edward Adams, has been even more radical, questioning the consensus that Christians almost always met in houses and exploring the evidence for a wide range of alternative settings where meetings may have been held: in workshops, warehouses, rented dining rooms, gardens and other outdoor spaces.[19]

Further insight into the character of the Pauline churches may also be gained from comparing them with religious groups in other times and places, particularly those labelled by sociologists as 'sects'. Indeed, since its first detailed application to the New Testament in 1975, by Robin Scroggs, the model of the New Testament Church as a 'sectarian' movement has been widely employed.[20] By employing this model, scholars have been able to understand some of the features of early Christianity as characteristics typical of such sectarian movements, like the stark distinctions drawn between insiders and outsiders (see, e.g., 1 Thess 5.5), the intensity of fellowship and love, the egalitarianism and lack of organized hierarchy, and so on. Nevertheless, criticisms have been raised concerning the use of the sect model as a means of understanding the early Christian churches: Does the model distort the evidence and squeeze it into the mould of a modern sociological category? Cross-cultural and cross-disciplinary comparisons can be highly illuminating, but there are always critical questions to be asked about the particular way in which such comparisons shape our perspective on the ancient evidence.

So what does the evidence from Paul's letters themselves reveal about the character of the Pauline assemblies, and specifically about Paul's attempts to shape that character? There is certainly some evidence to suggest that the Pauline churches were communities in which established distinctions between Jews and Gentiles, slaves and free persons, men and women, were transcended through the adoption of a new unity and identity in Christ, communities where all could participate fully according to whatever gift the Spirit gave them (Gal 3.28 – see further below). But it also seems clear that life in the churches fell short of the ideal vision, expressed in baptism and the Lord's Supper, that many different people had become one body in Christ. At Corinth, for example, the believers were divided in their loyalties to different missionary figures (1 Cor 1.10–17); they took one another to court to settle what Paul regards as petty differences (1 Cor 6.1–11); and the Lord's Supper had become an occasion for division and social distinction (1 Cor 11.17–34). Further examples of tension and division in the early churches, and of Paul's attempts to address and resolve those situations, could easily be listed (see, e.g., Gal 2.11–21; Rom 14.1–15.13). It is also clear that, whatever the equality supposed to exist between all Christians, some people held positions of power and authority, not least Paul himself, who claims his apostolic calling by God as the basis for his position of leadership (cf. 2 Cor 10.8ff; Gal 1.1 etc.; see below).

Leadership in the Pauline communities

In the preceding sections the subject of power and authority has already cropped up from time to time, and a social-scientific investigation into the character of the Pauline churches can hardly avoid it. New Testament scholars have long noted the apparent lack of formal Church offices in the communities to which Paul wrote, combined with Paul's emphasis on the Spirit's gifts of prophecy, teaching, and so on, which seem to be viewed as distributed to individual persons without regard for any established position or office they might or might not hold (1 Cor 12–14). Also well documented is the emergence of a somewhat more formal structure of named leadership positions (bishops, presbyters/elders, deacons) in the Pastoral Epistles, which most scholars believe to have been written some decades after Paul's death (see below, pp. 191–94). The change has often been expressed in terms of a development (or even a 'decline') from Spirit-led freedom to ecclesiastical order and law.

Studies employing social-scientific resources have looked afresh at the evidence and suggested new ways of interpreting it. Bengt Holmberg, for example, surveys the evidence in the Pauline epistles relating to the structures of power and authority in the earliest churches, and then interprets this evidence using categories derived from Max Weber's sociology of authority.[21] Holmberg sees that there are relationships of power and authority at work at various levels, right from the very earliest years of Christianity: in Paul's relationships with the leaders in Jerusalem, in Paul's leadership over his own congregations and within those congregations themselves. There is a circle of apostolic leaders, among whom Paul certainly claims that he belongs, and a wide group of co-missionaries and workers who also travel to visit various churches. Within the congregations themselves there are evidently people with some local leadership responsibility, though the precise nature of their role and authority is not specified in Paul's letters (see, e.g., Gal 6.6; 1 Thess 5.12). Adopting Weber's terminology, it may be suggested that this stage in the development of Christian leadership patterns represents a time when authority is still essentially 'charismatic'[22] – that is, based on people's acknowledgment of the extraordinary qualities of particular individuals – but is already in the process of being 'routinized' and institutionalized. As Margaret MacDonald has shown, this process of institutionalization continues through the decades after Paul's death, and the establishment of more formal leadership offices is a part of this sociological process, spurred on not least by the death of the first generation of apostles, especially Peter, James and Paul. In this process, it may be suggested, the early Christian 'sect' becomes gradually more like a 'church'.[23]

Questions may remain about whether this framework of interpretation is convincing and whether to some extent it merely labels with new terminology what was already known, though expressed in different language, in previous studies. At the very least, it seems to me, social-scientific studies have helped to bring to our attention some of the ways in which power and authority were operative even in the loosely structured period of Paul's activity as apostle, even if the rhetoric of Paul's letters sometimes implies that authority is attributed only to God, working through the Spirit. A social-scientific perspective helps to make clear that there is generally a connection between speaking of God's authority and a human being's claim to power. Paul, for example, insists both that *God* has appointed apostles at the top of the Church's hierarchy, and, of course, that God has appointed *him* as an apostle, and thereby given him authority (1 Cor 12.28; cf. 1 Cor 9.1–2; 2 Cor 10.8).

Women in the Pauline assemblies

As we saw in the opening chapter of this book, modern-day debate about the position of women in society and in the Church has led to vigorous investigation of Paul's views on such matters. Questions have been asked both about the participation of women in the Pauline movement and about Paul's attitudes to women, his teaching concerning their place in marriage, worship and leadership. And contrary to a popular perception that Paul was quite plainly a male chauvinist, a good deal of this work has argued that Paul himself (leaving aside the letters whose authenticity is doubted – see Chapter 8) was rather more in favour of women's liberation and equality than is often supposed. Although the women's movement has been a major stimulus for such work, studies have been conducted not only by feminist writers, but by scholars from a wide range of persuasions and perspectives. Even when commitments are not openly declared, and even when the aim is explicitly a balanced and 'objective' investigation of the evidence, it is not hard to see that contemporary convictions often underpin the work on the Pauline letters – convictions for or against women's ordination, or equality in marriage, employment or whatever.

Feminist scholars do make their commitments clear. The perspective from which they interpret the Pauline evidence is one committed to the critique of male domination and women's exploitation and the promotion of liberation and equality. The best known and ground-breaking feminist study of early Christianity is Elisabeth Schüssler Fiorenza's book *In Memory of Her*, first published in 1983 and reprinted with a new introduction in 1995.[24] Although this book first appeared over thirty years ago, it remains an influential and agenda-setting work, which it is important to consider.

For some scholars, such an overtly committed stance – an explicitly feminist hermeneutic – runs the risk of distorting the evidence, of constructing a picture which is a reflection of its own values. Fiorenza responds, however, by insisting that all history writing is reconstruction, reflecting the values and commitments of the historian, and that those who claim objectivity for their work merely conceal their own position of commitment.[25] Certainly her book challenges its readers not only with a distinctive presentation of the historical evidence but also with its overt commitment to a particular contemporary vision of social and political liberation for women, and as such it has influenced a wide range of gender-critical and politically engaged approaches to Paul.[26]

Fiorenza spends the opening chapters of her book outlining and justifying her feminist interpretative perspective. Her aim is to reconstruct a history of early Christianity in which women's contribution and their struggles for equality against patriarchal domination are recovered from texts written largely from a male perspective and in which women are often silenced and excluded (sometimes implicitly, e.g., through the use of masculine language to denote the whole community). As she makes clear there are two levels of androcentrism ('male-centredness') to be exposed by the feminist critic. There is firstly that of the texts themselves, which were generally written by men (like Paul!); and secondly that of the traditions of those texts' interpretation, developed by male-biased commentators and translators over the years and through which the texts may come to be seen as more patriarchal than they really are.

Two good examples of this second level of androcentrism are found in translations of specific verses in Paul's letters. In Romans 16.7 Paul refers to two people as 'outstanding among the apostles' – which seems most likely to mean that they are regarded as part of the group of apostles. Their names are given in Paul's Greek text as *Andronikon* and *Iounian*. Since the nineteenth century, these names have often been translated as the names of two men (e.g. 'Andronicus and Junias', RSV), although it is much more likely that the latter name is that of a woman and should be rendered 'Junia', as in most older translations.[27] Not least because of Fiorenza's work, this is now widely accepted (cf. NRSV). For Christians for whom the Bible is an important source of authority and guidance, this is highly significant with regard to modern questions about women's ordination and access to positions of leadership and authority within the Church.

A second example concerns the translation and interpretation of 1 Cor 11.10. There, in a difficult and puzzling passage to which we shall return, Paul writes that a woman should have 'authority [Greek: *exousia*] on her head, because of the angels'. Because of their overall decisions (and assumptions?) about what the whole passage means, translators have often rendered this as implying that the woman is *under* authority. For example, the New Jerusalem Bible translation states that a woman should 'wear on her head a sign of the authority over her'. The Good News Bible has: 'a woman should have a covering over her head to show that she is under her husband's authority'. But this is an extremely unnatural way to interpret the Greek, which suggests that Paul is talking about the *woman's* authority and not someone else's authority over her. The comments of the scholars Archibald Robertson and Alfred Plummer, writing in 1914, are revealing in this regard. Robertson and Plummer are clear about what the apostle means, but puzzled as to what he actually writes: 'Why does St Paul say "authority" when he means "subjection"?', they wonder.[28] Once again, in recent scholarship it has come to be widely accepted that Paul means what he writes, and is talking in some sense about the woman's own authority, although his precise meaning nonetheless remains obscure; it may well be that Paul sees the woman's head-covering as a symbol of her authority to pray and prophesy in church.[29]

Fiorenza argues that in earliest Christianity, both in the Jesus movement and the early Pauline churches, we can see an attempt to articulate and live a vision of equality, equality in the Spirit, or 'the discipleship of equals', as Fiorenza labels it. This vision may be seen, for example, in the baptismal declaration of Gal 3.28: 'There is no longer Jew or Greek, there is no longer slave or free, there is no longer male and female; for you are all one in Christ Jesus'.

Evidence of the full and active participation of women in the Pauline churches, and of Paul's acceptance of it, can be found in Paul's letters. In Romans 16, for example, a number of women are commended or greeted by Paul, including: Phoebe, a leading figure in the church at Cenchreae (one of Corinth's ports); Prisca and Junia, missionary partners with Aquila and Andronicus respectively; Mary, Tryphena and Tryphosa, all of whom are described as workers for the Lord. Likewise in Phil 4.2–4, two women to whom Paul appeals to settle their differences are described as having struggled in the work of the gospel alongside Paul and the rest of his co-workers.

But while Paul appears warmly to welcome the full participation of women in the work of ministry alongside him, he also seems to introduce some modifications of the baptismal vision of Gal 3.28. In 1 Corinthians in particular he addresses various issues arising concerning the place of women in marriage and in worship. In 1 Corinthians 7 Paul begins to answer the Corinthians' questions concerning marriage and sexual relations. In outlining the mutual responsibilities which husband and wife owe to one another he consistently implies an equal and parallel status for both partners. The fact that Paul writes *both* parts of verse 4, for example, is particularly striking: 'For the wife does not have authority over her own body, but the husband does; likewise the husband does not have authority over his own body, but the wife does'. It has often been noted that Paul's view of marriage throughout this chapter is somewhat less positive than modern readers might like: it appears (though some would disagree) that Paul regards it as preferable to remain single and views marriage as an outlet for those who cannot control their passions. Fiorenza, however, highlights the positive possibilities for women implied by Paul's encouragement to remain unmarried, an encouragement which went strongly against the customs and imperial decrees of the time, when marriage and child-bearing was very much the approved norm. According to Fiorenza, 'Paul's advice to remain free from the marriage bond was a frontal assault on the intentions of existing law and the general cultural ethos'. Paul 'thus offered a possibility for "ordinary" women to become independent'.[30]

In 1 Cor 11.2–16, Paul turns to address his concerns about the proper conduct of the Corinthians in their communal worship. This whole passage is notoriously difficult to interpret. (However, the argument, occasionally proposed, that it was added later to the text of 1 Corinthians has too little evidence to substantiate it with any degree of plausibility.) Paul is clearly concerned that in worship meetings women should only pray and prophesy with their heads covered and that men should only do so with their heads uncovered (11.4–5, 13). In order to support this exhortation, Paul seems to present a created 'order' in which man has priority over woman:

> Christ is the head of every man, and the man is the head of woman,[31] and God is the head of Christ (v. 3) . . . A man ought not to cover his head, since he is the image and glory of God; but the woman is the glory of man. For man did not come from woman,

> but woman from man (cf. Gen 2.21–23); and man was not created
> because of woman, but woman because of man.
>
> (vv. 7–9, DGH; cf. Gen 2.18)

But, as if to correct any impression that he is thereby seeking to
subordinate women to men, Paul then insists:

> Nevertheless, in the Lord woman is not independent of man or
> man independent of woman. For just as woman came from man, so
> man comes through woman; but all things come from God.
>
> (vv. 11–12)

Many of the words and phrases in this passage have been discussed and
debated at length, especially the meaning of the word 'head', which Paul
uses in verse 3. Does it imply a relationship of authority, or rather one
of source (man being the source of woman in the creation account: Gen
2.21–23)? Also much debated is Paul's underlying intention here. Is he
primarily concerned, as many commentators have suggested, to ensure
that the created *differences* between men and women are retained and
reflected in the congregational gatherings? Or is he, as Fiorenza argues,
mainly concerned with decency and order in the congregation, to avoid
the possibility that it might appear like one of the cults which gathered
in Corinth?[32] Whatever his intentions, a major question, of course,
concerns the extent to which Paul has here introduced a hierarchical
distinction between the sexes, undergirded with theological and
scriptural arguments, into early Christianity.

One final passage in 1 Corinthians is also of relevance to this topic:
1 Cor 14.34–35. Here Paul instructs women to be silent during meetings
of the church; if they have any questions they should ask their husbands
at home. Once again there has been much discussion of these few verses
and their meaning. Many scholars have argued, on the basis of textual
and contextual evidence, that they have been added later to the text of 1
Corinthians and are not authentically Paul's.[33] Those who accept them
as authentic have to find some way of explaining the apparent tension
with 1 Cor 11.2–16, where it is clearly assumed that women have the
right to pray and prophesy in church. Fiorenza's suggestion is that it is

wives in particular whom Paul instructs to be silent, and that the women who may pray and prophesy are the unmarried, whom Paul regards as 'holy in body and spirit' (1 Cor 7.34).[34] Other proposals include the idea that Paul is again concerned with decency and order in the congregation, and seeks to prevent women from disrupting the meeting with questions or conversation. If the verses are authentic (which I personally doubt) then again we have to ask about the extent to which Paul has taken steps to exclude women from participation in the church's worship. Even if there is a local and contextual reason for his instructions (as in 11.2–16) they nevertheless play their part in shaping the developing rules of the Christian community, particularly as they come (somewhat later) to be regarded as scripture.

Whether we should take other evidence into account in determining *Paul's* attitudes to women depends on our decisions on debated questions of authorship (see Chapter 8). If Paul wrote Colossians and/ or Ephesians, then we must take account of the so-called 'household codes' (Col 3.18–4.1; Eph 5.21–6.9) where husbands are urged to love their wives and wives to submit to their husbands. And if Paul wrote the Pastoral Epistles, then we must consider the passages there where women are apparently excluded from positions of authority and from teaching in the Church (1 Tim 2.9–15), allowed to teach only other women (Titus 2.3–5), and urged to play their 'proper' role within the household (1 Tim 2.15; 5.14; Titus 2.4–5). Of course, whether Paul wrote these letters or not, they are in the New Testament and so have to be taken into account by those who accept some sense of the Bible's authority for the Church. Taking them into account, however, does not necessarily mean believing that their teaching needs to be seen as a legitimate and abiding expression of the gospel. Moreover, scholars take various positions as to the degree to which these various passages do subordinate women to an inferior and secondary position in church and society. Some stress the particular and contextual reasons why the instructions were given in that specific time and place, thus implying that they need not be taken as universal and binding Christian injunctions. Others maintain that these texts do give strong backing to the opinion that the Church's ministry should be male and that the man should be the head of the household.

Fiorenza adopts the common (though by no means universally held) position that Colossians, Ephesians and the Pastoral Epistles were written after Paul's death, the Pastoral Epistles some time later than Colossians and Ephesians. For Fiorenza, these epistles reveal the increasing 'patriarchalization' within the Pauline churches, the gradual assertion of male dominance and the marginalization of women, though there continues to be an ongoing struggle between patriarchy and those who keep alive the vision of the discipleship of equals. In these post-Pauline letters there is a clear attempt to exclude women from ministry and authority, and to confine them to a subordinate role within both household and church.

What then should be our assessment of the evidence concerning the participation of women in the earliest Christian movement and Paul's attitudes to that participation? Scholarship has by no means provided a unanimous answer to that question, and even those who share a similar contemporary commitment (e.g., to feminism, or to evangelical Christianity) do not necessarily agree as to how to assess Paul. For some he is a voice for equality and liberation, for others a voice of male domination and women's oppression. This kind of stark polarity of extreme alternatives is, however, one that should probably be deconstructed, as Carolyn Osiek and Margaret MacDonald argue.[35] It seems clear enough that women played a significant role in the earliest Christian movement and that women occupied roles of significance and leadership, working along with men as missionaries, apostles and providers of various kinds of support. It seems clear that Paul regarded this as entirely acceptable, as is indicated by the various greetings and commendations he offers in his letters to named women as well as men. Yet it is also clear that Paul felt some need, particularly at Corinth, to regulate (and in some ways restrict) the participation of women in the Christian assemblies. Indeed, Osiek and MacDonald suggest that the 'greater social freedom for women' evidenced to some degree in the NT writings was a broader trend in Roman society at the time, and not a radically distinctive contribution of earliest Christianity.[36] There is also good reason to be suspicious of perspectives that depict a kind of radical 'feminist' Paul liberating women from a patriarchal Judaism. As in many other aspects of Pauline studies, that can too easily represent an assumption of Christian superiority more than historical evidence. Perhaps Florenza is right to stress that any assessment of Paul in this regard must accept the ambivalent legacy which his letters represent; otherwise he may be somewhat one-sidedly claimed either as 'chauvinist', or as 'feminist' and 'liberationist'. Fiorenza's own conclusions on Paul are worth quoting:

> Paul's impact on women's leadership in the Christian missionary movement is double-edged. On the one hand he affirms Christian equality and freedom. He opens up a new independent lifestyle for women by encouraging them to remain free of the bondage of marriage. On the other hand, he subordinates women's behaviour in marriage and in the worship assembly to the interests of Christian mission, and restricts their rights not only as 'pneumatics' but also as 'women' … The post-Pauline and pseudo-Pauline tradition will draw out these restrictions in order to change the equality in Christ between women and men, slaves and free, into a relationship of subordination in the household which, on the one hand, eliminates women from the leadership of worship and community and, on the other, restricts their ministry to women.[37]

Paul and the Roman Empire

Until relatively recently, the subject of Paul's relationship to the Roman Empire was somewhat neglected, especially compared with the dominant (and important) topic of Paul's relationship to Judaism (see Chapter 6). Much earlier in the twentieth century, however, scholars like Adolf Deissmann had insisted on the importance of the imperial context of the New Testament, but this interest rather dwindled as the century went on. According to Deissmann, unless we imagine that 'St. Paul and his fellow believers went through the world blindfolded' we must consider how the terms and images that confronted them every day formed the conscious backdrop against which the Christian message was formulated: 'the New Testament is a book of the Imperial age'.[38] Indeed, Deissmann proposed, Christian claims about Christ were expressed using terms also familiar from their application to the deified emperors or from the context of emperor worship: 'Thus there arises a polemical parallelism between the cult of the emperor and the cult of Christ'.[39]

Recent years, however, have seen a renewed interest in the subject of Christianity and the Roman Empire, and more specifically the New Testament and the imperial cult. The 'cult of the emperor', or the 'imperial cult', describes the wide variety of practices and customs whereby the emperor was the recipient of prayer, devotion and cultic worship. Indeed, the variety of practices means, as some have suggested, that it is probably better to speak of 'imperial cults' in the plural.[40] Ancient historians have come to emphasize the importance of this phenomenon in the Empire of Paul's time, thus encouraging a reconsideration of its significance for Paul and the early Christians.[41] In addition, just as contemporary factors (such as the post-Holocaust reassessment of the relations between Christianity and Judaism) help to explain the intense interest in Paul's view of Judaism, so here too there are contemporary social factors that help to explain the renewed interest in Paul's stance towards the Roman Empire, not least a growing and often critical awareness of the globalized operations of what may be seen as a modern equivalent of empire.[42]

Of particular interest and influence is the work of the 'Paul and Politics' group at the annual meetings of the US-based Society of Biblical Literature, published in a series of volumes edited by Richard Horsley. Paul's political stance is often assumed to be rather conservative and conformist, with Romans 13.1–7 and its call to submit to the governing authorities the most influential text. Here Paul seems to urge Christians to quiet submission to the state, and regards the imperial authorities positively as instruments of God's justice in the world. A different perspective, however, is presented in the work of Horsley and his colleagues, notably in the 1997 collection entitled *Paul and Empire*.[43] Here and in subsequent works Horsley and others have sought to show how we should understand Paul as engaged in a thoroughly political task, one which showed his 'adamant opposition to Roman imperial society': he was building exclusive communities 'of a new society, alternative to the dominant imperial society'.[44] Paul, for example, urged the Corinthian converts to avoid eating meat sacrificed to idols (1 Cor 8–10) and in doing so pressed them to withdraw from 'participation in the fundamental forms of social relations in the dominant society'. And their household-based assemblies were to be independent communities in which patterns of solidarity and economic exchange were 'diametrically opposed' to those of the wider political society.[45] Paul's critical perspective on the Roman Empire may be conveyed in 1 Thess 5.3: 'When they say "There is peace and security", then sudden destruction will come upon them . . . and there will be no escape!' Here Paul seems to be deliberately echoing the established way of talking about the achievements of the Empire, the *pax Romana* (the 'Roman peace'), and announcing that the destruction of this supposedly eternal empire will come soon.

Particular significance has also been found in the ways Paul talks about Christ. As we have seen above (pp. 83–92), Paul's Christology has been much discussed, particularly in terms of its relation to Jewish monotheism and its possible elevation of Christ to divine status. But recent interest in the imperial cults has drawn attention to the parallels – recognized long ago by Deissmann – between Paul's depictions of Christ's identity and those of the Roman emperors. For example, Augustus (the first Roman emperor, 31 BCE–14 CE) was acclaimed as the 'saviour' who had brought good news by his establishment of peace. He and other emperors were addressed as 'lord' (Latin: *dominus*, Greek: *kurios*) and acclaimed as 'son of god' (Latin: *divi filius*, Greek: *huios theou*). Seen against this backdrop, Paul's declaration that Jesus is the saviour (Phil 3.20), the exalted Lord, and the one to whom every knee shall bow (Phil 2.9–11) may be seen to have a polemical and political force.[46] This may also help to explain why the early Christians, Paul included, were not infrequently regarded as dangerous political rebels, proclaiming 'another king' but Caesar (Acts 17.7).

However, reading Paul as adamantly and intentionally anti-imperial has not gone unchallenged. For example, Karl Galinsky, an ancient historian, warns about the ways in which historical analysis may be skewed by contemporary political and religious convictions, and stresses that the imperial cult(s) were a flexible and diverse set of phenomena that cannot be isolated from the worship of other gods in Roman religion.[47] Seyoon Kim and John Barclay, in rather different ways, have questioned whether Paul's stance should really be seen as anti-imperial in the manner claimed by Horsley and others. Barclay – criticizing N.T. Wright in particular – points out the lack of explicit reference in Paul's letters to the emperor and the cultic activity focused on him, and suggests that Paul is 'subversive', not in consciously and polemically juxtaposing Christ and Caesar but rather in simply leaving the Empire and the Emperor 'off the stage', treating them as insignificant in the wider drama of God's battle against evil and plan of salvation: 'Paul's theology is political precisely in rendering the Roman empire theologically insignificant'.[48] It is certainly the case, it seems to me, that we need carefully nuanced and historically detailed analyses of the ways in which the early Christians responded to the Roman Empire, analyses that are not too heavily shaped either by convictions that value Christianity positively and thus depict the Empire as a contrast in solely negative terms, or by contemporary political convictions about the negative impact of (e.g.) American imperialism. Nonetheless, I think it clear that Horsley and others have brought an important dimension back to studies of Paul, namely the focus on the most significant 'given' in Paul's social and historical context: the domination of Rome. What that domination meant in practice and how it impinged on the earliest Christians needs to be carefully explored, and should certainly not be ignored.

Conclusion

This chapter has outlined some of the areas of contemporary Pauline studies where the focus is not so much on the theological ideas which Paul expressed but on various aspects of the socio-political context and social realities of the earliest Christian communities. Whether we focus on meeting places and ancient associations, on leadership structures and socio-economic composition, on the participation of women or on the imperial context, these issues take us beyond the figure of Paul and into the broader social and political world in which Paul operated. The topics surveyed here generally entail some direct engagement with material and literary evidence from the Roman world (e.g., on types of housing or the imperial cults), but scholarly treatments of them often draw also on various contemporary theoretical and interpretative perspectives (e.g., social-scientific theory or feminist criticism). One thing this chapter should make clear – not least when juxtaposed with Chapters 5 and 6 – is the diversity of contemporary Pauline studies, in which different scholars focus on very different themes and approaches. While some may regard the approaches outlined in this chapter as relatively marginal and unimportant to the key issues in the study of Paul, others may feel that the questions raised by such methods are of greater relevance to the world in which we now live than debates over, say, the meaning of the word 'righteousness' in Paul's letters.[49]

The approaches surveyed in this chapter, albeit very selectively, offer methods by which we may gain greater insight into the everyday worlds the early Christians inhabited, rooting the study of their theology in its concrete social context. Such socially-orientated questions, especially when informed by critical theory, also help to focus attention on the questions without which theology can be naive and unself-critical: How does Paul's teaching shape social relationships among members of the churches? How is power in the churches distributed and in whose interests is it used? How are women regarded and treated? What stance did Paul and the early Christian groups take towards the Roman Empire?

Depending on your own commitments and beliefs, you may or may not find such perspectives and questions congenial and engaging. What is important, in my opinion, is an openness to listen (or rather, to read!) with a desire to understand the arguments, to appreciate the issues raised and perhaps to change one's point of view. Just as an openness to learn and perhaps to change is important in our attempts to listen to Paul's letters themselves, so it is important too in listening to the different voices of those who interpret Paul, whatever their perspective and however different it may be from our own.

Further reading

The best places to begin further study of Paul and his churches from a social-scientific perspective are the classic treatments by W.A. Meeks, *The First Urban Christians* (London and New Haven: Yale University Press, 1983) and G. Theissen, *The Social Setting of Pauline Christianity* (Edinburgh: T&T Clark, 1982). Meeks' book in particular gives a wide-ranging and engaging presentation of the Pauline communities. For discussions of developments in this areas since the publication of Meeks' work, see T.D. Still and D.G. Horrell (eds), *After the First Urban Christians: Social-Scientific Study of Pauline Christianity Twenty-Five Years Later* (London & New York: T&T Clark, 2009). See also the works of Malina and Neyrey mentioned in Chapter 1, in the section listing further reading and also in note 4. For examples of the range of social-scientific methods employed, together with an introduction to the discipline and suggestions for further reading, see D.G. Horrell (ed.), *Social-Scientific Approaches to New Testament Interpretation* (Edinburgh: T&T Clark, 1999); A. Blasi, J. Duhaime and P.-A. Turcotte (eds), *Handbook of Early Christianity: Social Science Approaches* (Walnut Creek: Alta Mira, 2002). Among the brief introductions to the area are B. Holmberg, *Sociology and the New Testament* (Minneapolis: Fortress, 1990); D. Tidball, *The Social Context of the New Testament* (Carlisle: Paternoster, 1997, first published as *An Introduction to the Sociology of the New Testament* in 1983); J.H. Elliott, *What is Social-Scientific Criticism?* (Minneapolis: Fortress, 1993).

Along with Fiorenza's classic *In Memory of Her* (London: SCM, 1983, 2nd edn 1995), feminist perspectives on Paul and his letters (as well as on other biblical and extra-biblical texts) can be found in E.S. Fiorenza (ed.), *Searching the Scriptures, Vol. 2: A Feminist Commentary* (London: SCM, 1995) and in L. Schottroff, *Let the Oppressed Go Free: Feminist Perspectives on the New Testament* (Louisville: Westminster/ John Knox, 1993). An initial orientation to feminist perspectives may be found in C.B. Kittredge, 'Feminist Approaches: Rethinking History and Resisting Ideologies', in J.A. Marchal (ed.), *Studying Paul's Letters* (Minneapolis: Fortress, 2012), pp. 117–33. A clear and valuable overview of the relevant texts and main interpretative options is provided by T.G. Gombis, *Paul: A Guide for the Perplexed* (London & New York: T&T Clark, 2010), pp. 117–32. Other useful books on the subject of Paul and women include B. Byrne, *Paul and the Christian Woman* (Homebush, NSW: St Paul Publications, 1988); B. Witherington, *Women and the Genesis of Christianity* (Cambridge: CUP, 1990); and C.S. Keener, *Paul, Women and Wives* (Peabody: Hendrickson, 1992). An important study exploring the place of women in Roman households and society more generally, as the setting to understand their contribution to the early Christian movement, is C. Osiek and M.Y. MacDonald, with J.H. Tulloch, *A Woman's Place: House Churches in Earliest Christianity* (Minneapolis: Fortress, 2006).

The best way to begin a study of Paul and the Roman Empire is with R.A. Horsley (ed.) *Paul and Empire* (Harrisburg: Trinity Press International, 1997). For a collection of essays on the imperial cult and the New Testament, see the March 2005 issue of the *Journal for the Study of the New Testament* (volume 27). To develop critical perspectives on the 'Paul and Empire' discussion, see the important collection of essays in J. Brodd and J.L. Reed (eds), *Rome and Religion: A Cross Disciplinary Dialogue on the Imperial Cult* (Atlanta: Society of Biblical Literature, 2011), as well as J.M.G. Barclay, 'Why the Roman Empire Was Insignificant to Paul', in *Pauline Churches and Diaspora Jews*

(Tübingen: Mohr Siebeck, 2011), pp. 363–87 and S. Kim, *Christ and Caesar: the Gospel and the Roman Empire in the Writings of Paul and Luke* (Grand Rapids: Eerdmans, 2008). A good example of sophisticated and nuanced appraisal of Paul's engagement with the Roman Empire (though focused primarily on the disputed letters Colossians, Ephesians and the Pastoral Epistles) is H.O. Maier, *Picturing Paul in Empire* (London & New York: Bloomsbury T&T Clark, 2013). A very valuable collection of primary materials is available in M. Reasoner, *Roman Imperial Texts: A Sourcebook* (Minneapolis: Fortress, 2013).

For a sense of the range of critical approaches in contemporary Pauline studies, see J.A. Marchal, (ed.), *Studying Paul's Letters: Contemporary Perspectives and Methods* (Minneapolis: Fortress, 2012). A valuable survey of the wide range of approaches currently practised in biblical studies as a whole can be found in S.L. McKenzie and S.R. Haynes (eds), *To Each Its Own Meaning: An Introduction to Biblical Criticisms and Their Application* (revised and expanded edn., Louisville: Westminster/ John Knox, 1999) and a subsequent volume that explores new methods since 1999, S.L. McKenzie and J. Kaltner (eds), *New Meanings for Ancient Texts: Recent Approaches to Biblical Criticisms and Their Applications* (Louisville: Westminster John Knox, 2013). For the New Testament in particular, see also P. Gooder (ed.), *Searching for Meaning: An Introduction to Interpreting the New Testament* (London: SPCK, 2008).

Questions for further study

- How far can reconstructions of the socioeconomic situation of the recipients of Paul's letters help us to understand those letters better?
- Do you agree with Fiorenza that Paul's 'impact on women's leadership' is 'double-edged' (p. 169 above), in some ways liberating, in other ways suppressing? What is your assessment of the ongoing legacy of Paul's teaching in this regard?
- How far are you convinced by the view that Paul was adamantly opposed to the Roman Empire and to the cult of the emperor? To

what extent does an awareness of the imperial context lead us to read Paul's letters differently?

Notes

1 I make this qualification since it has been pointed out that the depiction of an 'old consensus' is not entirely true to what was in fact presented in earlier scholarship on this subject. See, e.g., G. Theissen, 'The Social Structure of Pauline Communities: Some Critical Remarks on J.J. Meggitt, *Paul, Poverty and Survival*', *Journal for the Study of the New Testament* 84 (2001), p. 66.

2 E.A. Judge, *The Social Pattern of Christian Groups in the First Century* (London: Tyndale, 1960), pp. 49–61.

3 G. Theissen, 'Social Stratification in the Corinthian Community', in *The Social Setting of Pauline Christianity* (Edinburgh: T&T Clark, 1982), pp. 69–119.

4 Theissen, *The Social Setting of Pauline Christianity*, p. 69.

5 W.A. Meeks, *The First Urban Christians* (London and New Haven: Yale University Press, 1983).

6 J.J. Meggitt, *Paul, Poverty and Survival* (Edinburgh: T&T Clark, 1998).

7 For responses to Meggitt's book, see Theissen, 'The Social Structure of Pauline Communities'; G. Theissen, 'Social Conflicts in the Corinthian Community: Further Remarks on J.J. Meggitt, *Paul, Poverty and Survival*', *Journal for the Study of the New Testament* 25 (2003), pp. 371–91; D.B. Martin, 'Review Essay: Justin J. Meggitt, *Paul, Poverty and Survival*', *Journal for the Study of the New Testament* 84 (2001), pp. 51–64; J.J. Meggitt, 'Response to Martin and Theissen', *Journal for the Study of the New Testament* 84 (2001), pp. 85–94.

8 S.J. Friesen, 'Poverty in Pauline Studies: Beyond the So-Called New Consensus', *Journal for the Study of the New Testament* 26 (2004), pp. 323–61 (a discussion article with responses by John Barclay and Peter Oakes). Friesen's approach is further discussed and amended in B.W. Longenecker, *Remember the Poor* (Grand Rapids: Eerdmans, 2010), pp. 36–59.

9 Theissen, *The Social Setting of Pauline Christianity*, pp. 145–74.

10 Meggitt, *Paul, Poverty and Survival*, pp. 118–22, 189–93.

11 See P. Oakes, *Reading Romans in Pompeii* (London/Minneapolis: SPCK/ Fortress, 2009).

12 See further D.G. Horrell, 'Pauline Churches or Early Christian Churches? Unity, Disagreement, and the Eucharist', in A. Alexeev *et al.*, *Einheit der Kirche im Neuen Testament* (Tübingen: Mohr Siebeck, 2008), pp. 185–203.

13 See Meeks, *The First Urban Christians*, pp. 150–62.

14 Meeks, *The First Urban Christians*, pp. 75–84. See further R. Ascough, *What Are They Saying About the Formation of the Pauline Churches?* (New York: Paulist, 1998).

15 For an overview, see E. Adams, 'First-Century Models for Paul's Churches: Selected Scholarly Developments since Meeks', in T.D. Still and D.G. Horrell (eds), *After the First Urban Christians* (New York & London: T&T Clark, 2009), pp. 60–78.

16 P.A. Harland, *Dynamics of Identity in the World of the Early Christians* (London & New York: T&T Clark, 2009).

17 For more on this, see, e.g., R. Gehring, *House Church and Mission* (Peabody: Hendrickson, 2004); C. Osiek and M.Y. MacDonald, with J.H. Tulloch, *A Woman's Place: House Churches in Earliest Christianity* (Minneapolis: Fortress, 2006).

18 See, e.g., Oakes, *Reading Romans*; D.G. Horrell, 'Domestic Space and Christian Meetings at Corinth: Imagining New Contexts and the Buildings East of the Theatre', *New Testament Studies* 50 (2004), pp. 349–69.

19 E. Adams, *The Earliest Christian Meeting Places: Almost Exclusively Houses?* (London & New York: Bloomsbury T&T Clark, 2013).

20 R. Scroggs, 'Earliest Christianity as Sectarian Movement', in J. Neusner (ed.), *Christianity, Judaism and Other Greco-Roman Cults: Studies for Morton Smith at Sixty. Part Two: Early Christianity* (Leiden: Brill, 1975), pp. 1–23; reprinted in D.G. Horrell (ed.), *Social-Scientific Approaches to New Testament Interpretation* (Edinburgh: T&T Clark, 1999), pp. 69–91.

21 B. Holmberg, *Paul and Power* (Lund: CWK Gleerup, 1978; reprinted Philadelphia: Fortress, 1980).

22 We should note that Weber intends this category as a general sociological type, and not specifically as a description of the Spirit-gifted leadership which Paul describes.

23 M.Y. MacDonald, *The Pauline Churches: A Socio-Historical Study of Institutionalization in the Pauline and Deutero-Pauline Epistles* (Cambridge: CUP, 1988).

24 E.S. Fiorenza, *In Memory of Her: A Feminist Theological Reconstruction of Christian Origins* (London: SCM, 1983; 2nd edn 1995).

25 See the introduction to the second edition of *In Memory of Her*, esp. pp. xxii–xxix.

26 For a recent survey of such approaches, see J.A. Marchal (ed.), *Studying Paul's Letters: Contemporary Perspectives and Methods* (Minneapolis: Fortress, 2012).

27 On this, see the detailed study by E.J. Epp, *Junia: the First Woman Apostle* (Minneapolis: Fortress, 2005).

28 A. Robertson and A. Plummer, *A Critical and Exegetical Commentary on the First Epistle of St. Paul to the Corinthians* (2nd edn, Edinburgh: T&T Clark, 1914), p. 232.

29 Of some influence here is the article by M.D. Hooker, 'Authority on Her Head: An Examination of 1 Cor. XI. 10', *New Testament Studies* 10 (1964), pp. 410–16, reprinted in *From Adam to Christ: Essays on Paul* (Cambridge: CUP, 1990), pp. 113–20.

30 Fiorenza, *In Memory of Her*, pp. 225–26.

31 The Greek words *anēr* and *gunē* can mean man or husband and woman or wife respectively. The NRSV translates them in this phrase as husband and wife, but I am not convinced that this more restricted meaning is implied by Paul here.

32 See Fiorenza, *In Memory of Her*, pp. 227–30.

33 For an argument to this effect, see D.G. Horrell, *The Social Ethos of the Corinthian Correspondence* (Edinburgh: T&T Clark, 1996), pp. 184–95.

34 Fiorenza, *In Memory of Her*, pp. 230–33.

35 Osiek and MacDonald, *A Woman's Place*, pp. 1–3.

36 Osiek and MacDonald, *A Woman's Place*, p. 2. For example, they discuss in detail the evidence for the extent of women's authority and autonomy in the household (pp. 144–57) as the backdrop for the evidence for women leading early Christian house-groups (pp. 157–63).

37 Fiorenza, *In Memory of Her*, p. 236; see also p. 241 note 99.

38 G.A. Deissmann, *Light from the Ancient East* (London: Hodder & Stoughton, 1910), p. 344.

39 Deissmann, *Light*, p. 346.

40 See, e.g., S.J. Friesen, 'Normal Religion, or, Words Fail Us: A Response to Karl Galinksy's "The Cult of the Roman Emperor: Uniter or Divider?"', in J. Brodd and J.L. Reed (eds), *Rome and Religion: A Cross-Disciplinary*

Dialogue on the Imperial Cult (Atlanta: Society of Biblical Literature, 2011), p. 24.

41 Particularly influential is the work of S.R.F. Price, *Rituals and Power: The Roman Imperial Cult in Asia Minor* (Cambridge: CUP, 1984).

42 See, e.g., R.A. Horsley, *Jesus and Empire* (Minneapolis: Fortress, 2002), esp. pp. 137–49.

43 R.A. Horsley (ed.) *Paul and Empire* (Harrisburg: Trinity Press International, 1997). See also R.A. Horsley (ed.), *Paul and Politics* (Harrisburg: Trinity Press International, 2000); R.A. Horsley (ed.), *Paul and the Roman Imperial Order* (Harrisburg: Trinity Press International, 2004).

44 See Horsley, '1 Corinthians: A Case Study of Paul's Assembly as an Alternative Society', in *Paul and Empire*, pp. 242, 244.

45 Horsley, '1 Corinthians', pp. 247, 251.

46 See e.g. N.T. Wright, 'Paul's Gospel and Caesar's Empire', in Horsley (ed.), *Paul and Politics*, pp. 160–83.

47 See K. Galinsky, 'The Cult of the Roman Emperor: Uniter or Divider?' and 'In the Shadow (or Not) of the Imperial Cult: A Cooperative Agenda', in J. Brodd and J.L. Reed (eds), *Rome and Religion: A Cross-Disciplinary Dialogue on the Imperial Cult* (Atlanta: Society of Biblical Literature, 2011), pp. 1–21 and 215–25.

48 J.M.G. Barclay, 'Why the Roman Empire Was Insignificant to Paul', in *Pauline Churches and Diaspora Jews* (Tübingen: Mohr Siebeck, 2011), p. 387. See also S. Kim, *Christ and Caesar: The Gospel and the Roman Empire in the Writings of Paul and Luke* (Grand Rapids: Eerdmans, 2008).

49 A good sense of the contrasting priorities and perspectives may be gained by comparing two recent edited handbooks: Westerholm's focuses heavily on Paul's influence on Christian theology, in figures such as Origen, Augustine, Luther, Calvin and Barth, while Marchal's offers, among others, economic, postcolonial, queer, feminist and African American approaches. See S. Westerholm (ed.), *The Blackwell Companion to Paul* (Chichester: Wiley-Blackwell, 2011); J.A. Marchal, (ed.), *Studying Paul's Letters: Contemporary Perspectives and Methods* (Minneapolis: Fortress, 2012).

8

Paul's Legacy in the New Testament and Beyond

Introduction

It is beyond dispute that Paul was a figure significant enough to leave a legacy after his death, unquestionable that his writings continued to have an influence on the ongoing life of the Christian churches. What is rather more open to dispute is where Paul's work ends and his legacy begins. In other words, where does Paul's writing stop and that of his successors commence? There are thirteen letters in the New Testament that explicitly claim to be written by Paul. (In addition, early tradition included the letter to the Hebrews – which nowhere mentions its author's name – among the Pauline letters. But no one today argues that Paul wrote Hebrews.[1]) In the opening chapter of this book, I outlined very briefly the position among scholars: that there are seven letters unanimously accepted as being by Paul himself and six letters which are frequently regarded as pseudo-Pauline, that is, written in Paul's name by someone other than Paul (Colossians, Ephesians, 2 Thessalonians, 1 Timothy, 2 Timothy, Titus; see pp. 8–9 above). Throughout the book, I have by and large used only the undisputed letters as primary sources of Paul's own views. However, as I made clear in Chapter 1, opinions on the authorship of the other letters vary, with some scholars – especially those of a more conservative evangelical persuasion – arguing that all the epistles attributed to Paul in the New Testament are probably authentic. The weight of scholarly support for the hypothesis of pseudonymity (see p. 8) also varies according to which letter(s) we are discussing: most scholars agree that the Pastoral Epistles (1–2 Tim,

Titus) are highly unlikely to have been written by Paul; the size of the majority decreases, broadly speaking, as we turn to Ephesians, and then to 2 Thessalonians and Colossians. Not all will agree, therefore, about whether some or all of the letters we shall examine in this chapter should be seen as part of Paul's own literary output, or rather as part of Paul's legacy, showing how Paul's successors sought to imitate Paul's teaching or to claim his authority for their own.

We shall therefore turn first to look briefly at the content and character of each of the six disputed letters, since this information will mostly stand as valid whatever view you take of the authorship of any particular letter. Then we shall turn to the matter of decisions about authorship, looking at some of the bases on which scholarly judgements are formed. Consistent with the aim throughout this book, by showing you some of the evidence and the ways in which evidence is assessed, I hope to provide you with some tools with which you can begin to work your way towards your own decisions on these matters. Thirdly, we shall consider some of the important areas of interest, study and debate arising from the content of these disputed letters. Finally, moving on to what is indisputably Paul's legacy, we shall cast a very quick glance at the impact of Paul after the New Testament period up to the present day.

The letters and their circumstances

1. Colossians

The letter to the Colossians, addressed to Christian believers in the city of Colossae in Asia Minor, states, as does Ephesians (Eph 3.1; 6.20), that it was written by Paul from prison (Col 4.10, 18). We shall consider some of the evidence relating specifically to its authorship below. Particularly significant features of its content are its expressions of a high and cosmic Christology (1.15–20), its sense of 'realized' eschatology (2.12; 3.1; see below), its appeal to believers to live as the new people that they are in Christ (2.11–3.17) and its so-called 'household code' – a list of duties and responsibilities addressed in turn to various groups within the Greco-Roman household: wives and husbands, children and fathers, slaves and masters (3.18–4.1). Most scholars (though not all) agree that Colossians was written to confront the dangers of a rival 'philosophy', to which some of the Christians were being attracted (see 2.8–23). What exactly this rival philosophy was is more disputed, with scholars disagreeing as to whether it was some form of Jewish mysticism, a non-Jewish philosophy or some syncretistic blend of various religious and philosophical traditions. What we can glean from the letter is that this philosophy seemed to involve the worship of angels, visions, and submission to rules concerning foods, festivals, sabbaths etc. (2.16–23).

2. Ephesians

The letter to the Ephesians is closely related in form and content to Colossians, notably in its Christology (1.20–23), its realized eschatology (2.6), its vision of Christians' life in Christ (4.14–5.20) and its household code (5.21–6.9). But all of this material is given distinctive treatment in Ephesians – for example, in the household code there is an extended reflection on the parallel between a husband's love for his wife and Christ's love for the Church (5.25–33; cf. Col 3.19). Most scholars favour the view that the author of Ephesians used Colossians as a basis for his letter, though some propose that the relationship was the other way around, Colossians using Ephesians, or that both letters drew on a similar stock of traditional material. Unlike Colossians, however, Ephesians does not seem to address any particular heresy or danger in the Church, and may have originated as a circular letter rather than as one addressed to the city of Ephesus. Among the distinctive features of Ephesians are its inspiring prayers (1.17–23; 3.14–21), its imagery of the armour of God (6.10–17) and its reflections on the unity in Christ of Jew and Gentile: in Christ the two become one people, the dividing wall between them having been broken down (2.11–22). Like Colossians, Ephesians emphasizes that God's work in Christ is an act of reconciliation, but whereas Colossians relates this to 'all things, whether on earth or in heaven' (Col 1.20), Ephesians relates it specifically to the reconciliation between Jew and Gentile (Eph 2.16).

3. 2 Thessalonians

The second letter to the Thessalonians is closely related, in style, content and plan to 1 Thessalonians: it seems most likely that the second letter was based upon the first. However, while 1 Thessalonians was written in part to address concerns arising because the Day of the Lord had not yet come, 2 Thessalonians confronts quite the opposite problem: 'we beg you, brothers and sisters, not to be quickly shaken in mind or alarmed, either by spirit or by word or by letter, as though from us, to the effect that the day of the Lord is already here' (2 Thess 2.1–2). This suggestion cannot be true, the author insists, because the 'lawless one' is being 'restrained' and has not yet been revealed (2 Thess 2.3; see 2.1–15). The author's references here are obscure and enigmatic – referring perhaps to an emperor or a false prophet – but depict an eschatological scenario influenced by Jewish apocalyptic literature (e.g., Dan 8.19–25; cf. 1 Macc 1.54–57; Mark 13.14; Rev 20.1–15). The problem then, in the author's view, is not the problem of delay but the problem of an 'over-realized eschatology' (cf. below on the authorship of Colossians). It is interesting that 2 Timothy condemns two 'heretics' who are 'claiming that the resurrection has already taken place' (2 Tim 2.18), a similar problem to that which 2 Thessalonians confronts. The author of 2 Thessalonians also exhorts Christians not to be idle, and not to support any who refuse to work to earn their food (2 Thess 3.6–13). While the 'signature' at the end of the letter (2 Thess 3.17) may indicate Paul's own authorship (cf., e.g., 1 Cor 16.21), it may be that the author here 'protests too much', trying hard to present his letter as a real one from Paul. Other verses in the letter (2 Thess 2.2, 5, 15) may imply that some time has passed since Paul was around (there are now false letters written in his name – 'a letter as if from us'; 2.2) and that here a follower of Paul is seeking to 'remind' people of Paul's teaching. (How far the teaching of the letter, if pseudonymous, was actually true to Paul is of course open to debate.)

4. The Pastoral Epistles: 1–2 Timothy and Titus

The Pastoral Epistles have been so named since the eighteenth century, a name based on the fact that all three epistles are addressed by Paul to two of his co-workers, Timothy and Titus, who have been left with a pastoral responsibility for the Christian communities in Ephesus (1 Tim 1.3) and Crete (Titus 1.5). The three letters are generally treated together, as a small collection of writings from the same author and location, though I shall here give a very brief overview of each one separately. (A few scholars argue that 2 Timothy is rather distinctive within this group of three epistles, and may have a better claim than the other two to have been written by Paul.[2])

The first letter to Timothy is presented as Paul's instructions to Timothy about his own conduct (1 Tim 4.7–16; 6.11–16) and about what he should teach and expect from members of the Christian congregations (1.3; 3.14–15; 4.11 etc.). The author, whoever he was,[3] clearly considers there to be a threat from 'false teachers' who are leading people astray, though there is little agreement among scholars as to exactly what the false teaching was. The author's response to this situation is essentially twofold. On the one hand, he engages in negative polemic against anyone and anything which stands contrary to what he regards as sound teaching – everything else is wicked and corrupt (see 1.3–11; 4.1–3; 5.11–15; 6.3–5). On the other hand he gives positive instruction about the kind of conduct which is to be expected from various groups within the congregation. Leaders are to be respectable men who govern their households well (3.1–13; 5.17–22); women are to be silent and submissive, dressing modestly and not extravagantly (2.9–15); slaves are to honour their masters and be willing slaves, especially if their masters are Christians (6.1–2). Thus the Church may remain sound and faithful to the gospel. There are also indications of financial and charitable responsibilities being undertaken by the Church: elders who govern well are to be given 'double honour' (5.17), which many commentators take as a reference to the payment of Church leaders; widows who lack family to care for them, who are over sixty and worthy in character, may be enrolled on a list, which presumably entitles them to support from the Church (5.3–16). In view of this it is understandable that we also find warnings that those who take up a Church office must not be 'greedy for money' (3.8) and against people who want to become rich (6.6–10).

The second letter to Timothy shares a number of these features of 1 Timothy: a concern to preserve sound teaching (2.1–2, 11–26; 3.14–4.5) and harsh polemic against false teaching and its proponents (3.1–9; 4.3–4). What is emphasized and developed more in 2 Timothy is the theme of Paul's own sufferings for the gospel, to the point of death, which is portrayed as imminent (4.6–8; cf. 1.11–18; 2.8–10; 3.10–11). Timothy too is reminded that loyalty to Christ will mean persecution and suffering (2.1–7; 3.12); 2 Timothy is thus perhaps the most personal in tone of the three Pastoral letters, and it is notable that the most detailed references to Paul's personal circumstances in the Pastorals are found in 2 Timothy (2 Tim 4.9–21).

The letter to Titus shares characteristics with both letters to Timothy, especially 1 Timothy. Like Timothy, Titus is given instructions about the qualities required of leaders in the Church (Titus 1.5–9). He is urged to 'appoint elders in every town' (1.5). As in 1 Timothy, there is both instruction for various groups within the churches – older men, older women, younger women, slaves (2.1–10; cf. 3.1–2) – and warnings about the threat from wicked false teachers (1.10–16). As in 1 Timothy there is little firm evidence from which to construct a picture of exactly what the false teachers were teaching, but there is some indication that they were from a Jewish background (1.10). Notable in Titus are the number of references to both God and Christ as 'our saviour' (1.3–4; 2.10; 3.4, 6; cf. 1 Tim 1.1; 2.3), and especially the one reference to 'our great God and Saviour Jesus Christ' (2.13) – though that translation is somewhat open to debate (see NRSV footnote at Titus 2.13).

Deciding about authorship

So why should anyone begin to doubt that a letter that begins 'Paul, an apostle of Christ Jesus ... to Timothy' (1 Tim 1.1-2) was really written by Paul? Before answering that question, it is worth noting that disagreement about which apostolic writings were genuine is not only a modern phenomenon. The early Church (c. second to fourth century) debated which writings should and should not be accepted, during the lengthy process of establishing what eventually became the 'canon' of writings that we know as the New Testament.[4] Broadly speaking, modern scholars' doubts about the authenticity of some of the letters attributed to Paul are based on some or all of the following features of a letter: its vocabulary and style, its theological and ethical content, and the context both in church and society which it assumes and reflects. Since scholars often mention differences between the 'genuine' and the 'pseudo' Pauline letters as grounds for the pseudonymity of the latter, it is worth pointing out – as a cautionary note in assessing the evidence – that even the undisputed letters of Paul vary widely in their vocabulary, content and the situations they address. For example, the language of 'wisdom' (Greek: *sophos, sophia*) is heavily concentrated in 1 Corinthians, especially in Chapters 1–3; it does not appear at all in Galatians, Philippians or 1 Thessalonians. The word *charisma* ('gift') appears often in Romans and 1 Corinthians, once in 2 Corinthians (once also in 1 Timothy and in 2 Timothy), but nowhere in the other Pauline letters. Despite attempts to use modern techniques such as computer analysis of the style and language in the epistles, which do indeed yield important information relevant to these issues, decisions about authorship are unavoidably somewhat subjective. One may perhaps compare them with arguments in the world of literature or art: is this sonnet really by Shakespeare, or this painting really by Rembrandt, or might they be the product of students of the master's school, attempting to follow in their hero's footsteps? In some cases, the evidence pointing towards a different author living in a different time seems to be strong; but in other cases, like Colossians, the extent of differences from the 'genuine' Paul is much harder to assess.

It is worth asking yourself how your own beliefs and commitments affect your thinking with regard to these questions about authorship. Does it *matter* whether Paul wrote 1 Timothy or not? And if it matters, *why* does it matter? Just as some people have paid a lot for a painting on the basis that it is by Rembrandt, and so have a financial investment to defend if its genuineness is questioned, so some Christians feel they have a sort of theological investment in the genuineness of the letters ascribed to Paul in the New Testament. Does it detract from the Bible's authority or integrity if some of the claims to authorship made in its writings are not genuine? Or can we accept Ephesians, or 1 Timothy, as presentations of Pauline teaching which are just as valuable – and just as open to criticism – whether or not Paul wrote them? Certainly theological commitments can influence judgements about authenticity. But scholars may also be influenced by other commitments. For example, if they have developed a certain view of the development of early Christian history, they may be strongly inclined to date the letters in a certain way, such that they reveal the evolution of the Church over several decades. There are therefore no entirely objective, disinterested decisions on such matters. But that does not mean that any viewpoint is as defensible as any other. Any view of Paul and his writings has to do justice to the content of those writings; and judgements, whether by scholar, student or any interested person, stand or fall according to how well they make sense of what is actually in the letters.

It is also worth being cautious about assuming a modern view of 'pseudonymity' – namely that a book which makes a false claim about its authorship is essentially deceptive, its author guilty of lying. For some Christians, this is a major reason why it is hard to accept that a letter in the Bible which claims to be by Paul might actually have been written by someone else. Some scholars would agree with this reasoning, and argue against any compromise concerning the authenticity of the Bible's writings.[5] Others, however, point out that writing in the name of an esteemed predecessor was a common and probably more acceptable practice in the ancient world, and that attempting to present someone's teaching and authority afresh to a new generation may be seen as a worthy and important, and not a deceptive, undertaking.[6] Indeed, there are many Jewish and Christian texts dating from the centuries around the time of Christian origins which were written in the name of a figure long since (or more recently) dead. Jewish examples include writings in the name of Enoch, Abraham, Moses, Ezra and Solomon; Christian texts of the second and third century include gospels attributed to Peter, Philip, Thomas, Mary, records of the 'Acts' of Peter, Paul and John, and letters such as the undoubtedly inauthentic third letter of Paul to the Corinthians.[7] Whether any of these non-canonical writings offers a precise parallel to the suggested pseudepigrapha in the New Testament is, however, debated: some may have been excluded from the canon precisely because they were deemed to be inauthentic. Yet they were certainly writings valued and used by early Christians. Moreover, a judgement about whether a writing was theologically 'sound', sufficiently orthodox to count as truly 'apostolic', may have been more influential in its acceptance than a conviction as to who was actually its author.[8]

Let us then look briefly at some of the evidence on which a decision about authorship must be based. I shall examine two examples, one of which concerns a letter, Colossians, which most agree is close in style to the undisputed Pauline letters and which is held as pseudo-Pauline by only a small majority of scholars.[9] (It is of course impossible to be exact about the distribution of scholarly opinion, since there are no polls taken of scholars' views! In any case, counting votes is not the best way to assess the strength of an argument; considering the evidence for yourself is.) The second example is that of the Pastoral Epistles, three short letters which most scholars group together and regard as written after Paul's death.

1. The authorship of Colossians

Although Colossians is clearly Pauline in character, the letter contains a number of words not found in the undisputed Pauline letters, and is generally agreed to exhibit some distinctiveness in its style, compared with the undisputed letters. Some aspects of its theology and ethics, moreover, reflect a degree of development from what we find in Paul's letters. For example, there is the great Christological poem in 1.15–20, and the statement that 'in him [Christ] all the fullness of deity dwells bodily' (2.9). How far, if at all, has this developed from the Christology which we find in Paul (see above pp. 88–92)? Paul's image of the Christian community as the body of Christ – including the head (1 Cor 12.27) – is clearly taken up and developed further in Colossians: here Christ is depicted as *the head over his body* which is the Church (Col 1.18; cf. 2.10, 19; Eph 1.22; 4.15; 5.23). In terms of eschatology too there may be some differences between Paul's perspective and that of Colossians. Compare the following two passages:

… we have been buried with him by baptism into death, so that, just as Christ was raised from the dead by the glory of the Father, so we too might walk in newness of life. For if we have been united with him in a death like his, *we will certainly be united with him in a resurrection* like his. (Rom 6.4–5)	… when you were buried with him in baptism, *you were also raised with him* through faith in the power of God, who raised him from the dead. (Col 2.12)

What is particularly interesting here – see the words I have italicized – is the different tenses used to refer to the Christians' resurrection. In Romans it is a future hope; in Colossians it has already (in some sense) happened. While the extent of difference on this point is debatable, Colossians seems to have what scholars sometimes call a more 'realized eschatology' than does Paul (cf. also Col 3.1). That is to say, Colossians presents the Christians' future hope as present and realized here and now: they are already raised with Christ! Colossians also presents Christ as having already (on the cross) triumphed over rulers and authorities (Col 2.15). Paul seems to see the final triumph as yet to occur, though the decisive battle has already been won (see 1 Cor 15.23–28). In deciding about the authorship of letters like Colossians it is important to try to assess the extent of development in theology, but another crucial question is: How far is it reasonable to think that Paul's theology might have developed and changed during the years when he was writing his letters? An answer to that question is of course somewhat subjective.

Another feature of Colossians not found in the undisputed Pauline letters is its ethical teaching in the form of a so-called household code (Col 3.18–4.1; see above, pp. 182–83). Again there are questions to be asked about how much of a development this code represents from the teaching found in Paul's letters (cf. e.g. 1 Cor 7.1–40; 11.2–16). We may also ask: If Paul did write Colossians, why did he not use some form of household code in letters like 1 Thessalonians and 1 Corinthians, where it might have seemed highly appropriate to the situation addressed?

These then are just some of the issues to be taken into account in deciding whether or not Paul wrote Colossians. We turn next to the Pastoral Epistles.

2. The authorship of the Pastoral Epistles

The differences in vocabulary and style between the undisputed Pauline letters and the Pastoral letters are significant. There are a number of words which appear in the Pastorals but are never used elsewhere by Paul. Examples include: *eusebeia* (godliness), *sōphrosunē* (modesty), *theosebeia* (piety, religion). There are also a number of words which seem characteristic of Paul but which do not appear in the Pastorals, such as *euangelizō* (to proclaim the gospel), *pneumatikos* (spiritual), *sōma* (body) etc.[10] Other features of the Pastorals' style have been held by many commentators to indicate non-Pauline authorship. On the other hand, however, there are a number of passages in the letters which seem to reflect Paul's personal circumstances (see esp. 2 Tim 4.9–21; also 1 Tim 5.23; Titus 3.12–13). These texts have been explained in various ways: for some they are strong evidence for the authenticity of the epistles; others have suggested that they are fragments of authentic Pauline writing woven into otherwise pseudonymous writings; others argue that they are simply part of the device of pseudonymity, fictional references intended to heighten the impression of genuineness.

Differences in theology and ethics also seem to be apparent. The Pastorals contain none of Paul's characteristic discussion of being 'righteoused' by faith and not by works of the law. Indeed, in contrast to Paul's emphasis on faith as trust and commitment, the Pastorals seem to treat faith more as a body of teaching and tradition which must be safely preserved (e.g. 1 Tim 4.6; 6.10; Titus 1.13). This is often seen as one indication of the later origin of these letters, some decades after Paul's death, when a major concern was to protect and guard the teaching which the original apostles had bequeathed to the Church (see 1 Tim 6.20; 2 Tim 1:14). Instead of extended theological argument (see, e.g., Gal 3.1–5.1; Rom 1.18–11.36) theology in the Pastorals seems to be expressed in concise credal statements, which are perhaps reflections of the ways in which crucial Christian beliefs were being summarized and recited. A good example is found in 1 Timothy 3.16:

> Without any doubt, the mystery of our religion is great:
> He was revealed in flesh,
>> vindicated in spirit,
>> seen by angels,
>> proclaimed among Gentiles,
>> believed in throughout the world,
>> taken up in glory.

The ethical teaching in the Pastoral Epistles reflects a strong concern with decent and proper conduct which is largely in conformity with what was regarded as respectable at the time. Elements of household-code teaching, as found in Colossians and Ephesians, are taken up in the Pastorals (e.g. Titus 2.1–10). Men who are the heads of their households are to manage those households well; women and slaves are to be submissive and to work faithfully at their tasks. Women are not permitted to be in positions of authority in the Church (1 Tim 2.9–15). Some contrast with the teaching found in Paul's letters seems apparent (see above pp. 161–69) – though our assessment of the degree of contrast will depend partly on decisions we make on other Pauline texts: for example, is 1 Cor 14.34–35 an original part of 1 Corinthians (see above, p. 166)? One clear contrast may be seen in the advice to widows concerning remarriage. Compare the following texts:

A wife is bound to her husband as long as her husband lives. But if the husband dies, she is free to marry anyone she wishes, only in the Lord. But in my judgment she is more blessed if she remains as she is. (1 Cor 7.39–40)	I would have younger widows marry, bear children, and manage their households, so as to give the adversary no occasion to revile us. (1 Tim 5.14)

Another characteristic of the Pastoral Epistles is their concern to protect 'sound' teaching in the face of threats from those whom the author regards as heretics. A distinctive feature of these letters is the polemic against such heretics, often in the form of long strings of negative adjectives, describing those who pose a threat with their wayward teaching:

> people will be lovers of themselves, lovers of money, boasters, arrogant, abusive, disobedient to their parents, ungrateful, unholy, inhuman, implacable, slanderers, profligates, brutes, haters of good, treacherous, reckless, swollen with conceit, lovers of pleasure rather than lovers of God, holding to the outward form of godliness but denying its power. Avoid them!
>
> (2 Tim 3.2–5)

Along with the concern to protect and preserve sound teaching, this polemic against deviant teachers may reflect a context some time after Paul's death, when diversity and disagreement are increasingly felt to be a problem in the Church. The suspicion that the Pastorals reflect a situation later than Paul's own lifetime may also be strengthened by the references to church leaders. The Pastorals show considerable concern over the kind of people who are fit for office in the Church (1 Tim 3.1–13; Titus 1.5–9). Moreover, it is clear that there are three named offices within the Church: bishops (*episkopoi*), elders (*presbuteroi*) and deacons (*diakonoi*). To many scholars it seems apparent that leadership structures have developed beyond the rather loosely organized time of Paul's own activity. Paul never – outside the Pastoral Epistles – discusses the appointment of people to the offices of bishop, elder and deacon. Indeed, nowhere in the undisputed letters does he mention 'elders', and the only reference to bishops (*episkopoi* – the Greek word means 'overseer', and may be used in a more general, non-official sense) is in Phil 1.1. The term *diakonos*, 'servant', is used a number of times by Paul to describe his own ministry and that of others (e.g. Rom 16.1; 1 Cor 3.5; 2 Cor 3.6). This would seem likely to represent an earlier stage of development, before the term *diakonos* began to designate a specific office within an emerging threefold order.

All of these factors and more lead the majority of scholars to conclude that Paul did not write the Pastoral Epistles. On this view these epistles reflect the concerns and context of an author writing some decades after Paul's death, and the apparently personal details about Paul's circumstances are simply part of the author's fictitious composition.[11] There are those, however, who argue that the changes in style, language, content and context have been somewhat exaggerated and can be envisaged as occurring within Paul's lifetime, specifically during a period of activity after release from captivity in Rome (cf. Acts 28.16–31; though there is no direct evidence to prove that such a period of activity took place – see above p. 53).[12] One further hypothesis, which falls somewhere between the alternatives of pseudonymity and authenticity, is that authentic fragments of Paul's own writing were put together and woven into the three epistles by a later author/editor.[13] This hypothesis, however, faces the difficulty of offering some coherent explanation as to how and why mere 'fragments' were preserved and why the proposed fragments are consistent in style with the rest of the Pastoral Epistles.

Important themes and issues

There are clearly a considerable number of issues and debates which emerge from a reading of the disputed Pauline letters. Some of these issues are linked closely with questions of authorship and dating, others less so. What follows is only a very brief sketch of some of the areas of discussion.

Earlier in this book we saw a little of the debate concerning Paul's Christology (pp. 83–92). The disputed Pauline letters raise further questions: How far has the Christology of Colossians and Ephesians developed from that in the undisputed Paulines? Do these letters represent a stage in the process of the development of a gradually higher Christology, one which ascribes an ever more exalted and divine status to Christ and which sees the scope of Christ's redemption in ever-wider cosmic terms? And is Titus 2.13 then a significant indication of where this development is leading: to Christ as 'our great God and Saviour'? Or is the implication of Christ's divinity already there in Paul's undisputed letters?

In terms of eschatology too, there seem to be some developments in the disputed Pauline letters, though by no means along a single trajectory. Colossians and Ephesians appear to reflect a somewhat more realized eschatology than is found in the earlier Pauline letters, but 2 Thessalonians and 1 Timothy seem to oppose those who teach a realized eschatology. To what extent are there tensions and differences here and to what extent was the revision of eschatological hope a major issue in early Christianity (cf. 2 Pet 3.8–10)?

Another distinctive feature of Colossians and Ephesians is their presentation of a carefully structured 'household code'. The Pastoral Epistles nowhere contain such a concise and structured table of duties, but they do clearly repeat and develop various aspects of the household-code teaching. To what extent is this social teaching a change from what is found in the undisputed Pauline letters? And how is it to be understood and explained? Are these later letters promoting an essentially conservative form of Christian social teaching, urging all social groups to remain quietly 'in their place'? Was it right for such teaching to be used to justify slavery in the colonial history of the West? Is it right for such teaching to be used to justify male leadership in the home and the Church?

The extensive attacks against false teaching in the Pastoral Epistles clearly raise questions about the nature of the opposition. But the author's strong polemic makes it difficult to discern with confidence what the opponents' message actually was. What kinds of teaching were being promoted and developed, and how might these link with the various doctrines attacked by the anti-heretical writers (such as Irenaeus) of the immediately following centuries? There are some hints, as we saw, that some forms of Jewish mysticism or of Jewish Christianity lay behind some of the beliefs and practices which were attacked. One reference in 1 Timothy has often been regarded as a hint that the opponents were moving in the direction of a form of Gnosticism[14]: 'Avoid the profane chatter and contradictions of what is falsely called knowledge (*gnōsis*)' (1 Tim 6.21).

Also clear in the Pastoral Epistles is the concern with Church leadership, and the emerging roles of bishop, elder/presbyter and deacon. This structure of leadership was to develop further, into what is known as a monepiscopal pattern – a single bishop presiding over a group of presbyters (elders) and deacons.[15] This threefold order of ministry remains a basic pattern for many major churches today. Again there are clearly questions concerning the extent to which this marks a development from the leadership patterns evident in Paul's undisputed letters and how the developments are to be explained (cf. above pp. 160–61).

Each of these areas of debate – and more besides – could be investigated in their own right. But what of the overall picture? Is there any evidence from these disputed letters that the Pauline churches are developing in a certain direction, and if so, how is that to be explained? Many scholars, taking these letters as pseudonymous compositions written some years after Paul's death, have argued that there is indeed a process of development taking place here; they have labelled the kind of Christianity emerging in the Pastoral Epistles 'early catholicism'. This 'early catholic' form of Christianity is said to be characterized by three main features: the disappearance of the hope for Christ's imminent return; the crystallization of the faith into creeds and set forms; and increasing institutionalization, especially regarding the development of fixed leadership offices.[16] Thus, the fading of the hope for Christ's imminent return is seen as a driving force behind the Church's establishment of formal leadership patterns and its more conformist social teaching: it had to reckon with existing in the world for some time to come (cf. 2 Pet 3.8–10). In recent years, however, there have been a number of voices critical of this 'early catholic' interpretation. In part this is because of a suspicion that it represents Protestant prejudice against Catholicism, dressed up in the guise of historical explanation. But it is also because it is felt by many to fail to do justice to the content and diversity of the later Pauline letters (and others such as Jude and 1–2 Peter). New perspectives have offered some different ways of interpreting and explaining the evidence, such as the social-scientific analysis of 'Institutionalization' we encountered briefly in Chapter 7 (see pp. 160–61). Whether old or new perspectives offer satisfying explanations I must leave to you to decide, but what is clear is that the whole collection of Pauline letters raises enormous and fascinating questions, not only about authorship and date, but about patterns in the development of Christianity in its first century of existence.

Paul's legacy through the centuries

Any attempt to cast an eye over Paul's legacy through the centuries is of course bound to be highly sketchy and selective but may perhaps serve to give us some indications as to Paul's impact on the generations of Christians who followed him, as well as his impact more broadly. An interest in the impact and 'afterlives' of biblical texts has indeed become prominent in recent biblical studies. Before we leave the New Testament behind, we should pause to mention one of the earliest writers (leaving aside the disputed Pauline letters) for whom Paul was a hero: the author of Luke-Acts. Paul is the dominant figure in the latter half of the Acts of the Apostles, with the rest of the apostles rather fading from view. In the earliest post-New Testament writings, Paul, along with Peter, is seen as an outstanding apostle and martyr. For example, in 1 Clement, written from Corinth to Rome towards the end of the first century, we find Paul and Peter described in these terms:

> Let us set before our eyes the good apostles: Peter, who because of unrighteous jealousy suffered not one or two but many trials, and having thus given his testimony went to the glorious place which was his due. Through jealousy and strife Paul showed the way to the prize of endurance; seven times he was in bonds, he was exiled, he was stoned, he was a herald both in the East and in the West, he gained the noble fame of his faith, he taught righteousness to all the world, and when he had reached the limits of the West he gave his testimony before the rulers, and thus passed from the world and was taken up into the Holy Place – the greatest example of endurance.
>
> (1 Clement 5.3–7)[17]

It was Peter, however, whom tradition came to regard as the first bishop of Rome, the first in a long line of papal authorities.

It is sometimes argued that Paul's influence in the early Church came more through his status as a heroic figure – apostle and martyr – than through his theology and writings, which, it is suggested, were often misunderstood. It was certainly recognized early on that Paul's letters were difficult to understand and subject to various interpretations (2 Pet 3.15–16). Evidently, Paul's influence did not extend only over what came to be regarded as orthodox Christianity. His persona and writings were also influential, perhaps more influential, within a wide range of what came to be seen as 'heretical' early Christian groups. The Gnostics, for example, found much inspiration in his letters[18] and the legendary stories about Paul in the second-century Acts of Paul and Thecla reveal his importance among Christian groups where women seem to have continued to take leading roles – perhaps not unlike those 'silly women' seen from a very different perspective by the author of the Pastoral Epistles, who criticizes them as gossips and busybodies (1 Tim 5.13; 2 Tim 3.6).[19] And then there was Marcion, the second-century heretic who maintained that the loving God of the Christian gospel was completely different from the cruel God of the Old Testament. Paul was a hero of Marcion's, even if Marcion misunderstood him. Yet it also seems to be true that Paul was of major influence in the dominant, 'orthodox' forms of early Christianity: in the writings of the 'Apostolic Fathers' such as Clement, Ignatius and Polycarp, in the theology of the anti-heretical writer Irenaeus, and so on. Indeed, William Babcock argues 'that Paul may have been one of the critical factors giving Christianity its distinctive identity within and over against its late-antique cultural environment'.[20]

We could continue – given unlimited space and expertise – to survey the whole sweep of Church history, noting Paul's influence on different groups and individuals at different times and places. Indeed, a full assessment of the impact and legacy of Paul would need to take account of all sorts of things beyond the realm of theology and the Church. However, since both space and expertise are unavoidably limited, let us conclude with just a few selected cameos which illustrate Paul's continued legacy through the centuries.

Augustine (354–430), bishop of Hippo in North Africa and a theologian of immense and continuing influence, was deeply influenced by Paul's letters. Augustine found in Romans 7 'a self-portrait of Paul with a divided mind uncommonly like his own';[21] he perceived in Paul's writing a powerful depiction of his own spiritual state, and in turn Augustine's reflections exerted a powerful influence on how Paul was understood for many centuries thereafter.[22] Around the time of his conversion, when he wrestled with the decision to live in chastity, Augustine found that Paul's words convinced him of the path he should choose (Rom 13.13–14).[23]

Martin Luther's theology, so central to the Protestant reformation, is unimaginable without Paul. For Luther (1483–1546) Paul's gospel of justification by faith provided both the answer to his personal struggle with sin and guilt and the critique of a Church which had quantified grace as a commodity to be purchased or earned.[24] The question of whether Luther's interpretation does justice to Paul and to the Judaism contemporary with Paul has already been raised (pp. 128–29). But what cannot be denied is the impact of Paul's letters upon Luther and the continuing influence of Luther's theology within the Protestant Churches.

Indeed, it might well be said that Luther and Paul combined to bring about the conversion of John Wesley (1703–1791), the founder with his brother Charles of Methodism. It was while listening to a reading of Luther's preface to Paul's letter to the Romans that Wesley felt his heart 'strangely warmed'. He wrote of that experience: 'I felt I did trust in Christ, Christ alone for salvation; and an assurance was given me that he had taken away *my* sins, even *mine*, and saved *me* from the law of sin and death'.[25]

If we move rapidly on to the twentieth century, and to almost certainly the most influential theologian of that century, Karl Barth (1886–1968), we find again the profound influence of Paul. The publication in which Barth announced his new theological programme to the world was his commentary on Romans, that most influential letter of Paul's. It was 'the mighty voice of Paul', the gospel Word of which Paul wrote, that Barth sought to understand and to express.[26]

That is only a cursory glance at just a few major figures in theology through the centuries. An examination of Paul's legacy could encompass so much more, beyond as well as within the walls of the Church: Paul's ambivalent impact on the history of slavery and its formal abolition; Paul's impact on Western attitudes to sex and sexuality; Paul's impact on Christian attitudes to self-sacrifice, charity and love. It is particularly interesting to note the recent engagement with Paul among (non-religious) philosophers, notably socialist writers such as Slavoj Žižek and Alain Badiou, who find in Paul's ideas the basis for radical political theory.[27] The list could continue almost indefinitely. Nevertheless, our passing glance at just a few prominent figures in Church history may be enough to suggest that there is some truth in Ernst Käsemann's comments on Paul. Käsemann argues that 'the real Paul' is all too often concealed beneath an ecclesiastical image of Paul. But whenever the real Paul is 'rediscovered – which happens almost exclusively in times of crisis – there issues from him explosive power ...'.[28]

Conclusion

Each of the letters attributed to Paul deserves careful attention, even if the undisputed Pauline letters understandably retain their central position in studies of Paul. For most scholars, the disputed letters provide evidence of how Paul's legacy began to be taken up by his successors, how his teaching and authority were brought to bear upon the changing situation of the developing Church. Even for those who take all these letters as genuinely from Paul there are important questions to be addressed about how their theology and ethics have developed from the earliest Pauline letters and about the new issues and problems which they seek to confront. But no matter where Paul's legacy actually begins, it is clear even from our hasty glance that his persona and his letters continued to shape the Church decisively right from the earliest times to the present day. Indeed, the impact and influence of Paul's thought extends beyond specifically Christian circles, to Western culture more generally and its traditions of philosophy and ethics.

Further reading

A very useful treatment of all of the letters discussed in this chapter can be found in R.F. Collins, *Letters That Paul Did Not Write: The Epistle to the Hebrews and the Pauline Pseudepigrapha* (Good News Studies 28, Wilmington: Michael Glazier, 1988). See also J.C. Beker, *Heirs of Paul: Paul's Legacy in the New Testament and in the Church Today* (Minneapolis: Fortress, 1991). Good introductions to the individual letters include the following: M.J.J. Menken, *2 Thessalonians* (London and New York: Routledge, 1994); J.M.G. Barclay, *Colossians and Philemon* (Sheffield: SAP, 1997); E. Best, *Ephesians* (Sheffield: SAP, 1993); M. Davies, *The Pastoral Epistles* (Sheffield: SAP, 1996). Also valuable, especially on the theology of the letters is the Cambridge University Press series, *New Testament Theology*: K.P. Donfried and I.H. Marshall, *The Theology of the Shorter Pauline Letters* (Cambridge: CUP, 1993) – this volume covers 1 and 2 Thessalonians, Philippians and Philemon; A.T. Lincoln and A.J.M. Wedderburn, *The Theology of the Later Pauline Letters* (Cambridge: CUP, 1993) – this book covers Colossians and Ephesians; F.M. Young, *The Theology of the Pastoral Letters* (Cambridge: CUP, 1994).

Questions of authorship are also dealt with in the standard 'introductions' to the New Testament (see the further reading listed in Chapter 1) and in the commentaries on particular letters. For a more conservative perspective, see D. Guthrie, *New Testament Introduction* (4th edn; Leicester & Downers Grove: Apollos/IVP, 1990). The best way to make a decision for yourself is undoubtedly to read the letters themselves and get to know them as well as you can, and also to read some commentaries or introductions which give contrasting points of view. A helpful discussion of the issue of pseudonymity may be found in J.D.G. Dunn, *The Living Word* (London: SCM, 1987), pp. 65–85.

On Paul's legacy in early Christianity, a concise overview is provided in J.A. Harrill, *Paul the Apostle: His Life and Legacy in their Roman Context* (Cambridge & New York: Cambridge University Press, 2012), pp. 97–162. See also W.S. Babcock (ed.), *Paul and the Legacies of Paul* (Dallas: Southern Methodist University Press, 1990). On the collection of Paul's letters and the formation of the New Testament see H.Y. Gamble, *The New Testament Canon: Its Making and Meaning* (Philadelphia: Fortress, 1985); A.G. Patzia, *The Making of the New Testament: Origin, Collection, Text and Canon* (Leicester: Apollos, 1995). For detailed discussion of Paul's influence on the history of Christian theology, see S. Westerholm (ed.), *The Blackwell Companion to Paul* (Oxford: Wiley-Blackwell, 2011). The most comprehensive discussion of the recent philosophical interest in Paul is W. Blanton and H. de Vries (eds) *Paul and the Philosophers* (New York: Fordham University Press, 2013).

Questions for further study

- What are the issues at stake, historically and theologically, in determining whether or not Paul wrote the letters whose authorship is disputed?

- How far is it legitimate to trace processes of doctrinal or ecclesiastical development over time through the genuine and disputed Pauline epistles? To what extent do you think there are changes or developments?
- Do you think, considering Paul's legacy, that there is truth in Käsemann's remark (p. 200 above) that when the 'real' Paul is 'rediscovered' – generally in times of crisis – 'there issues from him explosive power'? If this is true, is it a good thing, a bad thing, or a mixed blessing?

Notes

1 See R.F. Collins, *Letters that Paul Did Not Write: The Epistle to the Hebrews and the Pauline Pseudepigrapha* (Good News Studies 28; Wilmington: Michael Glazier, 1988), pp. 19–21, 47–55.

2 See, e.g., M. Prior, *Paul the Letter-Writer and the Second Letter to Timothy* (Sheffield: JSOT, 1989); J. Murphy-O'Connor, '2 Timothy Contrasted with 1 Timothy and Titus', *Revue Biblique* 98 (1991), pp. 403–18.

3 It seems reasonable to assume that the author was a man, particularly in view of the teaching contained in the epistle (see 1 Tim 2.9–15; 5.13–15 etc.).

4 See further H.Y. Gamble, *The New Testament Canon: Its Making and Meaning* (Philadelphia: Fortress, 1985).

5 E.g. J.I. Packer, *'Fundamentalism' and the Word of God* (Leicester: IVP, 1958), p. 184: 'pseudonymity and canonicity are mutually exclusive'. See further pp. 182–86.

6 See further J.D.G. Dunn, *The Living Word* (London: SCM, 1987), pp. 65–85; Collins, *Letters That Paul Did Not Write*, pp. 75–86. A more detailed discussion of this subject may be found in D.G. Meade, *Pseudonymity and Canon* (Grand Rapids: Eerdmans, 1987).

7 For some of the Jewish texts, see J.H. Charlesworth (ed.) *The Old Testament Pseudepigrapha* (2 vols, London: Darton, Longman & Todd, 1983, 1985); for Christian examples, see B.D. Ehrman, *The New Testament and Other Early Christian Writings* (Oxford: OUP, 1998); J.K. Elliott, *The Apocryphal New Testament* (Oxford: OUP, 1993).

8   Cf. H.Y. Gamble 'Pseudonymity and the New Testament Canon', in J. Frey *et al.* (eds), *Pseudepigraphie und Verfasserfiktion in frühchristlichen Briefen* (Tübingen: Mohr Siebeck, 2009), pp. 347–55.

9   Cf. Collins, *Letters That Paul Did Not Write*, p. 178; J.M.G. Barclay, *Colossians and Philemon* (Sheffield: SAP, 1997), pp. 18–36.

10 See A.T. Hanson, *The Pastoral Epistles* (New Century Bible Commentary; London: Marshall, Morgan & Scott, 1982), pp. 2–3, with further examples listed there.

11 See further Collins, *Letters That Paul Did Not Write*, pp. 88–131; J.C. Beker, *Heirs of Paul: Paul's Legacy in the New Testament and in the Church Today* (Minneapolis: Fortress, 1991), pp. 36–47.

12 See for example the defences of Pauline authorship in G.W. Knight III, *The Pastoral Epistles* (New International Greek Testament Commentary; Grand Rapids: Eerdmans, 1992), pp. 4–54; D. Guthrie, *New Testament Introduction* (4th edn, Leicester & Downers Grove: Apollos/IVP, 1990), pp. 607–49.

13 The classic statement of this position is by P.N. Harrison, *The Problem of the Pastoral Epistles* (London: OUP, 1921).

14 Gnosticism is the name given to a form of theology based on insight into divine knowledge (*gnōsis*) which developed among certain Christian groups in the second century and which the early Church Fathers branded as heretical. The origins and definition of Gnosticism are, however, subject to much debate and uncertainty. For an overview, see P. Perkins, *Gnosticism and the New Testament* (Minneapolis: Fortress, 1993); and on issues of definition, K.L. King, *What is Gnosticism?* (Cambridge, MA: Harvard University Press, 2003).

15 This monepiscopal structure is clearly the pattern which Ignatius urges as essential for the Church in his letters written early in the second century. For the text and translation of Ignatius' letters, see B.D. Ehrman, *The Apostolic Fathers, vol. 1* (Loeb Classical Library 24, Cambridge, MA/ London: Harvard University Press, 2003).

16 See J.D.G. Dunn, *Unity and Diversity in the New Testament* (London: SCM, 1990), p. 344.

17 For text and translation, see Ehrman, *Apostolic Fathers, vol. 1*.

18 See E.H. Pagels, *The Gnostic Paul: Gnostic Exegesis of the Pauline Letters* (Philadelphia: Fortress, 1975).

19 See further D.R. MacDonald, *The Legend and the Apostle: The Battle for Paul in Story and Canon* (Philadelphia: Westminster, 1983). Note

Tertullian's (160–220 CE) comments: 'But if certain Acts of Paul, which are falsely so named, claim the example of Thecla for allowing women to teach and to baptize, let men know that in Asia the presbyter who compiled that document . . . was found out, and though he confessed that he had done it for love of Paul, was deposed from his position' (*On Baptism*, 17; quoted from E. Evans, *Tertullian's Homily on Baptism*, London: SPCK, 1964, p. 37). On the basis of 1 Cor 14.34–35, Tertullian finds it incredible that Paul could have permitted women to teach and baptize, when he urged them to learn in silence.

20 W.S. Babcock, 'Introduction', in W.S. Babcock (ed.), *Paul and the Legacies of Paul* (Dallas: Southern Methodist University Press, 1990), p. xxvii.

21 H. Chadwick, *Augustine* (Oxford: OUP, 1986), p. 68.

22 Cf. K. Stendahl, 'The Apostle Paul and the Introspective Conscience of the West', in *Paul Among Jews and Gentiles* (London: SCM, 1977), pp. 78–96.

23 See M.T. Clark, *Augustine* (London: Geoffrey Chapman, 1994), p. 8; Chadwick, *Augustine*, p. 26.

24 For an introduction to Luther, see B. Lohse, *Martin Luther: An Introduction to His Life and Work* (Edinburgh: T&T Clark, 1987).

25 John Wesley, Journal for Sunday, May 21, 1738. Quoted from *The Journal of John Wesley*, abridged by C. Idle (Tring: Lion Publishing, 1986), p. 46.

26 The first edition of Barth's commentary was published in 1918; a thoroughly rewritten second edition appeared in 1921. For an English translation (of the sixth edition) see K. Barth, *The Epistle to the Romans* (trans. E.C. Hoskyns, London: OUP, 1933). The phrase quoted above is from p. 2.

27 For a helpful initial orientation to this engagement, see P.T. Kroeker, 'Recent Continental Philosphers', in S. Westerholm (ed.), *The Blackwell Companion to Paul* (Chichester: Wiley-Blackwell, 2011), pp. 440–54, and the essays in J.D. Caputo and L.M. Alcoff (eds), *St. Paul among the Philosophers* (Bloomington: Indiana University Press, 2009).

28 E. Käsemann, 'Paul and Early Catholicism' in *New Testament Questions of Today* (London: SCM, 1969), p. 249.

9

Coming Full Circle: Why Study Paul Today?

We began this introduction to the study of Paul by noting Paul's enormous influence and by mentioning some of the issues and questions that arise from our modern context and motivate our studies of Paul. As times change and new issues arise, so of course there will be new questions to put to Paul, new challenges in interpreting his letters. But now that we have completed our introduction to various aspects of Paul's life and letters and the ways in which these are studied and interpreted, we can perhaps stand back and consider the wider picture. After what we have seen of Paul in this short book, what are the main reasons to study him today?

I want to suggest three basic reasons – though there are surely others too – why studying Paul is important: historical, literary and theological. No one who wishes to understand the modern world can do so without some understanding of Christianity, and specifically of Christian origins. And that means some understanding of Paul. As we have seen, Paul's thought was crucial to the process by which Christianity eventually came to be separated from its Jewish parent and became a religion in its own right. That momentous separation led to the creation of what would gradually become a world faith, favoured and adopted by the Roman emperor Constantine in the early fourth century, and spread – sometimes with violent force – 'to the ends of the earth' (Acts 1.8) since then. By its very nature the Christian gospel, not least under Paul's influence, also led to tensions between Christians and Jews, tensions which still reverberate in the world of today. So there are good *historical* reasons for studying Paul.

Secondly, there are *literary* reasons for studying Paul. Ranked alongside the classics of Greek and Latin literature, Paul's letters may not come too near the top of the chart. Yet they are nevertheless powerful and artistic compositions which have been recognized as 'weighty and strong' (2 Cor 10.10) ever since they were written. In places they are also beautiful, lyrical and poetic. Those who watched the funeral of Diana, Princess of Wales, in 1997, saw Tony Blair, the British prime minister, reading 1 Corinthians 13 with great feeling and style. A friend of mine in Australia pointed me to an article written in *The Age*, one of Australia's leading broadsheet newspapers, in which the writer commented that 'Blair's ... eulogy at her [Diana's] funeral consolidated and confirmed his capacity to tap into contemporary society's need to feel that it is understood'.[1] Apparently another reporter made a remark to the effect that Tony Blair must have been pleased with his speech writers! Those comments not only suggest a certain lack of knowledge of Paul's letters (one good reason to study them!) but also reveal that Paul's poetry can still inspire admiration and stir emotions, can still seem appropriate to the needs of a contemporary society. Furthermore, without a knowledge of Paul's letters and the rest of the biblical literature, a whole host of allusions, metaphors and phrases in the works of literary giants through the ages will be lost on us.

Last, but by no means least, there are *theological* reasons for studying Paul. Indeed, studying Paul *without* seeking to understand his thought and consider its significance would be rather like investigating the date of a Beethoven manuscript, analysing the arrangement of the notes on the page, but never getting to hear the music. What drove Paul to write his beautiful and not-so-beautiful phrases, his encouraging and his angry words, was his enduring conviction that the God of Israel had acted in Jesus Christ for the salvation of the world. As we have seen, understanding exactly what Paul means by that and how that relates to his Jewish religious identity is not at all easy, but we do justice to Paul's historical and literary significance only when we struggle to grasp the meaning of what he wrote. Wrestling with Paul's theology does not necessarily imply agreeing with it, believing it, or considering it important for the world today – though it may include all of those things, to greater or lesser extent. As Daniel Boyarin's book shows well, engaging with Paul's central convictions can be done from a perspective which is critical as well as appreciative of Paul, and from perspectives other than Christian.[2] And, as we noted above (p. 200), some non-Christian philosophers have found Paul's ideas a stimulating and important resource for their own reflections and political theories. For Christians, of course, Paul's letters form part of their scriptures and thus have a claim to be studied with seriousness and care, with an expectation that within them the word of God may be discerned. Christians differ as to how to hear that 'word' from the Bible – is every sentence of the Bible to be regarded as the word of God, or is it a case of discerning critically the word of the gospel for today amidst the varied words of scripture? – but at root they share the conviction that what Paul wrote about God's act of reconciliation in Jesus Christ (2 Cor 5.19) remains important for Christian faith and action today.

Whatever our motivations for studying Paul, whether we share Paul's faith or not, hopefully this book will have provided some resources and tools to help that study to begin. The end of this book can only be a beginning . . .

Notes

1 S. Carney, 'Searching for Human Shapes in Politicians', *The Age*, Saturday 20 December 1997, p. 8.
2 D. Boyarin, *A Radical Jew: Paul and the Politics of Identity* (Berkeley and Los Angeles: University of California Press, 1994).

Bibliography

Note: the Bibliography lists items cited in the notes, but does not repeat works listed only in the sections recommending further reading.

Adams, E., 'First-Century Models for Paul's Churches: Selected Scholarly Developments since Meeks', in T.D. Still and D.G. Horrell (eds), *After the First Urban Christians* (New York & London: T&T Clark, 2009), pp. 60–78.

Adams, E., *The Earliest Christian Meeting Places: Almost Exclusively Houses?* (London & New York: Bloomsbury T&T Clark, 2013).

Anderson, R.D. Jr., *Ancient Rhetorical Theory and Paul* (Kampen: Kok Pharos, 1996).

Arnold, B., *Christ as the Telos of Life: Moral Philosophy, Athletic Imagery, and the Aim of Philippians* (Tübingen: Mohr Siebeck, 2014).

Ascough, R., *What Are They Saying About the Formation of the Pauline Churches?* (New York: Paulist, 1998).

Babcock, W.S. (ed.), *Paul and the Legacies of Paul* (Dallas: Southern Methodist University Press, 1990).

Barclay, J.M.G., *Colossians and Philemon* (Sheffield: SAP, 1997).

Barclay, J.M.G., *Pauline Churches and Diaspora Jews* (Tübingen: Mohr Siebeck, 2011).

Barrett, C.K., *Paul: An Introduction to His Thought* (London: Geoffrey Chapman, 1994).

Barrett, C.K., *A Critical and Exegetical Commentary on the Acts of the Apostles* (Vol. 1, Edinburgh: T&T Clark, 1994).

Barth, K., *The Epistle to the Romans* (trans. E.C. Hoskyns, London: OUP, 1933).

Bassler, J.M. (ed.), *Pauline Theology. Vol. 1: Thessalonians, Philippians, Galatians, Philemon* (Minneapolis: Fortress, 1991).

Bauckham, R., 'The Worship of Jesus in Apocalyptic Christianity', *New Testament Studies* 27 (1981), pp. 322–41.

Bauckham, R., *Jesus and the God of Israel: 'God Crucified' and Other Studies on the New Testament's Christology of Divine Identity* (Milton Keynes: Paternoster, 2008).

Beker, J.C., *Paul the Apostle: The Triumph of God in Life and Thought* (Edinburgh: T&T Clark, 1980).

Beker, J.C., *The Triumph of God: The Essence of Paul's Thought* (Minneapolis: Fortress, 1990).

Beker, J.C., *Heirs of Paul: Paul's Legacy in the New Testament and in the Church Today* (Minneapolis: Fortress, 1991).

Betz, H.D., 'The Literary Composition and Function of Paul's Letter to the Galatians', *New Testament Studies* 21 (1975), pp. 353–79.

Betz, H.D., *Galatians* (Philadelphia: Fortress, 1979).

Bockmuehl, M., *Jewish Law in Gentile Churches* (Edinburgh: T&T Clark, 2000).

Boyarin, D., *A Radical Jew: Paul and the Politics of Identity* (Berkeley and Los Angeles: University of California Press, 1994).

Bultmann, R., *Theology of the New Testament. Vol. 1* (London: SCM, 1952).

Bultmann, R., *New Testament and Mythology and Other Basic Writings* (trans. and ed. S.M. Ogden, London: SCM, 1985).

Butler, H.E., *The Institutio Oratoria of Quintilian* (4 vols, Loeb Classical Library; London: Heinemann, 1920–22).

Campbell, D.A., *The Quest for Paul's Gospel* (London and New York: T&T Clark, 2005).

Campbell, D.A., *The Deliverance of God: An Apocalyptic Rereading of Justification in Paul* (Grand Rapids: Eerdmans, 2009).

Caputo, J.D. and Alcoff, L.M. (eds), *St. Paul among the Philosophers* (Bloomington: Indiana University Press, 2009).

Carson, D.A., O'Brien, P.T. and Seifrid, M. (eds), *Justification and Variegated Nomism, Vol. 1: The Complexities of Second Temple Judaism* (Tübingen: Mohr Siebeck; Grand Rapids: Baker Academic, 2001).

Carson, D.A., O'Brien, P.T. and Seifrid M. (eds), *Justification and Variegated Nomism, Vol. 2: The Paradoxes of Paul* (Tübingen: Mohr Siebeck; Grand Rapids: Baker Academic, 2004).

Casey, P.M., *From Jewish Prophet to Gentile God* (Cambridge: James Clarke, 1991).

Chadwick, H., *Augustine* (Oxford: OUP, 1986).

Charlesworth, J.H. (ed.), *The Old Testament Pseudepigrapha* (2 vols, London: Darton, Longman & Todd, 1983, 1985).

Clark, M.T., *Augustine* (London: Geoffrey Chapman, 1994).

Clarke, F.K.T., 'God's Concern for the Poor in the New Testament. A Discussion of the Role of the Poor in the Foundation of Christian Belief (Early to Mid First Century CE)' (PhD thesis, University of Exeter, 2000).

Collins, R.F., *Letters that Paul Did Not Write: The Epistle to the Hebrews and the Pauline Pseudepigrapha* (Good News Studies 28, Wilmington: Michael Glazier, 1988).

Das, A.A., *Paul and the Jews* (Peabody: Hendrickson, 2003).

Das, A.A., *Solving the Romans Debate* (Minneapolis: Fortress, 2007).

Davis, C.A., *The Structure of Paul's Theology* (Lampeter: Edwin Mellen, 1995).

Deissmann, G.A., *Light from the Ancient East* (London: Hodder & Stoughton, 1910).

Deming, W., *Paul on Marriage and Celibacy: The Hellenistic Background of 1 Corinthians 7* (Cambridge: CUP, 1995).

Dodd, C.H., *New Testament Studies* (Manchester: Manchester University Press, 1953).

Dodd, C.H., *The Epistle to the Romans* (London: Fontana, 1959).

Donfried, K.P. (ed.), *The Romans Debate: Revised and Expanded Edition* (Edinburgh: T&T Clark, 1991).

Downing, F.G., *Cynics, Paul and the Pauline Churches* (London and New York: Routledge, 1998).

Downs, D.J., *The Offering of the Gentiles: Paul's Collection for Jerusalem in Its Chronological, Cultural, and Cultic Contexts* (Tübingen: Mohr Siebeck, 2008).

Dunn, J.D.G., *Christology in the Making* (London: SCM, 1980, 2nd edn 1989).

Dunn, J.D.G., *The Living Word* (London: SCM, 1987).

Dunn, J.D.G., *Unity and Diversity in the New Testament* (London: SCM, 2nd edn 1990).

Dunn, J.D.G., *Jesus, Paul and the Law* (London: SPCK, 1990).

Dunn, J.D.G., *The Theology of Paul the Apostle* (Edinburgh: T&T Clark, 1998).

Ehrman, B.D., *The New Testament and Other Early Christian Writings* (Oxford: OUP, 1998).

Ehrman, B.D. *The Apostolic Fathers, vol.1* (Loeb Classical Library 24, Cambridge, MA/London: Harvard University Press, 2003).

Eisenbaum, P., *Paul Was Not a Christian: The Original Message of a Misunderstood Apostle* (New York: HarperCollins, 2009).

Eisenbaum, P. 'Jewish Perspectives: A Jewish Apostle to the Gentiles', in J.A. Marchal (ed.), *Studying Paul's Letters* (Minneapolis: Fortress, 2012), pp. 135–53.

Elliott, J.H., 'Jesus the Israelite was Neither a "Jew," nor a "Christian": On Correcting Misleading Nomenclature', *Journal for the Study of the Historical Jesus* 5 (2007), pp. 119–54.

Elliott, J.K., *The Apocryphal New Testament* (Oxford: OUP, 1993).

Engberg-Pedersen, T., *Paul and the Stoics* (Edinburgh: T&T Clark, 2000).

Engberg-Pedersen, T. (ed.), *Paul Beyond the Judaism/Hellenism Divide* (Louisville: Westminster John Knox, 2001).

Epp, E.J., *Junia: The First Woman Apostle* (Minneapolis: Fortress, 2005).

Esler, P.F., 'Review of C.C. Hill, *Hellenists and Hebrews*', *Biblical Interpretation* 3 (1995), pp. 119–23.

Esler, P.F., *Galatians* (London and New York: Routledge, 1998).

Esler, P.F., *Conflict and Identity in Romans* (Minneapolis: Fortress, 2003).

Evans, E., *Tertullian's Homily on Baptism* (London: SPCK, 1964).

Fee, G.D., *God's Empowering Presence: The Holy Spirit in the Letters of Paul* (Peabody: Hendrickson, 1994).

Fee, G.D., *Paul's Letter to the Philippians* (Grand Rapids: Eerdmans, 1995).

Fee, G.D., *Paul, the Spirit, and the People of God* (Peabody: Hendrickson, 1996).

Fiorenza, E.S., *In Memory of Her: A Feminist Theological Reconstruction of Christian Origins* (London: SCM, 1983, 2nd edn 1995).

Friesen, S.J., 'Poverty in Pauline Studies: Beyond the So-Called New Consensus', *Journal for the Study of the New Testament* 26 (2004), pp. 323–61.

Friesen, S.J., 'Normal Religion, or, Words Fail Us: A Response to Karl Galinksy's "The Cult of the Roman Emperor: Uniter or Divider?"', in J. Brodd and J.L. Reed (eds), *Rome and Religion: A Cross-Disciplinary Dialogue on the Imperial Cult* (Atlanta: Society of Biblical Literature, 2011), pp. 23–26.

Furnish, V.P., *Theology and Ethics in Paul* (Nashville: Abingdon, 1968), reissued with an introduction by Richard Hays (Louisville: Westminster John Knox, 2009).

Gager, J.G., *Reinventing Paul* (Oxford & New York: OUP, 2000).

Galinsky, K., 'The Cult of the Roman Emperor: Uniter or Divider?' in J. Brodd and J.L. Reed (eds), *Rome and Religion: A Cross-Disciplinary Dialogue on the Imperial Cult* (Atlanta: Society of Biblical Literature, 2011), pp. 1–21.

Galinsky, K., 'In the Shadow (or Not) of the Imperial Cult: A Cooperative Agenda', in J. Brodd and J.L. Reed (eds), *Rome and Religion: A Cross-Disciplinary Dialogue on the Imperial Cult* (Atlanta: Society of Biblical Literature, 2011), pp. 215–25.

Gamble, H.Y., *The New Testament Canon: Its Making and Meaning* (Philadelphia: Fortress, 1985).

Gamble, H.Y., 'Pseudonymity and the New Testament Canon', in J. Frey et al. (eds), *Pseudepigraphie und Verfasserfiktion in frühchristlichen Briefen* (Tübingen: Mohr Siebeck, 2009), pp. 333–62.

Gaston, L., *Paul and the Torah* (Vancouver: University of British Columbia Press, 1987).

Gathercole, S.J., *Where then is Boasting? Early Jewish Soteriology and Paul's Response in Romans 1–5* (Grand Rapids: Eerdmans, 2002).

Gehring, R.W., *House Church and Mission: The Importance of Household Structures in Early Christianity* (Peabody: Hendrickson, 2004).

Georgi, D., *Remembering the Poor* (Nashville: Abingdon, 1992).

Gorman, M., *Inhabiting the Cruciform God: Kenosis, Justification, and Theosis in Paul's Narrative Soteriology* (Grand Rapids: Eerdmans, 2009).

Guthrie, D., *New Testament Introduction* (4th edn, Leicester & Downers Grove: Apollos/IVP, 1990).

Haenchen, E., *The Acts of the Apostles* (Oxford: Blackwell, 1971).

Hanson, A.T., *The Pastoral Epistles* (New Century Bible Commentary, London: Marshall, Morgan & Scott, 1982).

Harland, P.A., *Dynamics of Identity in the World of the Early Christians* (London & New York: T&T Clark, 2009).

Harrill, J.A., *Paul the Apostle: His Life and Legacy in their Roman Context* (Cambridge & New York: Cambridge University Press, 2012).

Harrison, P.N., *The Problem of the Pastoral Epistles* (London: OUP, 1921).

Harvey, A.E., *Renewal Through Suffering: A Study of 2 Corinthians* (Edinburgh: T&T Clark, 1996).

Hay, D.M. (ed.), *Pauline Theology. Vol. 2: 1 and 2 Corinthians* (Minneapolis: Fortress, 1993).

Hay, D.M. and Johnson, E.E. (eds) *Pauline Theology. Vol. 3: Romans* (Minneapolis: Fortress, 1995).

Hay, D.M. and Johnson, E.E. (eds) *Pauline Theology. Vol. 4: Looking Back, Pressing On* (Atlanta: Scholars, 1997).

Hays, R.B., *The Faith of Jesus Christ: An Investigation of the Narrative Substructure of Galatians 3:1–4:11* (Chico: Scholars, 1983, 2nd edn, Grand Rapids: Eerdmans, 2002).

Hays, R.B., *Echoes of Scripture in the Letters of Paul* (London and New Haven: Yale University Press, 1989).

Hays, R.B., ' "The Gospel Is the Power of God for Salvation to Gentiles Only?" A Critique of Stanley Stowers' *A Rereading of Romans*', *Critical Review of Books in Religion* 9 (1996), pp. 27–44.

Hays, R.B., 'Is Paul's Gospel Narratable?', *Journal for the Study of the New Testament* 27 (2004), pp. 217–39.

Hengel, M., *Judaism and Hellenism* (2 vols, London: SCM, 1974)

Hengel, M., *Between Jesus and Paul* (London: SCM, 1983).

Hengel, M., *Acts and the History of Earliest Christianity* (in *Earliest Christianity*, London: SCM, 1986).

Hengel, M., *The 'Hellenization' of Judaea in the First Century after Christ* (London: SCM, 1989).

Hengel, M., *The Pre-Christian Paul* (London: SCM, 1991).

Hengel, M. and Schwemer, A.M., *Paul Between Damascus and Antioch* (London: SCM, 1997).

Hill, C.C., *Hellenists and Hebrews: Reappraising Division within the Earliest Church* (Minneapolis: Fortress, 1992).

Hillert, S., *Limited and Universal Salvation: A Text-Oriented and Hermeneutical Study of Two Perspectives in Paul* (Stockholm: Almqvist & Wiksell, 1999).

Holmberg, B., *Paul and Power* (Lund: CWK Gleerup, 1978, reprinted Philadelphia: Fortress, 1980).

Holmberg, B., 'Jewish Versus Christian Identity in the Early Church', *Revue Biblique* 105 (1998), pp. 397–425.

Hooker, M.D., 'Authority on Her Head: An Examination of 1 Cor. XI. 10', *New Testament Studies* 10 (1964), pp. 410–16.

Hooker, M.D., *From Adam to Christ: Essays on Paul* (Cambridge: CUP, 1990).

Horrell, D.G., *The Social Ethos of the Corinthian Correspondence* (Edinburgh: T&T Clark, 1996).

Horrell, D.G. (ed.), *Social-Scientific Approaches to New Testament Interpretation* (Edinburgh: T&T Clark, 1999).

Horrell, D.G. 'Domestic Space and Christian Meetings at Corinth: Imagining New Contexts and the Buildings East of the Theatre', *New Testament Studies* 50 (2004), pp. 349–69.

Horrell, D.G., *Solidarity and Difference: A Contemporary Reading of Paul's Ethics* (London & New York: T&T Clark, 2005).

Horrell, D.G., 'Pauline Churches or Early Christian Churches? Unity, Disagreement, and the Eucharist', in A. Alexeev *et al., Einheit der Kirche im Neuen Testament* (Tübingen: Mohr Siebeck, 2008), pp. 185–203.

Horrell, D.G., Hunt, C. and Southgate, C.C.B., *Greening Paul: Rereading the Apostle in an Age of Ecological Crisis* (Waco: Baylor University Press, 2010).

Horsley, R.A. (ed.), *Paul and Empire* (Harrisburg: Trinity Press International, 1997).

Horsley, R.A. (ed.) *Paul and Politics* (Harrisburg: Trinity Press International, 2000).

Horsley, R.A., *Jesus and Empire* (Minneapolis: Fortress, 2002).

Horsley, R.A. (ed.) *Paul and the Roman Imperial Order* (Harrisburg: Trinity Press International, 2004).

Hübner, H., *Law in Paul's Thought* (Edinburgh: T&T Clark, 1984).

Hunt, A.S. and Edgar, C.C., *Select Papyri I* (Loeb Classical Library, London: Heinemann, 1932).

Hurd, J.C., *The Origin of 1 Corinthians* (London: SPCK, 1965).

Hurtado, L.W., 'Convert, Apostate, or Apostle to the Nations: the "Conversion" of Paul in Recent Scholarship', *Studies in Religion/Sciences Religieuses* 22 (1993), pp. 273–84.

Hurtado, L.W., *One God, One Lord: Early Christian Devotion and Ancient Jewish Monotheism* (London: SCM,1988, 2nd edn, Edinburgh: T&T Clark, 1998).

Hurtado, L.W., *Lord Jesus Christ: Devotion to Jesus in Earliest Christianity* (Grand Rapids: Eerdmans, 2003).

Hvalvik, R., 'A "Sonderweg" for Israel. A Critical Examination of a Current Interpretation of Romans 11.25–27', *Journal for the Study of the New Testament* 38 (1990), pp. 87–107.

Jewett, R., *Dating Paul's Life* (London: SCM, 1979).

Johnson, E.E. and Hay, D.M. (eds), *Pauline Theology, Vol. 4: Looking Back, Pressing On* (Atlanta: Scholars Press, 1997).

Joubert, S., *Paul as Benefactor: Reciprocity, Strategy and Theological Reflection in Paul's Collection* (Tübingen: Mohr Siebeck, 2000).

Judge, E.A., *The Social Pattern of Christian Groups in the First Century* (London: Tyndale, 1960).

Käsemann, E., *New Testament Questions of Today* (London: SCM, 1969).

Kennedy, G.A., *New Testament Interpretation through Rhetorical Criticism* (Chapel Hill: University of North Carolina Press, 1984).

Kim, S., *The Origin of Paul's Gospel* (Grand Rapids: Eerdmans, 1982).

Kim, S., *Paul and the New Perspective* (Grand Rapids: Eerdmans, 2002).

Kim, S., *Christ and Caesar: The Gospel and the Roman Empire in the Writings of Paul and Luke* (Grand Rapids: Eerdmans, 2008).

King, K.L., *What is Gnosticism?* (Cambridge, MA: Harvard University Press, 2003).

Knight, G.W. III, *The Pastoral Epistles* (New International Greek Testament Commentary; Grand Rapids: Eerdmans, 1992).

Knox, J., *Chapters in a Life of Paul* (revised edn, London: SCM, 1989).

Kroeker, P.T., 'Recent Continental Philosphers', in S. Westerholm (ed.), *The Blackwell Companion to Paul* (Chichester: Wiley-Blackwell, 2011), pp. 440–54.

Lohse, B., *Martin Luther: An Introduction to His Life and Work* (Edinburgh: T&T Clark, 1987).

Long, A.A. and Sedley, D.N., *The Hellenistic Philosophers: Vol. 1: Translations of the Principal Sources with Philosophical Commentary* (Cambridge: CUP, 1987).

Longenecker, B.W. (ed.), *Narrative Dynamics in Paul* (Louisville: Westminster John Knox, 2002).

Longenecker, B.W., *Remember the Poor: Paul, Poverty, and the Greco-Roman World* (Grand Rapids: Eerdmans, 2010).

Lüdemann, G., *Paul, Apostle to the Gentiles: Studies in Chronology* (London: SCM, 1984).

Maccoby, H., *The Mythmaker: Paul and the Invention of Christianity* (London: Weidenfeld & Nicolson, 1986).

Maccoby, H., *Paul and Hellenism* (London: SCM, 1991).

MacDonald, D.R., *The Legend and the Apostle: The Battle for Paul in Story and Canon* (Philadelphia: Westminster, 1983).

MacDonald, M.Y., *The Pauline Churches: A Socio-Historical Study of Institutionalization in the Pauline and Deutero-Pauline Epistles* (Cambridge: CUP, 1988).

Malherbe, A.J., *Paul and the Popular Philosophers* (Minneapolis: Fortress, 1989).

Malina, B.J., *The New Testament World: Insights from Cultural Anthropology* (3rd edn, Louisville: Westminster John Knox, 2001).

Marchal, J.A. (ed.), *Studying Paul's Letters: Contemporary Perspectives and Methods* (Minneapolis: Fortress, 2012).

Marsh, C. and Moyise, S., *Jesus and the Gospels* (London: Cassell, 1999; 2nd edn, London & New York: T&T Clark, 2006).

Marshall, I.H., *Luke: Historian and Theologian* (Exeter: Paternoster, 1970).

Marshall, I.H., *Acts* (Leicester: IVP, 1980).

Marshall, I.H. *The Acts of the Apostles* (New Testament Guides, Sheffield: Sheffield Academic Press, 1992)

Martin, D.B., 'Review Essay: Justin J. Meggitt, *Paul, Poverty and Survival*', *Journal for the Study of the New Testament* 84 (2001), pp. 51–64.

Matlock, R.B., 'Sins of the Flesh and Suspicious Minds: Dunn's New Theology of Paul', *Journal for the Study of the New Testament* 72 (1998), pp. 67–90.

Matlock, R.B., 'Detheologizing the *PISTIS CHRISTOU* Debate: Cautionary Remarks from a Lexical Semantic Perspective', *Novum Testamentum* 42 (2000), pp. 1–23.

Matlock, R.B., 'Zeal for God but Not According to Knowledge: Douglas
    Campbell's War on Justification Theory', *Journal for the Study of the New
    Testament* 34 (2011), pp. 115–49.

Meade, D.G., *Pseudonymity and Canon* (Grand Rapids: Eerdmans, 1987).

Meeks, W.A., *The First Urban Christians* (New Haven and London: Yale
    University Press, 1983).

Meggitt, J.J., *Paul, Poverty and Survival* (Edinburgh: T&T Clark, 1998).

Meggitt, J.J., 'Response to Martin and Theissen', *Journal for the Study of the
    New Testament* 84 (2001), pp. 85–94.

Mitchell, M.M., *Paul and the Rhetoric of Reconciliation* (Tübingen: Mohr, 1991).

Mitchell, S., *Anatolia: Land, Men, and Gods in Asia Minor. Vol. II: The Rise of
    the Church* (Oxford: Clarendon Press, 1993).

Moyise, S., *The Old Testament in the New: An Introduction* (London and New
    York: Continuum, 2001).

Moyise, S., *Paul and Scripture* (London: SPCK, 2010)

Murphy-O'Connor, J., *St Paul's Corinth: Texts and Archaeology* (Wilmington,
    Delaware: Michael Glazier, 1983; 3rd edn, Collegeville: Liturgical Press,
    2002).

Murphy-O'Connor, J., '2 Timothy Contrasted with 1 Timothy and Titus', *Revue
    Biblique* 98 (1991), pp. 403–18.

Murphy-O'Connor, J., *Paul: A Critical Life* (Oxford: OUP, 1996).

Nickle, K.F., *The Collection* (London: SCM, 1966).

Novenson, M.V., *Christ among the Messiahs: Christ Language in Paul and
    Messiah Language in Ancient Judaism* (Oxford & New York: OUP, 2012).

Oakes, P., *Reading Romans in Pompeii: Paul's Letter at Ground Level* (London/
    Minneapolis: SPCK/Fortress, 2009).

Osiek, C. and MacDonald, M.Y. with Tulloch, J.H., *A Woman's Place: House
    Churches in Earliest Christianity* (Minneapolis: Fortress, 2006).

Packer, J.I., *'Fundamentalism' and the Word of God* (Leicester: IVP, 1958).

Pagels, E.H., *The Gnostic Paul: Gnostic Exegesis of the Pauline Letters*
    (Philadelphia: Fortress, 1975).

Perkins, P., *Gnosticism and the New Testament* (Minneapolis: Fortress, 1993)

Porter, S.E. and Stanley, C.D. (eds), *As It Is Written: Studying Paul's Use of
    Scripture* (Atlanta: Society of Biblical Literature, 2008).

Price, S.R.F., *Rituals and Power: The Roman Imperial Cult in Asia Minor*
    (Cambridge: CUP, 1984).

Prior, M., *Paul the Letter-Writer and the Second Letter to Timothy* (Sheffield:
    JSOT, 1989)

Radice, B., *Pliny the Younger, Letters and Panegyricus* (2 vols, Loeb Classical Library; London: Heinemann, 1969).

Räisänen, H., *Paul and the Law* (Tübingen: Mohr Siebeck, 1983).

Riesner, R., *Paul's Early Period: Chronology, Mission Strategy, Theology* (Grand Rapids: Eerdmans, 1998).

Robertson, A. and Plummer, A., *A Critical and Exegetical Commentary on the First Epistle of St. Paul to the Corinthians* (2nd edn, Edinburgh: T&T Clark, 1914).

Roetzel, C.J., *Paul: The Man and the Myth* (Columbia: University of South Carolina Press, 1998).

Rohrbaugh, R.L. (ed.), *The Social Sciences and New Testament Interpretation* (Peabody: Hendrickson, 1996).

Sanders, J.T., *Ethics in the New Testament* (London: SCM, 1975).

Sanders, E.P., *Paul and Palestinian Judaism* (London: SCM, 1977).

Sanders, E.P., *Paul, the Law and the Jewish People* (London: SCM, 1983).

Sanders, E.P. *Paul* (Oxford: OUP, 1991).

Schweitzer, A., *The Mysticism of Paul the Apostle* (2nd edn, London: A&C Black, 1953).

Scroggs, R., 'Earliest Christianity as Sectarian Movement', in J. Neusner (ed.), *Christianity, Judaism and Other Greco-Roman Cults: Studies for Morton Smith at Sixty. Part Two: Early Christianity* (Leiden: Brill, 1975), pp. 1–23, reprinted in D.G. Horrell (ed.), *Social-Scientific Approaches to New Testament Interpretation* (Edinburgh: T&T Clark, 1999), pp. 69–91.

Segal, A.F., *Paul the Convert* (New Haven and London: Yale University Press, 1990).

Seifrid, M., *Justification by Faith: The Origin and Development of a Central Pauline Theme* (Leiden: Brill, 1992).

Smith C.F., *Thucydides, History of the Peloponnesian War* (Loeb Classical Library, London: Heinemann, 1928).

Stanley, C.D., *Arguing with Scripture: The Rhetoric of Quotations in the Letters of Paul* (London and New York: T&T Clark, 2004).

Stanley, C.D. (ed.) *Paul and Scripture: Extending the Conversation* (Atlanta: Society of Biblical Literature, 2012).

Stendahl, K., *Paul Among Jews and Gentiles* (Philadelphia: Fortress, 1976).

Stowers, S.K., *A Rereading of Romans: Justice, Jews and Gentiles* (New Haven & London: Yale University Press, 1994).

Theissen, G., *The Social Setting of Pauline Christianity* (Edinburgh: T&T Clark, 1982).

Theissen, G., *Social Reality and the Early Christians* (Edinburgh: T&T Clark, 1993).

Theissen, G., 'The Social Structure of Pauline Communities: Some Critical Remarks on J.J. Meggitt, *Paul, Poverty and Survival*', *Journal for the Study of the New Testament* 84 (2001), pp. 65–84.

Theissen, G., 'Social Conflicts in the Corinthian Community: Further Remarks on J.J. Meggitt, *Paul, Poverty and Survival*', *Journal for the Study of the New Testament* 25 (2003), pp. 371–91.

Theissen, G. and Merz, A., *The Historical Jesus: A Comprehensive Guide* (London: SCM, 1998).

Thomas, R.S., *Later Poems: A Selection 1972–1982* (London: Macmillan, Papermac, 1984).

Thompson, M.B., *Clothed with Christ: The Example and Teaching of Jesus in Romans 12.1–15.13* (Sheffield: JSOT, 1991).

Tomson, P. J., *Paul and the Jewish Law: Halakha in the Letters of the Apostle to the Gentiles* (Assen & Maastricht/Minneapolis: Van Gorcum/Fortress, 1990).

Tuckett, C.M., 'Paul, Scripture and Ethics: Some Reflections' *New Testament Studies* 46 (2000), pp. 403–24.

Watson, F., *Paul, Judaism and the Gentiles* (Cambridge: CUP, 1986; revised and expanded edn, Grand Rapids: Eerdmans, 2007).

Watson, F., *Paul and the Hermeneutics of Faith* (London and New York: T&T Clark, 2004).

Wedderburn, A.J.M., *The Reasons for Romans* (Edinburgh: T&T Clark, 1988).

Wesley, J., *The Journal of John Wesley*, abridged by C. Idle (Tring: Lion Publishing, 1986).

Westerholm, S., *Israel's Law and the Church's Faith* (Grand Rapids: Eerdmans, 1988).

Westerholm, S., *Perspectives Old and New on Paul* (Grand Rapids: Eerdmans, 2004).

Westerholm S. (ed.), *The Blackwell Companion to Paul* (Chichester: Wiley-Blackwell, 2011).

Westerholm, S., *Justification Reconsidered: Rethinking a Pauline Theme* (Grand Rapids: Eerdmans, 2013).

Witherington, B. III, *Paul's Narrative Thought-World* (Louisville: Westminster/John Knox, 1994).

Witherington, B. III, *Conflict and Community in Corinth: A Socio-Rhetorical Commentary on 1 and 2 Corinthians* (Grand Rapids: Eerdmans, 1995).

Witherington, B. III, *The Paul Quest: The Renewed Search for the Jew of Tarsus* (Leicester: IVP, 1998).

Witherington, B. III, *Paul's Letter to the Romans: A Socio-Rhetorical Commentary* (Grand Rapids: Eerdmans, 2004).

Wrede, W., *Paul* (London: Philip Green, 1907).

Wright, N.T., *The Climax of the Covenant* (Edinburgh: T&T Clark 1991).

Wright, N.T., *The New Testament and the People of God* (London: SPCK, 1992).

Wright, N.T., *What Saint Paul Really Said* (Oxford: Lion, 1997).

Wright, N.T., *Paul: Fresh Perspectives* (London: SPCK, 2005).

Wright, N.T., *Paul and the Faithfulness of God* (2 vols; London/Minneapolis: SPCK/Fortress, 2013).

Zetterholm, M., *Approaches to Paul: A Student's Guide to Recent Scholarship* (Minneapolis: Fortress, 2009).

Ziesler, J., *The Meaning of Righteousness in Paul* (Cambridge: CUP, 1972).

Ziesler, J., *Pauline Christianity* (revised edn, Oxford: OUP, 1990).

Index of Biblical References

Note: only passages which are quoted, discussed, or otherwise deemed to be of particular significance are listed here. To locate discussions of specific epistles as a whole see subject index below (under 'Romans', 'Galatians', etc.).

Index of Subjects and Authors

Note: only modern authors mentioned in the main text, along with selected subjects and names, are listed here.